In Their Best Interest?

Laura M. Purdy

IN THEIR BEST INTEREST?

The Case against Equal Rights for Children

Cornell University Press

Ithaca and London

First published 1992 by Cornell University Press.

Library of Congress Cataloging-in-Publication Data

Purdy, Laura Martha.
In their best interest? : the case against equal rights for children / Laura M. Purdy.
p. cm.
Includes bibliographical references and index.
ISBN 0-8014-2662-6 (alk. paper). — ISBN 0-8014-9956-9 (pbk. : alk. paper)
1. Children's rights. 2. Child development. 3. Children—Legal status, laws, etc. I. Title.
HQ789.P87 1992
305.23—dc20 91-55550

Printed in the United States of America

∞ The paper in this book meets the minimum requirements of the American National Standard for Information Sciences–Permanence of Paper for Printed Library Materials, ANSI Z39.48-1984.

CONTENTS

ACKNOWLEDGMENTS

No intellectual product could, so goes the cliché, be what it is without the contributions (witting or unwitting) of many people. This book has benefited enormously from the comments and criticisms of William Aiken, Russell Blackwood, Virginia Held, Louis Pojman, Robert Simon, and Mary Anne Warren; its shortcomings are of course entirely my own. Margaret Briggs and Barbara Salazar helped me to say more clearly what I meant and Diana Edel spared me some of the mind-numbing dirty work that accompanies such projects. Thanks also to Wells College for the sabbatical leave in 1986–87 that enabled me to start work on this issue, and to Hamilton College for research time that accompanied the Irwin Chair I held there in 1988–89 and for material support in 1989–90. I am also indebted to Kathleen Kearns and John Ackerman of Cornell University Press, without whose enthusiasm, help, and encouragement this book might well never have seen the light of day.

Parts of the Appendix are based on my article "Feminists Healing Ethics," *Hypatia* 4 (Summer 1989): 9–14, and my paper "Do Feminists Need a New Moral Theory?" presented at the conference Explorations in Feminist Ethics, Duluth, Minnesota, October 1988.

On the personal front, credit must go to my husband, John Coleman, who listened patiently to the endless thinking aloud that accompanied the book's gestation, and whose own activities led me to think about the topic in the first place. Finally, this work constitutes belated appreciation for my parents, who will, I think, have the last laugh when they read it.

L. M. P.

In Their Best Interest?

INTRODUCTION

> We must include the oppression of children in any program for feminist revolution or we will be subject to the same failing of which we have so often accused men: of not having gone deep enough in our analysis, of having missed an important substratum of oppression merely because it didn't directly concern us.
>
> —Shulamith Firestone, *The Dialectics of Sex*

> I propose that the rights, privileges, duties, responsibilities of adult citizens be made *available* to any young person, of whatever age, who wants to make use of them.
>
> —John Holt, *Escape from Childhood*

Julie, fourteen, wants to quit school; her parents think she should stay. Their disagreement illustrates two complex and difficult questions: How much control should children have over their lives? Are they capable of making decisions about their own best interest?

Julie thinks she is. She has been studying ballet for seven years and her progress in the next two years will determine whether she is good enough to dance professionally, something her heart is set on. She considers school irrelevant to her future and would rather concentrate fully on her dancing. Her parents realize that staying in school does reduce her chances of success as a dancer. But they also know that most young women—even those as dedicated as Julie—drop out of ballet before they are twenty; they also know that most dance careers are short and unremunerative, so that continued schooling is in any case necessary. Julie is convinced, however, that she will persevere and have such a long and successful career that when she does finally quit, she will be in demand as a teacher.

She does not now have a right to leave school. Should she have it? A surprising array of people, not just budding fourteen-year-olds, agree that she should have, along with all other adult rights, the right to decide for herself whether to go to school or not.

Is this idea as ludicrous as some people think? Shouldn't we just laugh at our children's accusations of "adult chauvinism"?[1] But then why, over the years, has the belief that children are oppressed attracted such prominent followers as Shulamith Firestone and John Holt?[2] Furthermore, an astounding 43 percent of the adults surveyed by Daniel Yankelovich in 1976–77 said that they wanted to be free to live as they chose, and saw no reason to deprive their children of the same liberty.[3]

And if the idea is so preposterous, how can we explain recent legal history? *U.S. News & World Report*, for example, announced in 1974 that "as children get lawyers, lobbyists, and political sympathizers, the growing trend is to view them as at least semi-independent persons with their own rights—not automatically subservient to parental or official authority." The article points out that compulsory school attendance, juvenile courts, and even child-labor laws have deprived children of rights they once enjoyed.[4] More recent legal cases have supported children's bid for increased autonomy.[5]

Children's subordinate social place is reflected in both their moral and their legal positions. Children's lives may be controlled in many

1. See Youth Liberation of Ann Arbor, "We Do Not Recognize Their Right to Control Us," in *The Children's Rights Movement: Overcoming the Oppression of Young People*, ed. Beatrice Gross and Ronald Gross (New York: Anchor/Doubleday, 1977), p. 128.

2. Shulamith Firestone, *The Dialectic of Sex* (New York: Bantam, 1970); John Holt, *Escape from Childhood* (New York: Dutton, 1974).

3. See Vance Packard, *Our Endangered Children* (Boston: Little, Brown, 1983), p. 8.

4. *U.S. News & World Report*, cited in Gross and Gross, *Children's Rights Movement*, pp. 207–12.

5. Among the cases that began the trend toward recognizing more autonomy for children, one might look at Brown v. Board of Education, 347 U.S. 483 (1954), which granted children the status of rights-bearing persons. Subsequent landmark cases included In re Gault, 387 U.S. 1 (1967), Tinker v. Des Moines Independent Community School District, 393 U.S. 503 (1969), and Planned Parenthood of Central Missouri v. Danforth, 428 U.S. 52 (1976). The first reinstituted certain procedural protections for children in delinquency proceedings, the second limited school prohibitions of children's political expression, and the third recognized a girl's right to choose abortion without consulting her parents. These cases do not represent a consistent trend, however. Among the more notable exceptions are later attempts to limit girls' right to abortion, although these particular cases probably have more to do with the backlash against women's rights than with children. For further discussion of legal cases, see Laurence D. Houlgate, *The Child and the State: A Normative Theory of Juvenile Rights* (Baltimore: Johns Hopkins University Press, 1980), chap. 3.

ways. This control is legitimized by a complicated network of legal rights and duties. There is "one set of rights for adults, and another for children," as Howard Cohen points out. "Adults' rights mostly provide them with opportunities to exercise their powers; children's rights mostly provide them with protection and keep them under adult control."[6] At present children have a right to a proper home, subsistence, education, medical care, and an "appropriate" moral environment; they also generally have a right to rehabilitation rather than punishment if they are convicted of a crime. These benefits come at a price, however. The guardians who provide for children have a corresponding right to choose their names, religion, and type of education, as well as to determine where they live, what they eat, and how they dress. A guardian can censor books and movies, and even has a right to a child's wages. As schools are considered to be *in loco parentis*, they too can adopt a variety of regulations intended to ensure a good learning situation. Among those that the courts have found acceptable are dress codes, restrictions on hair length, and prohibitions of secret societies. More generally, children are also subject to curfews, as well as limits on their work, on visits to dance and pool halls, on driving, drinking, and access to pornography. Some acts, "juvenile status offenses," are crimes only when they are committed by minors. They include running away from home, being ungovernable, being truant, having sexual intercourse, and becoming pregnant. Children cannot marry, vote, make a will, or make a valid contract.[7]

Why are children in this special category? They are denied equal rights on the grounds that they differ from adults in morally relevant ways; as Cohen puts it, "children are presumed to be weak, passive, mindless, and unthinking; adults are presumed to be rational, highly motivated, and efficient."[8] But John Harris and other liberationists join Cohen in denying such differences: "Bold, quick, ingenious, forward and capable young people are by no means a rarity; neither,

6. Howard Cohen, *Equal Rights for Children* (Totowa, N.J.: Littlefield, Adams, 1980), p. 43.

7. Laurence Houlgate, "Children, Paternalism, and Rights to Liberty," in *Having Children: Philosophical and Legal Reflections on Parenthood*, ed. Onora O'Neill and William Ruddick (Oxford: Oxford University Press, 1979), pp. 18–29. For a longer discussion of the legal status of children, see Alan Sussman, *The Rights of Young People: The Basic A.C.L.U. Guide to a Young Person's Rights* (New York: Avon, 1977).

8. Cohen, *Equal Rights for Children*, p. 45.

unfortunately, are dull-witted, incompetent adults."[9] These counter-examples undermine the claim that there are consistent morally relevant differences between children and adults.

Are children wrongly stripped of their right to self-determination by ignorant or overbearing adults who ought to know better? Proponents of equal rights for children believe that they deserve the same control over their lives as adults and that they are unjustly treated when such control is withheld from them. In fact, these advocates feel, since current practice seriously limits and frustrates children, it constitutes oppression that should be rectified.

Although philosophers have paid some attention to the question of children's relation to adults, their concern has most often been subordinated to more general political interests. The relative unimportance of this topic in the general philosophical scheme of things is indicated by the failure of historians of philosophy to provide a comprehensive and systematic account of it.[10]

Influential philosophers have had interesting things to say about the rearing of children. In *The Republic*, Plato abolished the family, at least in the ruling class of guardians, in what he thought was the interest of society as a whole.[11] For Aristotle, the family was a utilitarian arrangement for meeting the prerequisites of the good society rather than the emotional haven we seek in it today.[12] In the early modern period, from the time of Jean Bodin to John Locke, the dramatic shift in political discourse from a patriarchal to a liberal-contractarian paradigm brought questions about children to the fore. Robert Filmer had argued that patriarchal authority should be the model for all authority relations in society.[13] The early liberals, among whom Locke was the most prominent, argued instead for a

9. John Harris, "The Political Status of Children," in *Contemporary Political Philosophy*, ed. Keith Graham (Cambridge: Cambridge University Press, 1982), p. 37.

10. See Jeffrey Blustein, *Parents and Children: The Ethics of the Family* (Oxford: Oxford University Press, 1982), p. 19. Blustein attributes part of this lack to the difficulties inherent in such work, ranging from such conceptual tangles as the lack of common referent for "family" to the fact that two quite different interests have motivated philosophers to think about the family, its relation to the state and the relationships between its members (pp. 20–21).

11. Plato, *The Republic*, in *The Collected Dialogues of Plato*, ed. Edith Hamilton and Huntington Cairns (Princeton: Princeton University Press, 1963), 423e, 462, 464.

12. Aristotle, *The Nichomachean Ethics*, bk. 8, 1162a, and *Politics*, bk. 3, 1277b, in *The Basic Works of Aristotle*, ed. Richard McKeon (New York: Random House, 1968).

13. Robert Filmer, *Patriarcha*, in John Locke, *Two Treatises of Government*, ed. Thomas I. Cook (New York: Hafner, 1947).

conception of human relations based on consent. The position of children, who neither consent to be born nor consent to the authority that parents exercise over them, therefore posed a special problem for those who "believed, at least abstractly, that the completion of the democratic ideal required bringing all of social life under the sway of a single democratic authority principle." Jean Bethke Elshtain notes liberals' discomfort with the apparent implications of their view: they sought to justify contractarianism in the public realm and engaged in "discursive maneuvering" to avoid its implications in the private.[14]

Locke himself argued against the view that authority must come in only one form: the authority of parents over children did not derive from consent, unlike justified authority in the civil realm.[15] It arose instead from taking on responsibility for their welfare. This responsibility created a duty not only to care for them but to see that they develop into reasonable beings.[16] The basis for this relationship was trust in parents' concern for their children's well-being.[17] Locke not only helped provide the philosophical basis for current protectionist attitudes toward children but firmly directed much of the subsequent discussion about children toward questions about their education.[18]

Nonetheless, the apparent contradiction between the claim that justifiable authority derives only from consent and the view that parents rightfully exercise authority over their children continued to vex liberals, who frequently returned to the question of family relationships.[19] Some contemporary philosophers, too, intrigued by the notion that their general political principles might require children's liberation, have been subjecting their rights to critical analysis.[20] In the last ten years or so, an increasing number of works have ad-

14. Jean Bethke Elshtain, "The Family, Democratic Politics, and the Question of Authority," in *Children, Parents, and Politics*, ed. Geoffrey Scarre (Cambridge: Cambridge University Press, 1989), pp. 58–59.

15. See ibid., pp. 59–60.

16. John Locke, *Second Treatise of Civil Government*, ed. Peter Laslett (Cambridge: Cambridge University Press, 1960), sec. 58.

17. Note the similarity here between Locke's view and Annette Baier's view of the need for trust in human relationships. See, e.g., Annette C. Baier, "Trust and Antitrust," *Ethics* 96 (1986): 231–60.

18. Blustein, *Parents and Children*, p. 81.

19. Elshtain, "Family, Democratic Politics," p. 60.

20. E.g., Blustein, *Parents and Children*; O'Neill and Ruddick, *Having Children*.

dressed the question of children, and almost no anthology on this topic is complete without an article arguing for converting children's submission to authority to the adult consent model.[21] A few scholars have attempted to provide sustained theoretical support for the equal rights implicit in such a move.[22] Although the details of their arguments vary, their basic position that there is no consistent morally relevant difference between children and adults is singularly elegant and appealing. It seems to have a compelling logic that is hard for good liberals to resist, and it's not obvious just where it goes wrong.

Hence there are good theoretical reasons for examining anew the foundations of parent-child relationships. Furthermore, it is morally risky to dismiss without examination any claim of oppression: humanity's shameful record with respect to the weak and powerless shows us that we cannot rely on our initial intuitions about whether a given group is being justly treated. So even if our first reaction to this claim about children is disbelief or outrage, it is necessary to consider what could be said in its favor. In short, the question about the moral status of children is urgent because of its practical ramifications: if our assumptions about this central feature of our lives (whether as children, parents, or teachers) are unfounded, then we contribute to serious oppression. And claims of oppression are among those that require immediate scrutiny and, if valid, action to rectify the situation.

No less important, doubt about the theoretical basis of parent-child relations undermines those relationships on a day-to-day basis. Jeffrey Blustein voices this concern when he points out that:

> many parents today are uneasy about their right to exercise authority over their own children. We believe that, as parents, we are entitled to command our children's obedience, but we worry that our use of au-

21. E.g., Gross and Gross, *Children's Rights Movement*; O'Neill and Ruddick, *Having Children*; William Aiken and Hugh LaFollette, eds., *Whose Child?: Children's Rights, Parental Authority, and State Power* (Totowa, N.J.: Littlefield, Adams, 1980); and Scarre, *Children, Parents, and Politics*.

22. For instance, Cohen, *Equal Rights for Children*; Ann Palmeri, "Childhood's End: Toward the Liberation of Children," in Aiken and LaFollette, *Whose Child?*; Harris, "Political Status of Children"; and Richard Lindley, "Teenagers and Other Children," in Scarre, *Children, Parents, and Politics*.

> thority may actually be inhibiting our children's growth to autonomy. As a result of this insecurity, parents are frequently inconsistent in their use of authority, alternately failing to set limits for their children when they need to have demands imposed on them and then reacting to their children's perceived rebelliousness with excessive discipline and other authoritarian measures.[23]

This kind of inconsistency undermines good relationships and fails to meet children's needs.

Some parents do not suffer from such insecurity. Among them are liberal intellectuals who justifiably pride themselves on their concern for the rights of others, great and small. Add to these numbers the parents convinced of the value of the laissez-faire permissive child-rearing that leaves children free to set their own agendas, and we can see that large numbers of children in the United States are growing up with the idea that they should have more say over their own lives, perhaps as much as if they were adults. Many of these children come from the more powerful classes from which American leaders have historically been drawn. Even more important, perhaps, because of the social visibility of its adherents, this general approach constitutes an authoritative model, not only for upwardly mobile working-class families but also for the Third World nations most subject to American influence. It is therefore critical to determine whether this movement represents the forward march of justice or a confused and undesirable detour.

The central issue here is this: Is the view that children need special protection and help, even at the cost of control they do not necessarily want, well anchored in reality despite the recurrence of doubts about it? Given the importance of this question, not only to children themselves but for human civilization as a whole, it deserves the most thorough and dispassionate scrutiny. Although the extremism inherent in the notion that children deserve equal rights may seem to undermine the inquiry at its start, it is sufficiently influential and interesting to warrant careful investigation. An extreme position is not, in any case, necessarily wrong.

Skeptics dismiss the liberationist position as too outlandish to warrant further examination; its flip side, protectionism, seems ob-

23. Blustein, *Parents and Children*, pp. 4–5.

vious. Why argue for what we think we know already? The answer is that in our more thoughtful moments, we recognize that not every bit of "common sense" is sound: we have believed all sorts of things that aren't true. How many people, for instance, have believed (and still believe) that it is just "natural" for women to be subordinated to men? How many people bridle at the thought of bright twelve-year-olds in college?[24]

A common-sense belief may of course turn out to be true. For practical questions such as this one, successful testing is useful, for it inspires the confidence necessary for appropriate action. The activity of evaluating, whether fully successful or not, can also be enlightening in itself—even if, as here, it raises nearly as many questions as it answers.

Deeper exploration of an issue where common sense seems so unequivocally to support one kind of answer is all the more important when it involves fundamental assumptions about family, human development, and the good society. Most of the contemporary debate has so far been conducted in polemical snippets and brief exchanges in journals.[25] These salvos are no substitute for the careful probing that may uncover and pursue questionable assumptions or incoherence; only such probing can help us see how a more moderate case may fall prey to the same errors.[26] The apparent narrowness of the question whether to liberate or protect children is more than com-

24. "Common sense" suggests that they will just be too far out of step to succeed; but there is good evidence that some children flourish in these circumstances. See W. C. George, S. J. Cohn, and J. C. Stanley, eds., *Educating the Gifted: Acceleration and Enrichment* (Baltimore: Johns Hopkins University Press, 1979).

25. See, e.g., Francis Schrag, "The Child in the Moral Order," *Philosophy* 52 (April 1977): 167–77; Geoffrey Scarre, "Children and Paternalism," *Philosophy* 55 (January 1980): 117–24; Roland Case, "Pulling the Plug on Appeals to Irrationality, Immaturity, and Expediency," and Dwight R. Boyd, "Of Adults and Bathwater: Response to a Case for Children's Liberty Rights," both in *Philosophy of Education Society Proceedings* 41 (1985): 455–59; Gross and Gross, *Children's Rights Movement*. Exceptions to this approach are M. D. A. Freeman, *The Rights and Wrongs of Children* (London: Frances Pinter, 1983); and Blustein, *Parents and Children*. Both are excellent books that are substantially broader in scope than this work, and therefore devote much less space to the specific question at hand. Blustein in particular, though a Rawlsian liberal, shares some of my assumptions and raises points similar to the ones I develop here. Another exception is Houlgate, whose *Child and State* is both more theoretical and somewhat broader.

26. E.g., Richard Lindley "Teenagers," has proposed liberating teenagers. Although this proposal is significantly more plausible than the more extreme views expressed by Harris, "Political Status of Children," and Cohen, *Equal Rights for Children*, some of the same objections still apply.

pensated for by the almost frightening breadth of the territory that must be explored if we are to make any real headway.[27]

Is there anything new to say? After all, the general outlines of the protectionist response to the liberationist argument were sketched long ago by Locke, and there are only so many possible positions to adopt. I contend that three centuries later, the question is worth another serious look. Circumstances have changed, and we have learned a great deal in the meantime. Other contemporary philosophers clearly concur in this opinion, as a spate of protectionist arguments have appeared in response to proposals for equal rights.

Why don't *those* responses suffice? First, because they've been on the short side and have generally stuck with some widely accepted but questionable assumptions, both empirical and moral. Second, because their approach has been chiefly theoretical.

An air of unreality pervades the otherwise philosophically straightforward liberationist arguments, and protectionist responses shy at deploying the full array of knowledge and arguments available to those who have been deeply involved in childrearing.[28] Taken together, these two factors seem to me to stand in the way of further progress toward resolution of the question.

Now, as I have suggested, the theoretical liberationist argument has enormous appeal: it has a way of stopping dead in their tracks people who think Julie's quitting school is unreasonable. One source of its power is that it appears to be a logical extension of principles already widely accepted, an extension we would have thought of ourselves if we had been more imaginative or even just more consistent. And the empirical claim is striking: we all know bright, enterprising children as well as hopelessly inept adults. Another source of its power is that, perhaps because of these facts, opponents of equal rights for children have accepted many of the parameters of debate set by liberationists.

Liberationists quite reasonably place the burden of proof on those who would limit freedom: who could disagree with that? Their examples appear to break down our notion that there is some neat

27. One might object that this way of putting the question is confusing, as not all adults have exactly the same rights. What I refer to here are such paradigmatic rights of ordinary citizens as the right to make contracts.

28. The sense of unreality I refer to has a way of dissipating as we get into the arguments, although it returns to haunt us at the triumphant liberationist conclusion.

dividing line between adults and children. Their choice of reason as the morally relevant criterion seems beyond reproach: after all, aren't humans the rational animals? The model of human development upon which their position is most plausibly predicated is optimistic and attractive. And finally, their suggestions for social change to accommodate liberated children sound like good ideas. Protectionists are left with little cover: they tend to respond by focusing on the question of children's rationality, and assume, but do not provide much evidence for, limits on their possible development.[29]

Liberationist assumptions demand further inquiry, however, not only because of their importance in this context but because of their implications for moral philosophy as a whole. Take the primacy of freedom, for instance. Presumably everybody agrees that, other things being equal, freedom is a good thing. But should it play the preeminent role in social life presupposed by liberationists? Contemporary liberal theories aim at leaving individuals free to pursue purely personal notions of the good. They posit a small set of minimally constraining principles that attempt to guarantee equal freedom to all; the restrictions recommended by such theories vary.[30] Even such liberty-oriented theories, however, don't necessarily support equal rights for children. Moderate liberals deny children's rights on the grounds that children need a period of learning before they can make the kind of autonomous decisions required for participation in adult society. If they were nonetheless treated like full citizens, they might never become autonomous.[31] And what, in any

29. See, e.g., Freeman, *Rights and Wrongs*. Freeman mentions social science studies that seem to set limits on the nature and rate of possible development, but does not really discuss them. Much of Houlgate's argument in "Children, Paternalism" depends on his assumption that we do not have sufficient developmental evidence about children to conclude that they are not capable of avoiding harm to themselves.

30. The most prominent proponents of this kind of view are Bruce Ackerman, *Social Justice in the Liberal State* (New Haven: Yale University Press, 1980); John Rawls, *A Theory of Justice* (Cambridge: Harvard University Press, 1971); Ronald Dworkin, "Liberalism," in *Public and Private Morality*, ed. Stuart Hampshire (Cambridge: Cambridge University Press, 1978); and Robert Nozick, *Anarchy, State, and Utopia* (New York: Basic Books, 1974). Of course, there are substantial differences among these writers with respect to both the limits they would place on freedom and the way they defend those limits.

31. What Rawls would say about children would depend largely on what information about human development could pass the veil of ignorance required by the Original Position in which the principles of justice are chosen. For discussion of a contractarian argument about children's rights, see Houlgate, *Child and State*, chap. 7. Ackerman regards

case, happens to the argument for equal rights if we are more often willing than mainstream liberals to judge that some other value—avoidance of harm, for instance—should take precedence over freedom?

Closely related to the question of an adequate moral theory is the choice of the capacity for instrumental reasoning as the morally relevant criterion that is to determine whether children should have equal rights or not. How do we decide which differences are morally relevant? Not every empirical difference makes a moral difference, and not every similarity warrants equal treatment. Before we start the philosopher's logical engine going on "the facts," we must be satisfied that the value questions implicit in our judgment about which facts are important have been thoroughly scrutinized. So although the principle of universalizability requires us to treat cases alike unless there are good reasons for treating them differently, we cannot apply it until we have chewed over the tacit moral questions raised by asking what such good reasons would be.

How does this point bear on the case at hand? Consider the argument that even if substantial psychological differences exist between children and adults, they are not morally relevant. At the least, this claim implies denial of any objection to equal rights based on the consequences of recognizing such rights for psychologically immature individuals. In other words, this apparently value-free approach turns out to involve a critical moral assumption, one that rules out a whole class of conceptions of the good society. Among such discarded ideals are those promoting particular kinds of equality or well-being.

Still another problem is the model of human development that might most plausibly be assumed by liberationist arguments: growth is internally driven and will be most successful if left to flower freely.[32] But more than one such model exists; consider, for example, the view that children are shaped primarily by the environment, as well

---

considerable parental control to be legitimate, as competence at dialogic neutrality is essential for full citizenship (*Social Justice*, p. 149). Nozick, the least restrictive in his conception of justifiable state controls, seems unwilling to commit himself to stating the consequences of his general principles for children. (*Anarchy, State, and Utopia*, pp. 330–31). This topic is explored further in chap. 2, below.

32. There is no necessary connection between the growth view and children's liberation, but the connection is plausible and, I think, historically valid.

as other possible views about the interaction between nature and nurture. Hence we are not at liberty to choose the model we prefer without argument.

Finally, liberationists recommend a variety of social changes to facilitate children's introduction into the adult world. They start from the characteristics of children. It is assumed that those characteristics determine their rights; they in turn dictate how the world should accommodate them. Protectionists tend, with a few exceptions, to accept this general approach although they deny one or more of the relevant claims.[33] One might reasonably ask here, as people are doing elsewhere in moral philosophy, whether this atomistic approach is appropriate. Children, like the rest of us, are embedded within a social context: it seems one-sided to try to deduce what their legal relation to the rest of society ought to look like without trying to grasp the complex interdependence of all the elements in the picture. I agree with liberationists that their place badly needs reexamination. But as we study it, we need to keep an eye on many factors other than children's intrinsic characteristics. What rights children should have ought to depend in part on what they need and want. But what they need and want depends in part on social conditions and social ideals. Furthermore, the kinds of general changes required to free children may be neither feasible nor, on balance, desirable.

Protectionist responses to the liberationist challenge have been limited, in part, by the short formats generally chosen. But, as I suggested earlier, they have also been hampered to a considerable degree by narrow contemporary assumptions about what good philosophy is. Despite the renewed interest lately in taking on practical problems, not only is the necessary empirical material still viewed with some suspicion, but so is the detailed attention to the concrete and down-to-earth fabric of daily life: nothing could be further from the models of great philosophy held up for us to admire.

I bring to bear on this discussion a variety of observations made in the course of child rearing. Recognition of their epistemological status is uncertain, of course, as such conclusions have not been welcomed into the realm of what "every philosopher knows," presumably at least in part because there have been so few women

33. See, e.g., Blustein, *Parents and Children*, pt. 2, chap. 3.

philosophers and their interests have had so little impact (until recently) on what philosophy is supposed to be.[34] My work here is offered in the spirit of Annette Baier's suggestion that resolving moral problems requires attention to a variety of practical issues to which little heed has in general been paid: "philosophers will have to get their hands a little dirtier, a little more officially familiar not merely with intellectual arguments but with the other forces that drive human life, for better or worse." She adds: "such moral philosophy would merge with other disciplines, and with the reflections of common life, and such a merger might help us to escape from that arrogance of solitary intellect which has condemned much moral theory to sustained self-delusions concerning its subject matter, its methods, and its authority."[35] Certainly the question of children's rightful status cannot be resolved without that kind of attitude, and it is the lack of it, among other things, that impedes the debate and contributes to the sense of unreality that pervades it.

Progress now depends on our willingness to adopt a somewhat rough-and-ready moral framework: waiting for the solution of the most general theoretical problems is neither desirable nor possible.[36] Doing theory first might not, as Baier suggests, lead to the best thinking; in any case, we would lose the opportunity to promote human welfare now.

The general moral grounding of this work is consequentialistic and broadly utilitarian.[37] Any tenable moral theory must recognize as well the value of equality, liberty, and justice. That they may at times conflict not only with each other but with pure utility poses serious problems, whether they can (on the grounds of their utility) be fitted within the hierarchy crowned by the principle of utility or

34. See Caroline Whitbeck, "The Moral Implication of Regarding Women as People: New Perspectives on Pregnancy and Personhood," in *Abortion and the Status of the Fetus*, ed. William B. Bondeson, H. Tristram Engelhardt, Jr., Stuart Spicker, and Daniel Winship (Dordrecht: Reidel, 1983).

35. Annette Baier, "Doing without Moral Theory," in *Postures of the Mind: Essays on Mind and Morals* (Minneapolis: University of Minnesota Press, 1985), pp. 243–44.

36. See Appendix for further discussion of both the place of moral theory in applied ethics and for elucidation of the approach used here.

37. For discussion of consequentialism, see Samuel Scheffler, ed., *Consequentialism and Its Critics* (Oxford: Oxford University Press, 1988). For a recent defense of a utilitarianism oriented more toward the elimination of suffering than toward the maximization of utility, see Anthony Quinton, *Utilitarian Ethics* (La Salle, Ill.: Open Court, 1989); for more details of my own view, see the Appendix.

are regarded as competing independent principles. I believe that for the present work, however, this perennial problem is relatively unimportant.[38]

I also make a number of assumptions about family life derived from this general moral framework. Thus I take it as given that children are appropriate subjects of moral attention and concern even before they are moral agents. I also take it for granted that children and adults may have competing interests, which may require case-by-case analysis to resolve. Some may not be resolvable in any wholly satisfactory way; for others, a variety of approaches might be acceptable. In some situations, political negotiation will have to play a role in decision making. A further premise, based on both theoretical and empirical assumptions, is that women and men should be equal partners in childrearing and that it is immoral to base the family on the subordination of women.[39]

On the more purely empirical front, I notice that although parents mostly love their children and children love their parents, there are many unhappy families. Some of this unhappiness arises as a result of undesirable social conditions, such as poverty or discrimination, over which parents as individuals can exercise little or no control. Others arise as a result of the natural stresses involved in living at close quarters in a nonvoluntary relationship with individuals who have evolving and sometimes conflicting needs and desires.

Much valuable preparatory work has already been done on the issue of children's rights. It seems time to try to advance the debate beyond arguments that we ought to take children's independent interests seriously,[40] that the central questions here are theoretical ones about the competing rights of children, parents, and the state,[41] or that evidence is required for sound decision making about children's place.[42] It is also time to attempt to get beyond discussions about

38. Again, see the Appendix. For a theoretical utilitarian account of children's rights, see Houlgate, *Parents and Children.* In his more recent, *Family and State: The Philosophy of Family Law* (Totowa, N.J.: Rowman & Littlefield, 1988), Houlgate discusses the problems inherent in this view and argues for a more consistently utilitarian approach (see chap. 2, esp. n. 2).

39. On this question, see Virginia Held, "The Equal Obligations of Mothers and Fathers," in O'Neill and Ruddick, *Having Children.*

40. See, e.g., Harris, "Political Status"; Robert Young, "In the Interests of Children and Adolescents," in Aiken and LaFollette, *Whose Child?*

41. See, e.g., Kenneth Henley, "The Authority to Educate," and Jeffrey Blustein, "Children and Family Interests," both in O'Neill and Ruddick, *Having Children.*

42. See, e.g., Houlgate, "Children, Paternalism," and Palmeri, "Childhood's End."

specific rights, such as the right to an education, based, for the most part, on conventional moral theory.[43] In short, there is need for reasonably broad exploratory work that takes some basic theoretical points as given, but that combines questioning of other such points with a sense of urgency about making progress on practical problems.

Plan of Attack

A comprehensive look at whether children should have equal rights involves investigation of a wide-ranging and disparate set of issues. Neither basic philosophical issues nor historical evidence nor current social conditions can be ignored. The interdisciplinary nature of the question takes us on a breathtaking roller coaster ride of analysis and synthesis, but the scope and importance of the question demands no less. We ask whether integrating children fully into adult society is desirable or possible under contemporary conditions. If not, under what conditions would it be so? Without answers to these questions, despite the claims of liberationists, I do not believe that we can even begin to argue about equal rights.

The radical argument for equal rights falls into two parts. First, it is argued that justice requires granting children equal rights. Second, it is argued that the consequences of doing so will not be catastrophic. Although these are two separate sets of claims, they are not so unrelated as they at first seem. On the one hand, the argument based on justice relies on certain conceptions of rationality and morality, conceptions that need evaluation within the larger context of human interests. On the other, the place of consequences in moral argument cannot be divorced from our conception of justice, as has so often been the case.[44] I maintain that the argument from justice is much less compelling than proponents of equal rights for children have claimed. Showing why it is not provides us with some reason to think that the consequences of liberation would be worse than they believe; bolstering this conclusion is an array of evidence drawn from historical and psychological studies as well as sociological observations.

43. See, e.g., Victor L. Worsfeld, "Students' Rights: Education in the Just Society," in Aiken and LaFollette, *Whose Child?*

44. For further discussion of their relationship, see chap. 2 and Appendix.

This work is divided into two parts. I start in Part I by inquiring whether justice truly requires children's liberation. In chapter 1 I ask whether equal rights are truly in children's own interest; before we can decide, we must think about the criterion of rationality offered by proponents of equal rights and ask whether it is sufficiently sensitive to capture essential features of a desirable criterion of difference. I then go on in chapter 2 to ask whether and to what extent the interests of others are relevant to the question at hand. Also considered is the question whether the argument for equal rights is compatible with an acceptable moral theory. The answers to both these questions bear upon whether the argument based on justice can stand on its own two feet.

Part II develops the arguments about children's liberation on the basis of consequences. Chapter 3 examines evidence from the social sciences about the consequences of situations such as those that would obtain if children had equal rights. It also considers what light that information might shed on the growth metaphor that most reasonably undergirds the case for equal rights. Systematic speculation about the consequences of liberation is continued in chapters 4 and 5, which look at the areas of living arrangements, education, and work. I investigate arguments about a pair of liberationist responses to claims about harm in chapter 6: first, the institution of agents that supply children with missing capacities, and second, the idea that because childhood is at least in large part socially constructed, it follows that children could rise to meet the challenge of liberation. Finally, in the Conclusion I lay out the overall argument and show how the process of clearing away the attractive nuisance of liberationism helps us see more clearly how to think about dealing with children.

In writing this book, I have had in mind several audiences. First, because it is a contribution to the newly burgeoning field of applied ethics, I hope it will interest moral and political philosophers as well as scholars of other disciplines who are concerned with the family. Second, because it raises questions that everyone who deals with children must face, I hope that it will engage both teachers and parents. To make the work accessible to this second group of readers, I have been at pains to write clearly and avoid jargon; those who find themselves bogged down in the more purely philosophical discussions of chapters 1 and 2 might start instead with chapter 3.

Let me emphasize that this work addresses only one aspect of the problem of children's rights. Proponents of equal rights for children hold that the set of justifiable rights recognized on their behalf cannot include protective rights; I deny that thesis. That is not to argue, however, that the current set of rights we recognize for them is justifiable; indeed, as I suggest in the course of this work, it is probably seriously deficient with respect to the civil rights of teenagers and perhaps in other ways as well. Nor would I want to suggest that I think that the justifiable rights we now recognize for children are adequately protected by contemporary society. On the contrary, it is clear that many children are now neglected and abused. It would be a serious misinterpretation of this work to argue on its basis for the continuation of such behavior or for instituting unjust new restrictions on children.[45]

It would be equally erroneous to suppose that my real concern here is to help middle-class parents make sure that their children continue to land the "best" jobs. My arguments should show that my aim is to press for practices that guarantee for all children the benefits now enjoyed only by the luckiest—practices that, in general, reduce class-based inequality altogether.

I have no illusions about having provided any final word. I hope I have advanced the debate and at least suggested further lines of inquiry. An attempt to apply philosophical insights to pressing social problems may violate the Cartesian tradition of starting from first principles and proceeding to application only when the foundations are firm. Such foundationalism is now coming into question even in theory; it is all the more dubious in the face of urgent practical problems that can benefit from philosophical investigation even now.[46] It is time to venture from the cave to do what we can. Our children are waiting.

45. I am indebted to David Lyons for pointing out the need to emphasize this point.

46. See, e.g., Richard Rorty, *Philosophy and the Mirror of Nature* (Princeton: Princeton University Press, 1979); and Don Herzog, *Without Foundations: Justification in Political Theory* (Ithaca: Cornell University Press, 1985).

PART I

The Argument from Justice

Chapter 1

CHILDREN'S INTERESTS

> Because what we consider to be rational behavior or a rational life plan may be very limited, it is in tension with the principle of accepting the different behavior of other people. One thing, though, is clear—children *do not fail* to make decisions and plans on matters that they know about. What we really think of them is not that they cannot make decisions but rather that they are *incapable* of making *good* ones.
>
> —Ann Palmeri, "Childhood's End: Toward the Liberation of Children"

As we have seen, the radical argument can be divided into two parts. First it is argued that justice requires us to grant children equal rights. Then it is argued that the consequences of doing so will not be harmful. Let us consider the first argument.

The Argument from Justice

The justice-based liberation argument goes like this. Society's treatment of children is based on delusions about how different they are from adults: we are much more alike in the morally relevant ways than most of us would care to admit. In particular, children are in general no less rational or competent than adults. The decisions they make are not, even if different, necessarily worse than the ones we would have made in their stead. Since children are burdened by the special rules that apply to them alone, their desires are frustrated in ways that adults' are not. Because there is no good reason for this state of affairs, simple justice requires us to eliminate such discrimination.

This appealing thesis seems simple and clear, and it extends the trend toward recognizing individuals' rights to choose their own destiny. It is also a useful focus for some overdue reassessment of social arrangements concerning children. Human societies have been going through a period of rapid change, leaving us, perhaps, with ways of life that fail to meet our needs; and now is an especially promising time to rethink our affairs, as research is revealing socially constructed aspects of human life hitherto assumed to be "natural" and hence immutable.[1]

Before we can address the argument from justice directly, we need to clear away a bit of the philosophical underbrush by taking a brief look at the notion of a right.

Rights and Justice

The appeal to justice is couched in terms of rights. Children have a right to be as free as adults; rights are the strongest moral claims we have, and violating a right is unjust.

How might one justify this claim about children's rights? That depends, in part, on what one thinks a right is. Some people believe that rights accrue to us naturally, as *human beings*. Such rights are thought to be embedded in nature, and knowledge of them is accessible to human reason. Theories of this general kind have been influential since the early days of philosophy, when the Greeks first debated whether morality is a creature of nature or of convention. The view that it is a matter of nature—that is, that certain moral truths hold independently of the society in which one lives—has evolved through a variety of shapes in the hands of such thinkers as Plato, Aristotle, Cicero, Aquinas, and Locke, whose work has been so central in American political thought.[2] Rights themselves have come to represent a particularly important concept in moral thinking, the idea that we are owed specific protections—that we are, in fact,

1. We will be looking at human development in much more detail later. It is important, however, to keep in mind that there is, in any case, no good reason to suppose that the allegedly "natural" truly is immutable.

2. See Plato, *The Republic*; Aristotle, *Politics*; Cicero, *De Re Publica*; Thomas Aquinas, *Summa Theologica*; and Locke, *Two Treatises of Government*.

entitled to them.[3] To say that someone is entitled to a given protection is then to say that she is seriously wronged if it is not supplied, and that steps should be taken to rectify the wrong. Not every protection from harm or benefit qualifies as a right, though: in other words, it is not the case that the failure to provide every protection is a matter of injustice that requires social action.[4]

Deciding which claims of entitlements should be viewed as rights is central to natural rights theories; it seems most sensible to attempt to confine the notion of "right" to the most fundamental and general protections we need.[5] None but the crudest natural law theory would hold that rights can be read from nature directly, even though that position would seem to avoid the question of determining what rights we have altogether; to take such a position, however, is to commit the naturalistic fallacy.[6] But disagreements among the proponents of natural rights also raise the epistemological question of the criteria for concluding that we have a given right. More sophisticated theories that suggest a less direct relationship between nature and rights succeed in avoiding the naturalistic fallacy, but only at the cost of raising even more insistent justificatory questions.[7] The less direct the relationship between nature and rights, the more obviously it is mediated by independent moral principles that are themselves in need of defense.

Moral rights are often the subject of controversy. In general, I take it that making claim of right is a matter of arguing for recognition of the priority of a given interest. Which interests are considered

3. I am using "protection" here very broadly to include duties on the part of others (both individuals and states) to refrain from given acts (such as killing me without good reason) and to provide help (such as education).

4. For elucidation of this view, see Richard Wasserstrom, "Rights, Human Rights, and Racial Discrimination," *Journal of Philosophy* 61 (1964), reprinted in *Human Rights*, ed. A. I. Melden (Belmont, Calif.: Wadsworth, 1970).

5. For further discussion of this point, see H. L. A. Hart, "Are There any Natural Rights?" *Philosophical Review* 64, no. 2 (1955), reprinted in Melden, *Human Rights*.

6. The naturalistic fallacy implies that a given state of affairs ought to hold just because it does hold.

7. The justificatory questions are both ontological and epistemological, and they are seriously intertwined: If rights are somehow embedded in the world, why do we have such difficulty agreeing upon them? Why is there so much disagreement about who has which rights? In particular, do some natural rights belong to us by virtue of our humanity? And if so, what criterion of "humanity" are we using, and which rights are we talking about? If not, then which subsets of individuals have which rights? This kind of disagreement undermines the most appealing aspect of natural rights theory—the clarity and universality that are supposed to provide guarantees that other theories cannot.

to have priority will depend to a considerable extent on which moral theory one prefers. Thus a Lockean theory that places the highest value on autonomy, for example, will have somewhat different priorities than a utilitarian one that stresses welfare. The basic divergence of moral theories means that reasonable people may often disagree about whether a given claim constitutes a right or not, although some such claims may be untenable.[8] This work leans toward the view that welfare is fundamental, following John Stuart Mill's analysis of "right" as an especially important moral rule.[9]

The debate about children's rights presupposes that the language of rights is appropriately used in this realm. Some writers have raised questions about the overall emotional, psychological, and moral implications of speaking in terms of rights here, as opposed to using exclusively the language of love, duty, and affection.[10] I will nonetheless be assuming without argument that such talk is both meaningful and useful, even in a generally consequentialist framework.[11]

A moral claim has implications for others. It may require them to refrain from interfering with you, or to act to provide you with some good. It does not, however, guarantee this behavior on the part of others. But if a moral right is enacted into law, the state is supposed to make sure that this forbearance or action on their part is put into

8. Of course, only if we can move beyond complete moral skepticism can we hope to garner any consensus about rights; one can, in any case, recognize the probable limits of agreement without succumbing entirely to such skepticism. Given that neither liberationists nor protectionists are full-fledged skeptics, the status of moral claims requires no particular attention here.

9. See John Stuart Mill, *Utilitarianism*, in *The Utilitarians* (New York: Dolphin, 1961), chap. 5. This view contrasts with Jeremy Bentham's famous rejection of the notion of a moral right in *Anarchical Fallacies*, in *The Works of Jeremy Bentham*, ed. John Bowring (Edinburgh, 1838–1843), 3:221.

10. See, e.g., Francis Schrag, "Children: Their Rights and Needs," in Aiken and La Follette, *Whose Child?*; Loren Lomasky, *Persons, Rights and the Moral Community* (Oxford: Oxford University Press, 1987).

11. On the relationship between utilitarianism and rights, see David Lyons, "Utility and Rights," in *Theories of Rights*, ed. Jeremy Waldron (Oxford: Oxford University Press, 1984); R. G. Frey, ed., *Utility and Rights* (Minneapolis: University of Minnesota Press, 1984); Alan Gewirth, "Can Utilitarianism Justify Any Moral Rights?" in *Human Rights: Essays on Justification and Applications* (Chicago: University of Chicago Press, 1982); Allan Gibbard, "Utilitarianism and Human Rights," and James Fishkin, "Utilitarianism versus Human Rights," both in *Human Rights*, ed. Ellen Frankel Paul, Jeffrey Paul, and Fred D. Miller, Jr. (Oxford: Basil Blackwell, 1984).

practice.[12] Governments themselves are supposed to respect legal rights and are not to override them except under the most unusual and pressing circumstances.[13]

Other important questions about moral rights include whether rights and duties are always correlated, whether or not we could redescribe rights in terms of moral principles without losing important meaning, and whether positive rights (which require action on the part of others for our sake) as well as negative rights (which require them only to refrain from interfering with us) exist. Although all these questions involve interesting debate, my discussion can easily go forward in the absence of a definitive answer to the first.[14] The moral theory used here assumes that such redescription of rights is possible and that positive rights exist.[15]

Rights (both moral and legal) can perform various functions. Michael S. Wald suggests in his discussion of children that we distinguish between "protective" and "liberating" rights.[16] "Protective" rights are divided into rights against the world and rights of protec-

12. Although the distinction between moral and legal rights seems relatively clear, there are questions about both the moral status and the nature of enacted law. Natural law theory, for instance, denies that immoral laws are really laws at all. And are claims about rights merely predictions about what the courts will do? Is a right really a right if the courts do not uphold it? For further discussion, see such classic sources as John Austin, *The Province of Jurisprudence Determined*, (1832) (New York: Noonday Press, 1954); Wesley N. Hohfeld, *Fundamental Legal Conceptions*, (1919) (New Haven: Yale University Press, 1964); Roscoe Pound, *Jurisprudence* (St. Paul, Minn., 1959), vol. 4; and Lon L. Fuller, *The Morality of Law*, rev. ed. (New Haven: Yale University Press, 1969).

13. For discussion of this point, see Ronald Dworkin, *Taking Rights Seriously* (Cambridge: Harvard University Press, 1977), pp. 184–205; and Joel Feinberg, *Social Philosophy*, (Englewood Cliffs, N.J.: Prentice-Hall, 1973), chaps. 4 and 5.

14. For good general treatments of the first issue, as well as moral general issues about rights, see W. D. Ross, *The Right and the Good*, (Oxford: Clarendon, 1930); S. I. Benn and R. S. Peters, *Social Principles and the Democratic State* (London: Allen & Unwin, 1959); and R. B. Brandt, ed. *Social Justice* (Engelwood Cliffs, N.J.: Prentice-Hall, 1962). There are also many more recent good treatments of rights.

15. For an interesting discussion of the first question, see Lomasky, *Persons, Rights*, and Neil MacCormick, *Legal Rights and Social Democracy: Essays in Legal and Political Philosophy* (Oxford: Clarendon, 1982), chap. 8. In general, I am much in sympathy with Patricia White's reluctance to recapitulate lengthy analysis where it fails to advance the argument. In defense of her own similar "rough-hewn notion of rights," she argues: "It is sufficient, though, to allow us to make some headway with the substantive issues. It is thus justified on the principle that one should not load oneself down with vast amounts of conceptual baggage, if one can manage with a conceptual toothbrush": *Beyond Domination: An Essay in the Political Philosophy of Education* (London: Routledge & Kegan Paul, 1983), p. 39. The trees will be grateful, too.

16. Michael S. Wald, "Children's Rights: A Framework for Analysis," *University of California at Davis Law Review*, 12 (Summer 1979): 255–82.

tion from inadequate care; "liberating" rights are divided into rights conferring adult legal status and rights against parents.

Children's rights against the world assert the general importance of providing them with the conditions they need to flourish, although no specific persons are entrusted with this duty. Rights against inadequate care, on the other hand, do assign duties to particular individuals. Both kinds of rights assume that children's incapacities warrant special protection. They protect by providing for goods and services normal adults must procure for themselves. They also protect by frustrating children's desires when they conflict with what we see as their long-term good.[17] Thus, for instance, children are compelled to attend school, regardless of their distaste for it, to prepare to become autonomous adults. Among the main characteristics of such autonomy are the capacities to estimate probable consequences and to resist the lure of immediate gratification in favor of their own welfare and that of others.

"Liberating" rights, on the contrary, open the way for children to act upon their desires. Such rights presuppose that their subjects know what they are doing when they choose to exercise them, even if doing so is risky to themselves or others. Many adult rights are of this kind, unlike the protecting (but limiting) rights we think are appropriate for children. Adults can legally vote, drink, engage in sex, choose medical treatment, and commit themselves to binding contracts concerning work, marital living, and financial arrangements. Lack of liberating rights precludes (or renders illegal) such acts for children.

Legal rights against parents are unique to children: they hold parents responsible for making sure children's needs are met. Thus at present parents are required to feed, clothe, shelter, and educate their offspring. A consistent liberationist position does not, I think, have any room for such a concept.

I suspect that our current distribution of rights—more protective rights for children, more liberating ones for adults—is widely considered appropriate for young children, if not necessarily for middle and late teens. The most radical proponents of equal rights for children, however, for reasons we will see later, assert that no age-based distinctions of this sort at all are justifiable. A somewhat less ex-

17. Elshtain, "Family, Democratic Politics," pp. 261–63.

treme view contends that age should always be considered a "suspect" classification. This legal term means that distinctions based on age are unjustifiable unless they can pass stringent constitutional tests.[18] Since the first position tends to raise the central issues best, we will concentrate on it here.

Proponents of equal rights for children contend that protective rights unjustly limit children's freedom: there are no morally relevant differences between children and adults that can bear the weight of depriving children of the good represented by full adult rights. Liberationists argue for a very weak conception of what is to count as rationality, the capacity to plan for goals; it therefore follows that it is wrong to withhold adult rights from children. I argue, however, that this weak criterion includes children who ought not yet to be running their own lives. A more attractive standard would be the capacity for planning systematic utility-enhancing projects or having a rational life plan. Properly understood, these possibilities make more sense but exclude from equal rights young children and quite possibly most older children as well.

Why is the requirement that we be able to plan systematic utility-enhancing projects likely to exclude many children? The implications of "systematic" and "utility-enhancing" are the key. They suggest a capacity to make solid judgments concerning not just what one wants in the short term but what is good for one in the long run. Moreover, they suggest character traits that enable one not only to know the good but to do it. Liberationists dislike this kind of stronger standard. It would exclude from equal rights not only many children but also some adults. Hence it is unsatisfactory as a sorting principle for equal rights, unless we are prepared to grant equal rights to some children and withhold them from some adults.

An initial reaction to this argument is that it assumes an overly pessimistic conclusion about how adults operate. Liberationists, however, do not need to rely on the inadequacy of all adults: they believe that even one incompetent would make their case, for we do not take away the rights of poorly functioning adults. This claim is not altogether true, of course: if adults fail in a sufficiently spectacular way to protect their own interests, society often does in fact at-

18. Wald, "Children's Rights," p. 267. Only a compelling government interest could justify enshrining such a distinction in law.

tempt to take them in hand. Adults, however, do have a good deal more leeway in this respect than children.

Why is this policy of preventing children from doing things we don't prevent adults from doing reasonable? I argue that their situations differ enough to justify some such differences in treatment. One way in which their situations differ is that we are trying to provide children with a protected period in which they can learn how to manage their life intelligently. Another is that it seems much easier to lay down a solid basis for doing so early in life rather than later. Hence even though it might seem as though we are treating similar cases differently, we are not.

The Liberation Argument

Proponents of equal rights assume that if no morally relevant differences could be found between children and adults, it would be unjust to recognize different rights with respect to them. The form of this appeal to justice is uncontroversial. Treating like cases alike and requiring a morally relevant difference if we are to treat them differently is the essence of formal justice or universalizability.[19] Universalizability is the thesis that if two cases are to be treated differently, it is necessary to show some morally relevant difference between them; it is generally taken as the bedrock of talk about justice. Once people agree about the criteria for morally relevant differences, it would be a gross violation of justice to deny like cases equal treatment.

The rub, of course, is that avoiding such violation merely requires us to provide a good argument that the criterion being used is not the morally relevant one. Although this is not a trivial demand, since some arguments clearly fail to pass muster, often enough there are credible and even good arguments on two or more sides of a contro-

19. For a recent discussion of universalizability, see Nelson Potter and Mark Timmons, eds., *Morality and Universality: Essays on Ethical Universalizability* (Dordrecht: Kluwer, 1985). The concept of justice is generally divided into two parts, formal and material. Formal justice has to do with the form of a justice claim—like cases are treated alike. Material justice argues for specific claims about how a given case should be treated. So material justice might require society to ensure that any jobless person be provided with sufficient help to keep from starving; formal justice would require all the jobless to be provided with such help.

versy. The real focus of debate is the decision about which differences are to count as morally relevant.

Among the criteria that might be considered in a given type of case are such factors as need, ability, achievement, effort, contribution, and utility.[20] Much energy has also been expended on arguing about the relevance of such characteristics as sex and race.[21] Age has recently come under increased scrutiny, as questions have arisen not only about the limits based on it now placed on children but also those endured by old persons.[22]

Once agreement is secured about which differences are morally relevant, further questions may arise about how to treat people who fall into the various classes marked by those differences. Answering those questions is the job of material justice. Thus once we have decided whether age is morally relevant in a given situation, it is considerations of material justice that allow us to determine exactly how individuals in the particular categories should be dealt with.

In this context, the central question about justice is what characteristic(s) should be considered a necessary condition for enjoying adult freedoms. In other words, the main argument arises about the criterion of difference between classes that do and do not have adult rights. Liberationists believe that the right criterion is rationality, which several of them define as some minimal capacity for getting what you want. So if individuals are able to plan projects, they have a right to do so without interference. Children, it is argued, have this

20. See, e.g., Mill, *Utilitarianism*; Nicholas Rescher, *Distributive Justice* (Indianapolis: Bobbs-Merrill, 1966).

21. For further discussion of whether or when sex is a morally relevant difference, see Jane English, ed., *Sex Equality* (Englewood Cliffs, N.J.: Prentice-Hall, 1977), esp. pt. 2; for more recent discussions, see Mary Midgeley, "On Not Being Afraid of Natural Sex Differences," in *Feminist Perspectives in Philosophy*, ed. Morwenna Griffiths and Margaret Whitford (Bloomington: Indiana University Press, 1988), and Alison Jaggar, "Feminist Ethics: Some Issues for the Nineties," *Journal of Social Philosophy* 22 (Spring/Fall 1989): 91–107. For further discussion of whether or when race is a morally relevant difference, see Bernard Boxill, *Blacks and Social Justice*, (Totowa, N.J.: Rowman & Allenheld, 1984); Peter Singer, "Is Racial Discrimination Arbitrary?" *Philosophia* 92 (July 1983): 347–67; and Richard A. Wasserstrom, "Racism, Sexism, and Preferential Treatment: An Approach to the Topics," *UCLA Law Review* 24 (1977): 581–622.

22. For a provocative discussion of the possible moral relevance of age, see Daniel Callahan, *Setting Limits: Medical Goals in an Aging Society* (New York: Simon & Schuster, 1987), and Nora Bell's review, "What Setting Limits May Mean: A Feminist Critique of Daniel Callahan's *Setting Limits*," *Hypatia* 4 (Summer 1989): 168–78.

capacity. Universalizability therefore yields the conclusion that it is wrong to prevent children from living as freely as adults.[23]

Rationality as the Criterion for Equal Rights

Talk about rationality tends to figure largely in discussions of equal rights for children. This is hardly surprising, given the importance attributed to rationality in the history of Western thought.[24] What *is* surprising is the ambivalence demonstrated by proponents of equal rights about its proper role here. In particular, although they tend to base their argument on the claim that rationality is the morally relevant difference upon which access to adult rights should be based, they often seem unsure of its nature or value.

We know well enough that there is a great deal of disagreement about the precise definition of rationality.[25] In an attempt to undermine appeal to anything but the most minimal notion of rationality, for example, the liberationist Bob Franklin points out the many possibilities here. Some have thought that rationality is entailed by a given IQ level, or by the ability to infer consequences of choices. Others emphasize thoughts and actions based on empirical knowledge and logic. Given these differences, he asks, how do we justify the choice of any given definition as a basis for granting rights?[26]

This question should not be the end of the line. Despite much argument on the part of philosophers and others, it seems to me that most of us have a rough working definition of what we mean by the concept. At its core is the notion that we need good reasons for

23. See, e.g., Harris, "Political Status of Children,"; Cohen, *Equal Rights for Children*.

24. See, e.g., Nicholas Rescher, *Rationality* (Oxford: Clarendon, 1988): "The ancients saw man as 'the rational animal,' set apart from other creatures by capacities for speech and deliberation. Under the precedent of Greek philosophy, Western thinkers have generally deemed the use of thought for the guidance of our proceedings to be at once the glory and the duty of *Homo sapiens*" (p. 1). The role of reason in morality has been especially emphasized from Plato on down.

25. See, e.g., Max Black, "Ambiguities of Rationality," in *Naturalism and Rationality*, ed. Newton Garver and Peter H. Hare (Buffalo, N.Y.: Prometheus, 1986). For a particularly useful discussion of various aspects of the concept, see Mario Bunge, "Seven Desiderata for Rationality," in *Rationality: The Critical View*, ed. Joseph Agassi and Ian Charles Jarvie (The Hague: Martinus Nijhoff, 1987). For other recent work on rationality see Rescher, *Rationality*; and Martin Tamny and K. D. Irani, eds., *Rationality in Thought and Action* (Greenwich, Conn.: Greenwood, 1986).

26. Bob Franklin, *The Rights of Children* (Oxford: Basil Blackwell, 1986), p. 28.

believing and acting. Furthermore, rational action involves some awareness of alternative courses of action together with a judgment about which are better and which worse. Definitions of rationality can be more or less demanding with respect to thoroughness, of course, as well as with respect to the moral quality of ends. But the necessity for ongoing debate about such matters needn't preclude adopting some such approach as the one described here. What matters is not the elaboration of some Platonic form of rationality but deciding what it should take to qualify for adult rights.

Liberationists favor weak definitions of reason. In fact, Howard Cohen, because he denies the necessity for any distinction between the rights of children and those of adults, cannot, strictly speaking, require of children any reasoning ability at all.[27] He believes that their desire to make choices would not, in general, outstrip their developing competence at using them well. What at first appears to be an argument for equal rights based on justice turns out to depend in a fundamental way upon a utilitarian judgment, the judgment that the possible harm would not outweigh the benefits provided by those rights.

John Harris, more typically—and somewhat more plausibly—suggests that a sufficient criterion for equal rights would be having "a life to lead." Having such a life means "to have decisions and plans to make and things to do, it is to be aware of doing it all, to understand roughly what doing it all involves and to value the whole enterprise." This position sounds quite demanding until he fleshes it out somewhat more by saying that it would be important to be able to "see the connection between action (and inaction) and consequence, and [to have] some rudimentary understanding of the nature of consequences." A requirement of this sort turns out, in his view, to entail only awareness of elementary survival facts, such as that "fire burns, knives and broken glass cut, roads are dangerous, not everything can be safely eaten and that these things hold for others too."[28] So the position to be evaluated seems to be that once children are capable of avoiding the obvious physical dangers, they should be left free to plan their lives, just as adults are. It is important to keep in mind here just what this position implies in reality. It implies,

27. Cohen, *Equal Rights for Children*, p. viii.
28. Harris, "Political Status of Children," p. 48.

among other things, that a six-year-old's announcement that she's not going to school today (or ever) should be respected. Isn't that a wildly implausible stand?

What could be said in its favor? Insofar as it is more demanding than Cohen's minimalist approach, it is likely to lead to less harm. Yet it is still weak enough to constitute an attractive escape from the very real difficulties inherent in making certain kinds of distinctions, difficulties that have in the past helped to rationalize serious injustice. The human track record with respect to such judgments is shameful: sex, color, and some other clearly irrelevant characteristics have all too often been used to deny people basic rights. Given this history, the appeal of erring on the side of generosity is understandable. It is reinforced by the general problem of defining boundaries: any given location may appear arbitrary and therefore vulnerable to slippery-slope arguments. This consideration is especially alluring in the case at hand, as children's gradual development over time makes extremely difficult the exact distinctions liberationists hold to be essential when basic rights are at issue. So there seem to be compelling reasons for adhering to the least demanding standard: only thus can the unjust inconsistent treatment of children and adults be avoided.

Nevertheless, the costs of retreating to such a weak criterion of rationality are so great that they undermine the case for liberation (as I will show in Part II). In general, refusing to make distinctions can cause us to treat unlike cases alike, ignoring differing needs, capacities, and desires. Consider the consequences for women if society grants equal rights to fetuses: most abortions would unjustifiably be prohibited. In general, then, despite the advantages of adopting more inclusive standards, we cannot be blind to the possibly overridingly bad consequences of doing so. The details of the particular question at hand ought to determine which path is chosen. Unlike the liberationists, I believe not only that there is a great deal to lose by opting for a low standard here but that we are able to justify and apply a more demanding one. In short, in some situations, such as this one, we must resist the charms of generosity and return to the hard labor of making distinctions trusting democratic discussion to protect against oppression.

At issue here is the question of minimum qualitative standards in decision making. Let us reflect for a moment on some of the differences between more or less competent decisions. A more competent decision about ends reflects some understanding of the variety of possible ends, as well as their probable consequences. Even if we doubt the possibility or wisdom of evaluating ends in terms of prudence or morality, a case can be made for emphasizing the importance of being aware of a wide range of possibilities before one chooses.[29] Such awareness is, after all, one of the central values of the kind of liberal moral theory most likely to undergird the argument for equal rights. Decisions about means require the same kind of awareness of alternative routes between one's starting position and a given end.

Such knowledge about the world as these inferences require is accumulated only gradually (as Hume reminds us), so that young children are less likely to be well equipped with it than people with more experience.[30] And general background knowledge is critical to intelligent behavior, as even those parents blessed with unusually bright children can observe. A course of action that looks perfectly reasonable given an inaccurate set of premises becomes comically inept given more accurate ones. The plans of even quite mature adolescents provide their parents with many a good laugh; were they to be carried out, however, this amusement would in some cases turn to horror. What if your fourteen-year-old daughter decided to celebrate Halloween by going trick-or-treating as a nudist?

Even college-age students can be deficient in background knowledge to a worrisome degree, though they generally are noticeably better provisioned than younger teens.[31] Howard Kahane emphasizes how important it is for them (and by extension for younger children) to learn that reasoning validly from premises to conclusions is not enough.[32] What you already believe determines how well you can evaluate new information: "Even the most brilliant person cannot successfully evaluate everyday rhetoric without bringing to bear sufficient relevant background information, and that is why the need to

29. I will be arguing shortly for the possibility and the desirability of some such judgments.

30. David Hume, *An Enquiry Concerning Human Understanding* (Oxford: Clarendon, 1748), sec. IV, pt. 1.

31. I argue in chap. 2 that such a difference in degree *is* morally relevant here.

32. In response to the liberationist "Aha!" in response to this point, it seems worth noting that this state of affairs could plausibly be attributed to American adolescents' general immaturity and inadequate education as compared to, say, the average European.

have accurate background beliefs should be emphasized at least as much as the rules of validity so dear to logicians."[33] According to Jean Piaget, the intellectual tools for reasoning logically are acquired around the age of puberty.[34] If he is right, then if background knowledge were not so important, it might be quite appropriate to recognize equal rights for children at the age of twelve or thirteen. But background knowledge is crucial, and in anything like the present circumstances it is hard to picture children acquiring enough of it to manage their lives well much before their late teens. When we imagine the various possible degrees of competence in choosing means and ends, we see a vast range of levels of accuracy in conceptions of the whole interlocking network of cause and effect created by sequences of decision making over the course of time. The differences in function these levels represent may be a matter of degree, but the degrees are of such magnitude that for all practical purposes they constitute differences in kind.

Surely these points should also help lay to rest worries about the gray area where individual judgment plays such a large role in defining rational behavior. There will undoubtedly always be room for disagreement about whether some choices are wise, but it doesn't follow that there are no guidelines for evaluating decision making. Such considerations should help to show why the weak criteria for rights espoused by liberationists won't do; there are others, as well. Harris seems to equate his notion of children's "having a life to lead" with having the capacity for planning systematic utility-enhancing projects.[35] The two seem to me to be quite different, however; the requirements for the latter would surely require far more of a child than the mere ability to avoid obvious physical threats.[36] It would, in fact, entail knowing a great deal more about the workings of the world than the average five- or even ten-year-old.

Why would fixing on the capacity for planning systematic utility-enhancing projects as the relevant criterion for equal rights change the picture so much? Background knowledge is only the beginning.

33. Howard Kahane, *Logic and Contemporary Rhetoric: The Use of Reason in Everyday Life*, instructor's manual (Belmont, Calif.: Wadsworth, 1988), p. vi.

34. See chap. 2 for a description.

35. Harris, "Political Status of Children," p. 41.

36. One might well question Harris's minimal criterion here, even on its own grounds. Contemporary life is full of subtle threats that it would be well beyond most children to discern or deal with; why discount them just because they are not so immediate as the kind of threat he mentions?

The decision to bake up a pan of brownies after school, for instance, constitutes a utility-enhancing project: one knows how to make brownies and one knows that one likes them.

It is undeniable that children routinely plan and successfully carry out projects of this sort. But does a series of such projects constitute a truly *systematic* approach to *utility enhancement*? The answer is clearly negative, on two counts. First, even if utility is defined only with an eye to our own pleasure, it must involve more than short-term gratification; enlightened self-interest, in fact. This point quickly leads to the second, that doing what is in our interest rather than what is immediately gratifying requires us to put our various goals into a broader context. So if a child bakes brownies every day and eats half the pan, she is not engaged in systematic utility enhancement.

In other words, a more sophisticated view of utility enhancement immediately suggests something like having a rational life plan, a criterion for equal rights proposed by Ann Palmeri. Now although Palmeri herself leaves us quite in the dark about what she means, the phrase hints at something rather more demanding than the criteria proposed by other liberationists, something more thought out and thorough, including perhaps some moral component.[37]

This notion presumably is borrowed from John Rawls, who says that we are "to suppose . . . that each individual has a rational plan of life drawn up subject to the conditions that confront him. This plan is designed to permit the harmonious satisfaction of his interests. It schedules activities so that various desires can be fulfilled without interference. It is arrived at by rejecting other plans that are either less likely to succeed or do not provide for such an inclusive attainment of aims." Rawls then goes on to argue, as will I, that although people's plans may have different ends, any such plan will require certain goods he describes as "primary goods." He is concerned mainly, however, with what he calls "natural goods," such as intelligence and health, and "social goods" that are supplied by society, such as wealth and opportunity.[38] I concentrate instead on individual characteristics that, although based on natural factors, develop as a result of personal and social effort.

What such primary goods might be implied by this notion of a

37. Palmeri, "Childhood's End," p. 112.

38. Rawls, *Theory of Justice*, p. 61. Rawls's "natural goods" seem to me also to depend significantly on personal effort and social support.

rational life plan? It would surely have to assume considerable competence at instrumental reasoning; it must also assume a capacity for evaluating ends and not just in terms of immediate pleasure. Evaluating ends requires both routine checks for coherence with respect to ends and the capacity to judge some ends to be more important than others. Thus the prerequisites for being able to plan systematic utility-enhancing projects and having a rational life plan look very much alike. Any difference between them might most plausibly be seen as a matter of degree, with a rational life plan requiring a better-organized and more comprehensive approach.

Before going any further here, it is important to notice that liberationists stress *capacities* much more than *actions:* they talk about the capacity for instrumental reasoning or the capacity for planning systematic utility-enhancing projects. Conspicuously lacking in emphasis is the carrying out of plans. Why is that? Tests of rational behavior rather than rational plans, they assert, would fail to differentiate adequately between children and adults: members of both classes would fail to pass any action-based test. Cohen suggests that we excuse adults who do not behave sensibly, without being tempted to withdraw their rights, by attributing their failures to circumstances beyond their control or to a conscious choice not to do so, whereas children are held to lack the ability to behave sensibly even when they want to.[39] He provides no real evidence for his assertion, but is relieved of the need to do so by his view that even if children did lack the ability to behave sensibly and adults had that ability, that difference would not be morally relevant. Cohen, as we shall see later, attempts to justify this unpromising claim by positing child agents who supply children with the necessary abilities.

Even if child agents could help children plan intelligently, however, they would be unable to make them behave intelligently. There is simply more to this question than Cohen is prepared to recognize. The capacity to make plans is one thing; acting on them is another. The first involves mainly cognitive capacities; the second, mainly character traits. Cognitive capacities help us figure out what to do, character traits are necessary to help us to do it.[40] Since planning, by

39. Cohen, *Equal Rights for Children*, p. 47.

40. This is a somewhat inaccurate description of the situation but it will do as a rough approximation for now. Once we add a moral dimension to this picture, which so far includes only prudence, the dichotomy will break down still further.

itself, is not a particularly valuable endeavor, it is hard to see why it should be regarded as triggering rights unless it is accompanied by appropriate action. Children's capacity for planning, if we assume for the sake of argument that it is on a par with that of adults, wouldn't therefore be a very persuasive reason for recognizing equal rights for them. What is required in addition is the character traits that enable children to *carry out* their plans. Even if some adults have such weak characters that they are relatively lacking in the ability to act on their plans, that is not, as I will argue later, sufficient reason to ask less of children. So the ability to carry out systematic utility-enhancing projects or having a life plan requires both the cognitive capacity to judge what is in one's own interest and the character traits necessary to act on it. Let us now go on to consider those qualities.

To say that *X* is in my interest is simply to assert that it is connected in some important way with my welfare, with my good. I may or may not desire the state of affairs in question. Some that are intrinsically unpleasant—visits to the dentist, for instance—may nonetheless be generally in my interest. In such cases we can surely say, however, that if we are rational we must recognize *X*'s value.

Having the capacity to plan systematic utility-enhancing projects or having a rational life plan assumes that it is possible to make good judgments about interests. Liberationists often express uneasiness about the soundness of such judgments, especially judgments about the interests of others. This uneasiness is, I think, a major source of their inclination toward weaker rather than more demanding conceptions of how to run a life. They also place a very high value on freedom, and believe that, if we were consistent, the diversity of life plans we respect for adults would entail our acceptance of children's life plans also. In other words, given the same life plan, we might unjustifiably prevent a child from going ahead while leaving an adult free to do so.

There is some tension between the views that judgments about interests are dubious and that freedom is the primary value, as Ronald Dworkin notes.[41] Furthermore, since proponents of equal

41. See Dworkin, "Liberalism."

rights tend to alternate between them, it is often hard to pin down their argument satisfactorily.[42]

Interests

Most people believe that there are better and worse ways of life. This is not to say, like Aristotle, that there is one best way of life. On the contrary, there are, many worthwhile and satisfying pursuits. Some choices, however, are likely to lead to frustration and unhappiness, and if we make too many of them, we will be quite miserable. Skeptics enjoy denying these claims, but it is impossible to live as if they weren't true. Even liberationists assume that there are better and worse ways of life, otherwise they would not be arguing that the free life is better. So the real issue here is what makes for a better life.

Some skeptics save their ammunition instead for the claim that we can *know* anything about better and worse ways of life. The world is so complicated, they say, that judgments about our interests are simply unreliable. It is undeniable that certainty about interests (or almost anything else) is virtually unobtainable. A course of action that could have been expected to be disastrous may have delightful consequences; the converse is also true. Likewise, a decision that didn't seem particularly significant might instead be a turning point. Yet I know that there are no fewer than five things I could do right now that would most probably begin to unravel my life in a destructive way, and anybody with some experience of the world could truthfully say the same. The least we can do for our children is to teach them about such matters.

Proof of these claims would take us far afield. Here I want simply to sketch out a reminder of how we make judgments about interests and why we can be reasonably confident about them.

Reasoning about interests involves our making instrumental judgments about how to reach goals and our evaluating goals in terms of needs and desires. As we have already seen, the relevant instrumental judgments require dispassionate assessments of how the world is

42. These two views are, strictly speaking, incompatible (see ibid.). Proponents of equal rights, perhaps because they are aware of this fact, usually avoid overt skepticism; their position nonetheless draws substantial strength from it.

and what makes it tick. Individuals with more experience and a fuller and more accurate understanding of the physical world and human psychology are more likely to make successful judgments about how to get to *B* from *A*. In particular, those who are able to separate what they wish were true from what really is true will reach their goals more certainly than those who do not. Thus we can be good or bad at these tasks.

We can make these judgments in our own case or in the case of others, if we are more experienced and clearheaded than they are, and can, by virtue of these facts, better predict the consequences of their acts. Thus wishful thinking may prevent a woman from seeing that a second child, unwanted by her husband, is likely to destroy the marriage. Inaccurate perceptions of the demands of a job may lead another to misallocate energy: university professors who enjoy teaching, for instance, sometimes fail to devote enough time to research. Likewise, a combination of wishful thinking and ignorance can lead to disastrous political decisions, as when Jimmy Carter gave asylum to the shah of Iran.

Of course, judgments of this sort cannot be certain: a husband's attitude may change, a short article whipped out at the last moment may become a classic, Iranian moderates might have gained the upper hand. It is unwise, however, to count on such unlikely developments if the outcome is important to us. The extent to which we can rationally do so will depend on our nature, too: some people are gamblers, others are not. But if I really don't wish to get pregnant, it is foolish to be whimsical about contraception. We do not need certainty to live sensibly; nor does living sensibly necessarily entail any one particular way of life. What is needed is realistic assessments of the likely consequences of given acts; only then can we decide whether they are consonant with our considered values. Although there is a lot of leeway in the values we can have and still live a good life, such a life does assume some common values because of how the world is.

Some liberationists argue that protectionists tend to overestimate the degree to which humans depend on such rational decision making. Bob Franklin, for example, admits: "I consider myself to be a fairly cautious, thoughtful person who tries to assess the likely outcome and consequences of my decisions . . . but I am none the less constantly aware of how few of my decisions derive from rational considerations. In confessing this I do not feel condemned to solitude."[43] I take it that he is saying two things here. First, he often acts without much conscious deliberation; second, he often chooses immediate gratification despite its probable negative impact on his interests.

In response to the first claim, I would argue that acting without much conscious deliberation is not necessarily irrational. On the one hand, many of our choices don't really matter: deciding to walk on the left rather than right side of the street or having lettuce rather than carrots is inconsequential and it would be irrational to agonize over it. On the other hand, we can behave rationally even when we are unaware of making any decision at all because we develop efficient routines that get us through the day without much thought. Otherwise, we would be overwhelmed by the constant need to make decisions. To take just one example: suppose you decide that you need three hours of aerobic activity every week and that it fits into your schedule best on Tuesday, Thursday, and Saturday at 4:30 P.M. Consequently, on any given Tuesday, you don't need to rethink the matter: you just go do it.

Franklin's second claim, that he quite often prefers immediate gratification to furthering his interests, can be answered in a variety of appropriate ways. I am tempted to say that succumbing to this temptation is sometimes reasonable: the interest in question may be trivial, or perhaps we choose wisely sufficiently often to permit us some latitude. If, for example, my income and retirement plan are adequate, I can splurge on little luxuries even if it would be better to put away more money for retirement. Or if I eat sensibly most of the time, there is nothing wrong with having a slice of fudge cake. It is, in fact, perfectly rational to indulge in these pleasures under such circumstances.

If, however, Franklin has in mind more seriously detrimental patterns of behavior, this conclusion does not hold. It is undeniable that a few people regularly disregard their own interests in destructive ways, and others do so less frequently. This kind of behavior, however, is not so universal as Franklin wants us to suppose: if it were, society could hardly function. Furthermore, even were this the case, that would not be grounds for the kind of fatalism to which he seems resigned, as I will argue shortly.

43. Franklin, *Rights of Children*, p. 30.

I have asserted that judging interests requires of us knowledge about the world and the will to act upon it. In addition, we must understand whatever common prerequisites there may be for human well-being, as well as what a given individual needs. Our knowledge of the prerequisites is a function of our general sophistication about human psychology; our knowledge of what someone needs depends on how well we know the specific person. It would be disingenuous to believe that we are completely in the dark about what humans need in general. Observation and experience, as well as literature, are fruitful sources of knowledge. The better we know ourselves, the sounder our judgments about our interests; the same is true of our judgments of others.

Liberal theorists, including liberationists, have a strong tendency to privilege individuals' judgments about their own interests. They have two basic reasons for doing so.[44] One is their belief that you are likely to know yourself better than anybody else does. As I have suggested, however, there clearly are whole classes of exceptions to that rule: some people may be poorly informed about the world, and others' opinions about themselves may be clouded by wishful thinking. In those cases we can quite often make better judgments about them than they can. College advisers, for instance, can often recognize well before their first-year pre-meds themselves who among them is not really cut out for a life in science.

The second reason liberals are wary of judging the interests of others is that doing so is often a prelude to forcing them to do what you think is in their best interest. To do so would be incompatible with the kind of respect for persons entailed by liberal theory. To the extent that we value liberty, caution is warranted here. It is important not to confuse the legitimacy of the judgment with that of any ensuing coercion, however.[45]

The extent to which psychological rather than philosophical considerations undergird this liberal position is an interesting question. My suspicion is that both the inclination to privilege individuals'

44. Mill, as we shall see in chap. 6, argues that making your own decisions is intrinsically valuable; he also believes that practice (even if it doesn't always lead to the greatest utility in a particular case) enhances our decision-making ability and results in the overall greatest utility. But given his distinction between children and adults, he must be depending on something like the statistical argument I rely on.

45. Nor should we accept as obvious the view that such coercion would never be justified. For discussion of this issue, see Joel Feinberg, *Harm to Self* (Oxford: Oxford University Press, 1986). See also n. 52 below.

assessments of their own interests and the overriding valuation of freedom could be traced to the male concerns that have so overwhelmingly been reflected in philosophy as a whole and therefore by moral and political philosophy in particular. If the findings and speculation of such writers as Nancy Chodorow and Carol Gilligan can be taken seriously, one might contend that the thrust of the whole liberationist argument issues from the need for separation and independence so integral to current patterns of male development.[46] Pursuing this line of reasoning would quickly take us into murky waters, however, and as the case against liberation can be made without any such assumptions, this aspect of the topic can safely be left for another day.

It does seem worth considering somewhat more at length the narrower question of assumptions about our knowledge of others' interests, though. What we philosophers take for granted as we argue (as opposed to what we consider in need of justification) depends to a considerable extent on our own background and experiences. To the extent that women pay more careful attention to other persons and to relationships between them, they will more often be in a position to fulfill at least one of the prerequisites for knowing what is in another's interest, knowing that person well. My sense is that women are therefore less reluctant to make such judgments, and that when the other prerequisites are met, they do so very accurately. If there were more women philosophers, the position espoused by Cohen (that we can't know much about the interests of others) would quite likely be considered even more questionable than it is now.

Because liberationists tend to buy this skeptical approach to interests, I contend that they are unrealistic about both adults' background knowledge of the world and their disposition to act intelligently. This is not to say that many adults could not do much better with respect to both these characteristics, but it is to say that some do quite well most of the time, and many do so some of the time. Likewise, this skepticism tends to cause liberationists to accept courses of action that reveal children's uninformed and ill-thought-out judgments as valid choices. The conjunction of these tendencies

46. See Nancy Chodorow, *The Reproduction of Mothering: Psychoanalysis and the Sociology of Gender* (Berkeley: University of California Press, 1978), and Carol Gilligan, *In a Different Voice* (Cambridge: Harvard University Press, 1982).

causes proponents of equal rights to underestimate the difference between most children and most adults.

Children's Interests

Cohen denies that we can know much about children's interests. As we have seen, he supports this claim by doubting that we can know much about *anybody's* interests. We have also seen, however, that there are some reasons for thinking that this general claim is implausible: we can, on the contrary, know a good deal about our own interests and, in some cases, those of others. That being the case, grownups are very often in a position to be able to make sound judgments about children's interests.

First, adults meet the conditions for being able to make good judgments about interests in general: they can be expected to have an adequate store of background knowledge about human psychology and the world, together with the requisite reasoning capacity. Second, good parents and teachers know their children well and are therefore in a position to know what they, as specific individuals, might need. Third, good parents and teachers care about the children entrusted to them so that they will make the effort to judge wisely and to act on those judgments. Now bad parents or teachers may be lacking in any of these respects. That is, they may lack background knowledge or reasoning capacity, they may not pay enough attention to a child, or they may not care enough to follow through on those judgments.

Does it follow that adults should abdicate decision-making responsibility with respect to children, as proponents of equal rights suggest? I don't think that would make sense. If only some parents fail their children in these ways, whereas most can and do guide them quite intelligently, then it would be irrational to alter the good situation of the majority in order to accommodate the worse-placed minority, especially when some of their problems stem from the same kind of inattention that would be promoted by the alleged remedy.

This conclusion is, I think, obscured by liberationists' assumption that the average child would do fine if equal rights were granted. They therefore focus on the worst-case scenario of the status quo, the case of children who are psychologically or physically abused by an ignorant, irresponsible, or sadistic adult. Statistics suggest that substantial numbers of children fall into this category. It is also well known that social responses to this problem have not been very satisfactory, partly because of a bias on the part of the law toward keeping children with their biological parents and partly because of a desire to spend as little money as possible on social needs of this sort. The solution to this problem is therefore fairly obvious, even if the practical details of removing a child from a problem home will often be difficult. If the general solution to this kind of problem is so clear, doesn't that undermine one of the main justifications for liberating children?[47] Furthermore, liberationists seem to think that wiser and more humane social services are beyond our reach, so they argue for letting children leave home. But if they are in despair about the possibility of better social services, isn't it contradictory to count on a warm reception for these children out in society at large?

So it seems to me that this appeal to the worst-off children to justify the general liberation of children fails. The call for liberation must therefore rest upon the claim that equal rights would benefit the average child. And it is just this contention that I argue against. Before I do so, however, it is important to explore somewhat further the reasons why we ought to have confidence in adults' ability to guide children's development. First, adults' experience helps them see what characteristics children need to develop if they are to live well. Second, there is such substantial consensus about those characteristics that diversity of values does not undermine the crucial importance of certain basic principles of action. Third, consideration of the issues would, in any case, lead reasonable people to agree to the importance of those basic principles, so that a case can be made for encouraging adults who deal with children to commit themselves to them even if they do not now do so.

In other words, the case for adults' ability to make judgments about children is strengthened by the kinds of decisions that are most often in question. Although both children and grownups must

47. The general solutions I have in mind are (1) removing the bias toward biological parents and (2) willingness to spend more money on social services designed to prevent such problems in the first place, such as education. The most comprehensive solution obviously involves major social reorganization of a sort not likely to occur soon, such as ensuring full employment and child care. But even the less demanding approaches I have suggested would go far toward improving these children's lives.

make many decisions in the course of each day, the nature and scope of the decisions the two groups make are rather different: a much larger percentage of the decisions children make are momentous in their consequences for the children's later life and at the same time revolve about values that ought to be regarded as uncontroversial.

What I mean is this. Adults quite often face difficult and important decisions: Where should I live? What kind of work would be best? Should I marry? This person? What about having a child? And so forth. They are operating, however, from a base of relatively settled questions—questions about who they are and what they can do. They have seen and experienced some of the temptations and pitfalls of life and are thus well placed to advise and guide children for whom these pitfalls remain a serious threat.

To the extent that children are as yet unformed, they have the potential to develop in a variety of ways, some much less promising of future well-being than others. Especially important to them is a certain class of skills, habits, and goals that play a large role in determining what choices will later be open to them as well as the satisfaction they will enjoy in life. I focus here on habits that help us get what we want, habits I call "enabling virtues"—such as rationality, hard work, and the desire for excellence. Some people believe that these traits are intrinsically valuable. I would not rule out their intrinsic value, but my emphasis here is only on their instrumental value.

Take reason, for instance. Even the bare instrumental conception of reason already described is essential if we are to achieve our goals: the best will in the world is powerless without reason. Likewise, common sense suggests that we will more probably achieve our goals if we work hard and strive for excellence. This is not to say that hard work is the only value, or that there are not appropriate limits to work, but only that it would be difficult to come up with a list of achievements in which hard work did not figure at some point. Nor does it seem that unfocused effort is often rewarded: a clear conception of one's goal coupled with consistent effort toward it appears to be a key to success in any endeavor. Not only does my own personal experience bear out this claim, but there is increasing evidence of its validity. Although accounts of the logic of discovery in science sometimes point out the importance of serendipitous findings, for example, they emphasize the hard work and persistence that laid the groundwork that made the findings possible. Benjamin Bloom documents this fact over and over.[48]

Now, except to the lucky few, these characteristics come neither easily nor naturally. Some never develop them to an adequate degree: most of us can point to friends or acquaintances whose ambitions are repeatedly frustrated by their deficient enabling virtues. In fact, if a sensible fairy godmother had to decide whether to give a child a solid set of enabling virtues or a fortune, she would choose the former.[49] Without such traits, her godchild is unlikely ever to experience the satisfaction that comes of excellence.

The value of these enabling virtues seems obvious; yet they often get bad press. If such criticism is tenable, that would, of course, undermine the case I am making for transmitting them to children even at the cost of some loss of freedom. I suspect that the main objection to such virtues stems from their unfortunate association with "middle-class values." This association is especially irritating to the liberal and left-wing critics of society who find the possibility of equal rights for children so appealing.

The bourgeois way of life is typically characterized as greedy, competitive, prudish. Yet it seems to me that a good deal of what critics have rightly objected to arises from the ends to which members of the bourgeoisie have historically devoted themselves, such as making money no matter what the cost to others or attempting to buy the obedience of family members. The means to those ends, however, enabling virtues, are to a large extent separable from them; we need not, for example, dedicate hard work and self-discipline to moneymaking or keeping up with the Joneses—we can apply them instead to social reform, as well as to unremunerative but worthwhile pursuits such as ballet and philosophy.

Social critics have, I think, often tarred means and ends with the same brush. It is easy to see how this happens, as means do tend to lose their distinctiveness in the real world, especially when our perception is clouded by the emotions aroused by injustice. We sometimes fail to notice, however, that by throwing out means along with ends, we deprive ourselves of the only tools available for achieving goals: very little can be attained without them.

48. Benjamin Bloom, *Developing Talent in Young People* (New York: Ballantine, 1985).

49. I would want to add others, such as caring and intelligence.

In sum, enabling virtues are valuable traits, necessary for the achievement of desirable goals. Achieving such goals is arguably one of the major components of a good and satisfying life.[50] By themselves, however, enabling virtues can be dangerous because they can be coupled with evil ends, so, helping children develop them is only part of our educational task.

I have provided neither a complete list of enabling virtues nor anything but the bare bones of an argument for them: fleshing out the details of this position will have to wait until the more general issues have been clarified and resolved. What I want to suggest here, though, is the importance of the underlying core virtue of self-control. By "self-control" I mean the capacity to resist temptations that interfere with a previously set goal.

Consider the many demands of life, demands that we satisfy in part by developing mindless routines and in part by the conscious subordination of our immediate desires to the acts necessitated by our goals. Each day brings with it the need to get out of a warm bed, eat a healthy breakfast, and get at the awaiting tasks. These tasks include not just short-term jobs such as changing diapers or walking through frozen streets to a bus stop, but those that must be seen to if we are to manage our lives efficiently, such as having clean, presentable clothes, making sure that there is gas in a car, and visiting the dentist once in a while. The less control we have over our lives because of poverty or prejudice, or the more ambitious we are, the more such projects eat into the discretionary portions of our lives. Thus it is evident that some measure of self-control is an essential accompaniment of virtually everybody's life: even in the absence of the additional demands of morality, none of us is able to enjoy the carefree life of a beloved domestic cat.

So although self-control is by no means the only good, conflicts between it and other goods will often have to be resolved in its favor. Only by emphasizing self-control can we avoid the unappealing prospect of a society peopled by individuals seriously lacking in that characteristic. Not only would this state of affairs lead to much personal frustration and misery, but the initial chaos would most likely

50. This rather Aristotelian conception of the good life is one to which many thoughtful individuals have come and is to be contrasted primarily with the image of Polynesian languor, which depends on a more forgiving environment than the one with which most of us must contend.

result in the imposition of authoritarian controls to maintain a semblance of order. With self-control, we can lay down the basis for the enabling virtues necessary if people are both to pursue their own enlightened self-interest and to further the welfare of others.

It would be a mistake to equate my plea for this kind of self-control with a demand for the kind of tight-lipped, prudish narrow-mindedness that finds intrinsic value in deprivation and suffering. Nothing could be further from what I have in mind. Any such leap would presuppose a false dilemma that forces us to choose between total freedom and total control. Arguing for the instrumental (not intrinsic) value of self-control makes it possible to limit the scope of its requirements and show why any particular call for it is justified.

It would be equally confused to suppose that this emphasis on self-control entails any of a number of other undesirable things, such as rigidity of outlook, lack of creativity, unthinking submission to authority, or a cold, perfectionistic childrearing methodology. Conflating self-control with rigidity or lack of creativity is a common error on the part of those who fail to understand that excellence arises out of discipline, not in spite of it.[51] Likewise, unthinking submission to authority is surely at least independent of, if not diametrically opposed to, self-control in adults.[52] Finally, there is no reason at all to assume that setting high standards for a child is incompatible with warmth and supportiveness: on the contrary, it is likely that this combination will, in general, be the most effective approach to childrearing.[53]

One might object, nonetheless, that self-control is not necessarily the fundamental virtue that I have suggested it is. First, self-control may itself depend on some still more basic condition(s) or trait(s). Second, children vary and some may naturally be endowed with substantial self-control. Third, different cultures may neither need nor value self-control or the virtues to which it can lead.

There is some truth to all these claims. It may well be that self-control can develop only in certain circumstances. If so, this circumstance would not undermine my emphasis on self-control itself: learning more about how to help individuals control themselves is

51. For an excellent discussion of this matter, see Paul Nash, *Authority and Freedom in Education* (New York: Wiley, 1966); also Bloom; *Developing Talent.*

52. This is one respect in which children and adults appear to differ profoundly.

53. This issue will be looked at in more detail in chap. 3.

an empirical matter appropriately left to child psychologists. It is also true that some children need less help in developing self-control than others. This doesn't mean that self-control is less important for them, but only that their parents and teachers are free to concentrate on other aspects of their progress. Finally, self-control may be more or less critical, depending on one's culture.

This last claim requires elaboration. One issue is that self-control is less crucial where other characteristics help individuals achieve the ends to which self-control is conducive; the other is that where the relevant ends are less valued, the means become less so as well. It is easy to see that if you live in a world where achievement is considered relatively unimportant, then self-control will become unimportant, too. It's also true that if you live in a world of diminished needs or abundant resources, then prudent or moral behavior will also require less self-control. You will also need less control if your society encourages individuals to develop the caring side of their personality so that you are naturally inclined to help others.

Neither of these considerations undermines the argument in favor of increased attention to self-control for American children. In general, our society does not emphasize caring for others to whom we have no special tie or make it psychologically easy for us to do. On the contrary, many circles are preoccupied with the advancement of individual self-interest. Thus moral behavior toward others must depend on a kind of self-control that would otherwise be less essential. And, as I have argued, many desirable forms of achievement also require self-control.

In sum, then, it is beneficial for children to develop enabling virtues and the self-control on which they are based. These are habits that help them achieve their goals and that therefore ought to be considered uncontroversial. Hence the case for limiting children's freedom in the interest of their acquiring self-control is very strong.

Liberationists might respond at this point that since it is equally beneficial for adults to acquire self-control, the desirability of this goal fails to distinguish between members of the two classes. There are good reasons, however, for distinguishing between children and grownups. In particular, it is plausible to believe that self-control is most reliably acquired early and that it is much more difficult to acquire it as an adult.

What grounds could one have for asserting these claims? An interesting study comparing Danish and American families supports the hypothesis that learning self-control early is beneficial. Danish families are strict with young children but permissive with adolescents. Yet the adolescents are more self-disciplined and autonomous than the more consistently permissively reared American youths. The researchers suggest that early strictness causes the children to internalize controls and hence to be able to use their later freedom wisely.[54] In addition, recent intriguing studies on brain development suggest a basis for thinking that some traits, such as the ability to pay attention, plan, organize, and persist at projects, develop best at specific "sensitive" phases of brain maturation.[55]

Such studies also suggest some connection between childhood learning and adult behavior as well. Most of us have probably witnessed the trials of adults struggling to overcome bad habits that stand in the way of success, or indeed threaten their lives, such as procrastination and smoking. Although other pressures may partially explain such behavior, it would be plausible to attribute a good deal of it to the earlier failure to develop self-control. It is surely an assumption of this kind that leads parents to try to help their children develop it. One of the more heart-rending experiences of parenting is seeing a child resist or fail to develop self-control and then having to watch the predictable failures and frustrations that follow. Consider the fate of bright kids who are insufficiently chal-

54. Denise Kandel and Gerald S. Lesser, "Parent-Adolescent Relationships and Adolescent Independence in the U.S. and Denmark," in *Influences on Human Development*, ed. Urie Bronfenbrenner, pp. 631–41 (Hinsdale, Ill.: Dryden, 1972).

55. See Jane M. Healy, *Endangered Minds* (New York: Simon & Schuster, 1990, esp. chaps. 1, 2, 3, and 9. Chap. 9 contains a striking description by a pediatric neurologist, Dr. Martha Bridge Denckla, director of the Kennedy Institute Neurobehavioral Clinic, who worries that "the growing phenomenon of inattention might be attributable to a lack of basic organization in children's lives." She says:

> I think clearly organic problems may account for about one-third of the cases, but I'm beginning to think many of the others relate to changing environments for young children. I see an awful lot of parents with a lack of knowledge about child development who don't have the ability to provide the structure children need. I had a couple in the other day who thought their three-year-old was hyperactive, and when I asked them about their daily routines, I found out they expected, among other things, this three-year-old to take her own bath. There was no one to say to the child, 'Now we get up, now we get dressed.' There are families nowadays that never have a family meal; they literally leave food out on the counters. (pp. 177–78)

This point of view should give serious pause to proponents of children's liberation as it reflects practices that such liberation would encourage and perhaps even require.

lenged in high school and who therefore never acquire adequate study habits. The price for many is a very rough time in college or even the collapse of ambition.[56] Conversely, my experience suggests that helping children develop self-control often leads to further success on their part, at least insofar as outside circumstances permit. We will be seeing more evidence for this position later.

Consider, in addition, the following train of reasoning. If you don't learn self-control when you are young, you need to learn it later, when there are obstacles in the way that weren't there earlier. First, when you are older, you have already developed bad ways of coping: to develop good ones, you have to unlearn the old. This learning, unlike learning self-control young, takes much conscious attention and effort. Second, when you are little, others are helping you; once you are on your own, it is more difficult to procure the same kind of support and encouragement. In particular, the more freedom you have, the easier it is for your weak side to take over. If, for instance, you go shopping with your father and he won't let you put a box of cookies in the cart, that's that. When you are in charge, an instant's loss of control puts the cookies in the cart. It is reasons of this kind that motivate people to arrange to have themselves locked away in rehabilitation programs.

If it is important to try to develop self-control young, and if self-control is central to a good life in human societies, then a case can be made that it is right to limit children's freedom (if that is what it takes) in order to help them develop it. And (as we shall see in chapter 3) there is good empirical evidence for the view that controlling children in certain ways, rather than letting them set their own agendas in every respect, fosters the kind of character we seek. Both historical and psychological studies strongly suggest that children who are rarely (if ever) subjected to adult limits do not develop in desirable ways, and help explain why this finding makes good sense.

56. Halbert B. Robinson writes: ". . . gifted children in an age-graded educational system are seldom encouraged to develop good study habits, habits of application and perseverance in the face of difficulty. The child for whom everything comes easily may learn to expect that everything *should* come easily. He or she may be made anxious and discouraged when faced with a degree of challenge or even a minor failure that a less capable student would take in stride. Encounters with adversity may have devastating effects, including avoidance of difficulty, feelings of self-abasement, and even withdrawal from college or graduate study": "A Case for Radical Acceleration," in *Academic Precocity*, ed. Camilla Persson Benbow and Julian C. Stanley (Baltimore: Johns Hopkins University Press, 1983), pp. 144–45.

The underlying assumption is that children must *learn* what good behavior is, and that unless they are firmly reminded of it by demands or punishment, their tendency will be to form habits on the basis of what is easiest rather than what is best. There are grounds for believing those claims about the desirability of developing self-control early, grounds that even many liberals would concede. Self-control opens up a range of desirable opportunities and choices in regard to occupations, pursuits, indeed, entire ways of life not otherwise available. If the price of developing it is special limits on children, it is worth paying.

In an attempt to refute this view, liberationists contend that the difference in functioning between children and adults is trivial. Given the injustice involved in our inconsistent treatment of the two classes, the barely noticeable improvement in functioning is not worth it. Just as we permit adults to be weak and idiotic, we should do the same for children: "A brief review of human history reveals a catalogue of blunders. It is adults who have chosen to pollute their environment with industrial, chemical and nuclear waste, fought wars, built concentration camps, segregated people because of the colour of their skin, and it is adults in developed countries who stupidly and insensitively eat their way to a premature death through coronary disease while many starve in the Third World."[57]

Liberationists such as Franklin and Cohen stress that we *learn* from our mistakes and we should let children do likewise. But Franklin's pessimistic assessment of adult behavior undermines his own case: if what he says is true, then we clearly don't learn very much this way. Furthermore, the adults who are doing so badly did have a protected period of learning. How would they be doing in its absence? Proponents of equal rights for children would have to assert that they would, on the whole, do at least as well without it. We have seen some reason to doubt any such claim, and more is forthcoming.

Despite the obvious appeal of Franklin's assessment of the state of the world, his position is difficult to evaluate. A great deal of evidence could be gathered to support it, but so could many counterexamples to refute it. It is also undeniable that our day-to-day experiences strongly influence our view here: on bad days we seem to be

57. Franklin, *Rights of Children*, p. 33.

surrounded by incompetence and selfishness; on other days people are kind and sensible. Our general outlook tends to fluctuate with these events.

What appears true to me is that many children live mostly in the present and demonstrate relatively low levels of self-control.[58] It may be, as liberationists contend, that children have the potential to do substantially better. This point of view will be considered later. It cannot be assumed, however, that such will automatically be the case.

At least one writer envisions much darker possibilities. In *Lord of the Flies* William Golding showed us what he thought would happen if children were left to their own devices: the collapse of civilized behavior.[59] Now perhaps he indulged in poetic exaggeration, and the presence of adults might in any case mitigate this picture (a consideration available only to those who see a significant difference between children and adults), but such a picture might also suggest that we could not be assured of a rosy outcome here.

Of course, as liberationists never tire of pointing out, the contemporary adult world quite often seems not much better. It does seem safe to claim that there is a difference in the average levels of children and adults, but the difference is not nearly so great as one would wish. Given the serious crises facing us, I'm not sure civilization (or life itself) would survive much longer if we behaved any more stupidly than we already do. In fact, such an outcome seems likely if we don't soon start behaving significantly *more* intelligently. The implications of this state of affairs will be examined in more detail shortly.

Conclusion

The liberationist argument that justice requires equal rights for children because they are as rational as we are depends on a minimally demanding instrumental conception of reason. Even given this low standard, there is a range of degrees of competence; we might on this basis argue for distinctions between children of different ages. More demanding conceptions of rationality, such as the ability

58. To what extent this is a result of our treatment of them will be considered later.
59. See William Golding, *Lord of the Flies*, (New York: Coward-McCann, 1962).

to plan systematic utility-enhancing projects and having a rational life plan, are plausible alternatives to this first view. But examination of these notions reveals that they presume substantial knowledge about the world and sensitivity to human interests. They also require certain character traits. It is doubtful that children, especially young children, could meet such demands. The extent to which older children (and for that matter adults) meet them generally increases by degrees. But some differences in degree are so significant as to be morally relevant.

Given the desirability of helping children to develop self-control and enabling virtues, and the likelihood that it is easier for them to do so when they are young and have help, there is at least a prima facie case for setting limits for children. Such a judgment is predicated on the view that good parents and teachers are in a position to make sound judgments about their children's welfare. Hence it is justifiable to treat children in ways that would be paternalistic were they adults in order to help them develop well.[60] This conclusion is derived both from direct consideration of children's own present and future welfare and from indirect considerations about the survival of civilization.

The general outline of my case is not new and it should not be especially controversial.[61] Filling in the supporting arguments that are in other versions left to the imagination of readers should allay any fears that they have been swept along by a supeficially plausible but nonetheless untenable position. By itself, it is a strong response to the case for equal rights for children; but a good deal more is to be said.

60. It should be noted that we are not absolutely strict about paternalism (nor is it clear that we should be), although it is difficult to find instances of the overriding of adults' decisions that couldn't also be justified by an indirect appeal to the general interest. Thus we require motorcyclists to wear helmets even if it is their own neck they save: if they were to break it, society would pay, too. Perhaps this sort of example should suggest reasons for wariness about the usefulness of the concept. Only the most libertarian society could let the chips fall where they may when others harm themselves.

61. See, e.g., Locke, *Second Treatise*; Mill, *On Liberty*; Blustein, *Parents and Children*; Joel Feinberg, "The Child's Right to an Open Future," in Aiken and LaFollette, *Whose Child?*; Schrag, "Child in the Moral Order"; Amy Gutmann, "Children, Paternalism and Education: A Liberal Argument," *Philosophy and Public Affairs* 9, no. 4, (1980): 338–56.

Chapter 2

MORAL ISSUES

> . . . the parents who raise their child in such a way as to promote his self-fulfillment most effectively will at every stage try to strengthen the basic tendencies of the child as manifested at that stage. . . . The child will even have very basic tendencies toward various kinds of attitudes from an early stage, at least insofar as they grow naturally out of his inherited temperamental propensities. He may be the naturally gregarious, outgoing sort, or the kind of person who will naturally come to treasure his privacy and to keep his own counsels; he may appreciate order and structure more or less than spontaneity and freedom; he may be inclined, *ceteris paribus*, to respect or to challenge authority. . . . The discerning parent will see all of these things ever more clearly as the child grows older, and insofar as he steers the child at all, it will be in the child's own preferred directions. At the very least he will not try to turn him upstream and make him struggle against his own deepest currents.
>
> —Joel Feinberg, "The Child's Right to an Open Future"

To recapitulate the argument so far: I have suggested that the purely instrumental conception of reason sometimes promoted by proponents of equal rights for children is not a desirable criterion by which to judge readiness for rights because it is too inclusive. Some liberationists seem to concede this point by proposing another test that they describe variously as the capacity to plan utility-enhancing projects and having a rational life plan. This criterion catapults us into a different realm, for it requires that the child make judgments about interests, not just seek immediate gratification and avoidance of pain. To make judgments about interests and act upon them, children must know a good deal about how the world and other people operate, and they must possess substantial self-control. It is plausible to hold that children develop such knowledge and traits over time, and that older children can reasonably be expected to manifest them more regularly and at a higher level of sophistication than younger ones. Furthermore, despite the views of some liberationists, adults are in a position to evaluate many of the plans children make and there are good reasons for putting pressure on children to pursue some but not others—even if our concern is limited to their welfare.

Moreover, we surely ought not to be concerned only about their welfare. Most of the debate about equal rights for children has been conducted within a liberal framework whose primary focus is the individual. Liberationists rarely raise the issue of moral development; when they do, it doesn't seem to play much of a role in their arguments. Even protectionists seem only slightly more aware of this dimension of human development. Typical is Joel Feinberg's emphasis on children's self-development.[1] His remarks are intended to suggest that simple self-determination is not an adequate goal and that limiting children's freedom is therefore justifiable even on individualistic grounds. Since he fails to address the equally important moral dimension, however, he seems to be saying that it is less important than learning to further one's own long-term self-interest.[2]

This lack of serious interest in children's moral development seems very odd. For like the rest of us, children are embedded in a web of human relations; the significance of their moral position is, after all, a central liberationist insight. Furthermore, they constitute the next generation of actors, those who will in the future be taking responsibility for the kind of world we have.

1. Joel Feinberg writes: ". . . a majority view [among philosophers] that seems to me highly plausible would identify a person's good ultimately with his *self-fulfillment* . . . It surely involves as necessary elements the development of one's chief aptitudes into genuine talents in a life that gives them scope, an unfolding of all basic tendencies and inclinations, both those that are common to the child and those that are peculiar to the individual, and an active realization of the universal human propensities to plan, design and make order": "The Child's Right to an Open Future," in Aiken and LaFollette, *Whose Child?* pp. 142–43.

2. This is not to say that by furthering one's own interests one is necessarily failing to further those of others. Enlightened self-interest requires us in some cases to pay attention to the interests of others, and if we have a caring nature, we will naturally be concerned about their interests. In many cases, however, it is possible to focus on our own interest to the exclusion of that of others, even though it would be morally better to concentrate on the latter. Blustein takes exception to this generalization; although he shares the liberal outlook overall, he properly sees children as enmeshed in a social context (*Parents and Children*, pp. 127–28).

Before going any further, I must lay out my moral assumptions in somewhat greater detail. It has so far been presupposed that interests have a critical role in moral reasoning. As I suggested in chapter 1, to assert that *X* is in my interest is to say something about my welfare; if I am rational, I have to concede that what is in my interest is things that contribute to my ultimate good. Applying the notion of "interest" in specific cases would require more fleshing out, but the foregoing will suffice for my purposes here.

Prerequisites for moral action are genuine caring for others, the capacity to decide what is in another's interest, as well as to compare the relative weight of interests, and the self-control and enabling virtues to act on those judgments. Without these characteristics we are unable to promote the interests of others when they conflict with our own. I take it as given that strong interests generally have priority over weaker ones; hence our own are not necessarily the most pressing. It is also assumed that relieving or preventing suffering is a major component of advancing the interests of others, as is fostering their overall well-being.

This approach is broadly utilitarian. I am drawn to it primarily because it seems to me to be the only way to recognize both needs and desires. I am all too aware of the drawbacks of the theory, but despair at finding a better one.[3] Some of the worst difficulties are avoidable, I think, if we concentrate less than traditional moral theorists on desert-island cases and are willing to put up with quite a bit of roughness at the edges. This loose approach should help us make substantial progress toward the goal of justifying children's place.

Among the assumptions made here are that preventing serious harm should generally take precedence over promoting happiness, and that we know quite well what basic harms are. Starvation, physical or mental abuse, discrimination on the basis of irrelevant characteristics: these are the kinds of harm I am talking about. Once we have eradicated some of the most egregious harms now affecting the world, we shall have to face a variety of questions I ignore here; we can wait to cross some bridges until we come to them, however.[4]

3. See Appendix for more details.

4. For a thorough discussion of harm, see Joel Feinberg, *Harm to Others* (Oxford: Oxford University Press, 1984), esp. chap. 1. Among the difficult questions we face about harm are (1) how to determine whether a given state of affairs constitutes harm or failure to benefit, (2) distinguishing mental harm from mere offense, (3) deciding how to deal

The very strongest interests are those protected by being designated "rights," and the central role of justice is to ensure that they are not violated; if they are, serious harm occurs. Moral individuals are persons who can be relied on to respect rights and be sensitive to the lesser interests of others. This framework is compatible with the existence of special commitments created by particular acts or agreements, but these commitments do not exhaust the sources of moral obligation.[5]

Although this theory is relatively simple, it is a good deal more demanding than popular moral views that stress the overriding importance of pursuing our own conception of the good without interference. This approach to morality can easily degenerate into preoccupation with the self. As Bob Franklin points out, it is not difficult to find examples of the collapse of the most elementary sense of consideration for others. Consider, for instance, the illustrations in Kate Leishman's recent account of the AIDS epidemic. In "Heterosexuals and AIDS" she describes the following kinds of behavior: Fabian Bridges was diagnosed as having AIDS but continued to work as a prostitute. Stan Borrman, a prostitute with ARC, the highly infectious precursor to AIDS, had over a thousand partners since his diagnosis several years before. Members of high-risk groups refuse to get tested but continue to engage in unsafe sex despite the possibility of infecting others. People imagine that they can "intuit" seropositivity. Couples who test positive knowingly have children who may well be infected and die. Couples one member of which is HIV-positive continue to have unprotected sex, even though repeated exposure is thought to increase the chance of transmitting the virus.[6] These things have happened even though becoming seropositive is thought to carry with it a high—perhaps 100 percent probability—of eventually getting AIDS, and AIDS so far appears to be invariably fatal. Consider, too, that no reliable vaccine or cure is in sight, and that the probability of exponential spread is high.

Many other examples of short-sighted, selfish behavior come easily to mind—we have only to consider recent domestic and foreign policy. Furthermore, whereas in the past, humanity as a whole could

---

with threat of harm, and (4) drawing some lines between direct and indirect harm.

5. This is a generally consequentialist framework with strong but not doctrinaire utilitarian leanings. For more discussion, see the Appendix.

6. Katie Leishman, "Heterosexuals and AIDS," *Atlantic*, February 1987, pp. 39–58.

afford localized environmental disasters (even though they caused great and unnecessary suffering), our immensely powerful technology and high population levels now render both the earth and the human population much more vulnerable to bad decisions. It is also becoming ever more clear that apparently "natural" disasters can be magnified or even caused by short-sighted political decisions.[7]

The case for higher levels of moral awareness and action—that is, greater sensitivity to the interests of others and more willingness to put them before our own—is buttressed by some recent developments in moral and social theory, developments that have considerable bearing on whether we should recognize equal rights for children.

One of the most interesting and persuasive arguments against social policies that accord primacy to freedom is offered by the sociologist Robert Bellah, who points out that societies whose explicit norms lean toward an undemanding liberalism rely on unrecognized nonliberal beliefs to help hold people together. Bellah argues that all the great political philosophers from Aristotle to Montesquieu thought that "a political regime is an expression of the total way of life of a people, its economics, its customs, its religion." The best society, a republic, will therefore have republican customs; "public participation in the exercise of power, the political equality of the citizens, a wide distribution of small and medium property with few very rich or very poor."[8] These customs lead to what Bellah describes as "public-spirited citizens," people willing to sacrifice their own interests for the common good. It is clear that the values underlying these assumptions go well beyond any Spartan individualism.

Republics are difficult to maintain, however: they "go against gravity" and tend to degenerate. To survive they must "root out corruption and encourage virtue." That goal requires the state to commit itself to what Bellah describes as "high ethical and spiritual values," and then it must get actively involved in "molding, socializing, and educating the citizens into those ethical and spiritual beliefs

7. For just one example, consider the current threat of the greenhouse effect. For discussion of such problems, see Eric J. Barron, "Earth's Shrouded Future: The Unfinished Forecast of Global Warming," *The Sciences*, September/October 1989, pp. 14–20; and Andrew Goudie, *The Human Impact on the Natural Environment*, 2d ed., (Cambridge, Mass.: MIT Press, 1986).

8. Robert Bellah, *Varieties of Civil Religion* (San Francisco: Harper & Row, 1980), p. 9.

so they are internalized as republican virtue." In the absence of such pressure, the people will become corrupt, and since people get the government they deserve, despotism will ensue.[9]

What is "corruption"? According to Bellah, it is to be found in

> luxury, dependence, and ignorance. Luxury is that pursuit of material things that diverts us from concern for the public good, that leads us to exclusive concern for our own good, or what we would today call consumerism. Dependence naturally follows from luxury, for it consists in accepting the dominance of whatever person or group, or, we might say today, governmental or corporate structure, that promises it will take care of our material desires. . . . And finally ignorance, that is, political ignorance, is the result of luxury and dependence. It is a lack of interest in public things, a concern only for the private, a willingness to be governed by those who promise to take care of us even without our knowledgeable consent.[10]

In chapter 1 I examined the role of self-control in the context of children's interests. Its importance, however, does not end there. We saw that those who are unwilling to work hard (an endeavor in which self-control plays a major role) are less likely to achieve their goals; perhaps still more important, they are also unlikely to contribute significantly to mutually chosen social aims. The implications of their failure to make such effort has repercussions both for their own satisfaction and for that of society at large: a community with a preponderance of such persons will be quite different from one composed of achievers. One might also reasonably expect more mistakes and sloppiness in communities where a significant proportion of individuals fail to take responsibility for their own actions. This might seem a trivial problem until we remember the interdependence characteristic of human societies, interdependence we take very much for granted but upon which our well-being is grounded. How much suffering and death have come of mishandling poisonous materials, bad engineering, or irreponsible diplomacy? Finally, self-control is a centrally important factor in moral, rather than selfish, behavior: without it, the minor irritation of stopping to put on a condom turns into willingness to put a partner at risk for AIDS.

9. Ibid., pp. 9, 16, 19.
10. Ibid., pp. 19–20.

Likewise, much can be said in favor of simple and frugal living, as Bellah contends.[11] Three general kinds of considerations support this judgment. One is that a luxurious life is likely to be focused on consumption, which by itself now appears to be singularly unsatisfying. Because it is unsatisfying, it fosters ever-increasing desires. And because resources are finite, these will at some point have to be unfulfilled. In general, it seems safe to say, however, that other values are more intrinsically satisfying and do not have this effect. A second problem with luxury is the question of equity. In a time of widespread poverty, justice requires us to share our wealth. A moderate way of life permits us to do so.[12] Overall, a society of luxury lovers will be quite a different affair from one composed of people more easily satisfied. A third concern is the effect of an affluent way of life on children and hence upon the future of the culture. Richard Flacks argues that there is an inherent conflict between effort and indulgence:

> Typical middle-class parents expect their offspring to strive and achieve and to understand the necessity for self-discipline and effort in attaining goals. Very often, however, such families have surplus incomes and try to provide their children with a sense of being well taken care of. Indeed, in many families parents indulge their children in order to demonstrate their love and care. . . . Such parental indulgence . . . tends to weaken the offspring's sense of necessity for self-discipline, sacrifice, and toil.[13]

In view of the points already made about self-control and enabling virtues, this fact has obvious consequences for both long-term personal satisfaction and the nature of the culture we can expect in the future.

A final necessity for Bellah's "republican" component of society is

11. Naturally, what constitutes simple living depends on circumstances; it could not be determined without a much fuller discussion than is appropriate here. Luxury may be a deeply relativistic term; I think it is no less useful for all that, although its relativeness creates special problems when we try to decide what does and does not constitute luxury.

12. Consider the simple and powerful arguments of Peter Singer, "Famine, Affluence, and Morality," *Philosophy and Public Affairs* 1, no. 3 (1972); and Erik Dammann, *The Future in Our Hands* (Oxford: Pergamon, 1979).

13. Richard Flacks, "Growing Up Confused: Cultural Crisis and Individual Character," in *Intimacy, Family, and Society*, ed. Arlene Skolnick and Jerome H. Skolnick (Boston: Little, Brown, 1974), p. 353.

the balance between individual and community concerns. Both he and the sociologists Brigitte and Peter Berger rightly disparage the view that if we concentrate on our own needs and desires, the community will take care of itself. The Bergers dub this approach "hyper-individualism" and attribute to it (at least in part) the disintegration of our society.[14] It is, of course, one thing to emphasize the importance of balance, as both Bellah and the Bergers do, and quite another to try to discern the point of equilibrium. It is a major step forward to acknowledge the need for community even if details of working it out lie before us.

Before we go on, it is important to distinguish between two contrasting meanings of "individualism." The first is preoccupation with one's individual interests. The second is the habit of thinking for oneself and standing up for one's conclusions. I have just been arguing against the view that our primary concern should be our own interests; however, to continue the case for rationality (broadly construed) as an enabling virtue important for the moral life, it is necessary to argue *for* the second view of individualism as the capacity to withstand the influence of the crowd.

The desirability of promoting this latter kind of individualism hardly needs elaborate justification. Properly applied, reason helps us both to reach our goals and to evaluate them. It functions as a brake to impulsive, ill-considered action whose consequences we would soon regret. As such, it has a significant moral dimension. William K. Clifford demonstrated convincingly the far-reaching implications of inadequately supporting one's beliefs.[15] Examples of the bad consequences of the failure to think things through are easily found. Spending less on prenatal care programs now, for instance, means spending much more on neonatal intensive care later.

Nor should the value of standing up for what we believe in need much argument. It seems clear, for example, that it would have been a good deal easier to stop Hitler early on if all those who disagreed with his policies had stood up to be counted. Critical thinking is almost pointless unless one is prepared to act in accordance with it.

14. Brigitte Berger and Peter Berger, *The War over the Family* (New York: Anchor/Doubleday, 1983).

15. William K. Clifford, "The Ethics of Belief," *Lectures and Essays* (London: Macmillan, 1879). See also Allen W. Wood's excellent paper on this subject, "The Immorality of Faith," presented at San Diego State University, February 1986.

Do we really want to live in a society where people are always carried along by their perceptions of public opinion, where no value is placed on questioning tradition, law, custom on the basis of individual conscience? Consider just for a start the chilling effect on intellectual life of the failure of academics to stand up against Joseph McCarthy.[16] In short, implicit in conceptions of republican virtue is a wide array of desirable values, values that ought to be promoted by society and perhaps even by its legal arm, the state.

Liberalism, despite its historical roots in the republican tradition, has an entirely different view of politics and education. It holds that in a well-designed state, the common good will be automatically furthered by the self-interested acts of its citizens. The exact details of such claims have varied, but among its most prominent proponents are Bruce Ackerman, Ronald Dworkin, and Robert Nozick.[17] Bellah calls this "the most wildly utopian idea in the history of political thought." The state itself is to have no aims or values: it is supposedly a "purely neutral legal mechanism." Bellah rightly points out that the freedom it is intended to promote "does imply a purpose and a value."[18]

These two antithetical models of political life—republicanism and liberalism—are the major strands in the American tradition and have been balanced in uneasy partnership. Bellah's point is that republicanism has tacitly supplied glue without which liberalism and American society could not have survived. That glue was, in his opinion, provided by the institutions of federalism and the churches. The insight about the churches was provided by Tocqueville, who saw that "naked self-interest is the surest solvent of a republican regime," one that religion could transmute into social consciousness by stressing the importance of "self-interest rightly understood," public-spirited and self-sacrificing. Bellah, like Tocqueville, is not sure about the staying power of this uneasy compromise. He wonders whether we have not lately been witnessing the disintegration of the republican element in American society, and whether we can survive without it. Doubting that we can, he argues that "a pure

16. See, e.g., Ellen Schrecker, *No Ivory Tower* (Oxford: Oxford University Press, 1986).

17. See Ackerman, *Social Justice*; Dworkin, "Liberalism"; Nozick, *Anarchy, State, and Utopia.*

18. Bellah, *Varieties of Civil Religion*, pp. 9, 12.

liberalism is a *reductio ad absurdum* and a sociological impossibility."[19] That is why a "pure" liberal state has never existed and why republicanism did not die out sooner.

A still more provocative analysis proposed by Annette C. Baier reaches much the same conclusion about the contribution of unacknowledged but essential belief systems. She locates the problem in the bifurcated moral tradition that emphasized the value of rights, autonomy, and justice only for some:

> The domestic work was left to women and slaves, and the liberal morality for right-holders was surreptitiously supplemented by a different set of demands made on domestic workers. As long as women could be got to assume responsibility for the care of home and children, and to train their children to continue the sexist system, the liberal morality could continue to be the official morality, by turning its eyes away from the contribution made by those it excluded. The long unnoticed domestic proletariat were the domestic workers, mostly female.[20]

A careful look at the political theorists most influential in American history supports these claims.[21] The real, but invisible keystones of our way of life are the assumptions that dependent individuals are mostly taken care of in the private sphere, as is the domestic labor necessary to keep the public world running. Yet "universal" rights and the moral assumptions upon which they rest play a relatively small role in this private domain. It is therefore plausible to infer that the public realm works only if many real human needs are taken care of somewhere else—a place where the individualistic conception of human relations predicated of that realm do not hold.

Feminist writers emphasize the peculiarity of a moral and political theory that has often failed to make room for many activities neces-

19. Ibid., pp. 16, 12.

20. Annette C. Baier, "The Need for More than Justice," in *Science, Morality, and Feminist Theory*, ed. Marsha Hanen and Kai Nielsen, *Canadian Journal of Philosophy* 13, suppl. (1987): 50.

21. Consider Aristotle, Hobbes, Rousseau, Kant. Not only did they believe that women were defective, but they posited entirely different moral virtues for them. Furthermore, they imagined that the basic human unit was the family, not the individual. The family was a private domain, where the much-vaunted virtues of justice, etc. penetrated not at all. See the recent feminist scholarship on the history of political philosophy, e.g., Susan Moller Okin, *Women in Western Political Thought* (Princeton: Princeton University Press, 1979); L. Clarke and L. Lange, *The Sexism of Social and Political Theory* (Toronto: University of Toronto Press, 1979).

sary for human life. Alison Jaggar, for instance, charges that the atomistic assumptions of classical political theories are unrealistic

> even if one conceives of all human beings as healthy adults, which most social contract theorists have done. As soon as one takes into account the facts of human biology, especially reproductive biology, it becomes obvious that the assumption of individual self-sufficiency is impossible. Human infants resemble the young of many species in being born helpless, but they differ from all other species in requiring a uniquely long period of dependence on adult care. This care could not be provided by a single adult; in order to raise enough children to continue the species, humans must live in social groups where individuals share resources with the young.[22]

Baier adds the more general problem that since Kant, at least, moral theory has emphasized relationships between equals. Relationships between unequals, such as "parents and children, earlier and later generations in relation to one another, states and citizens, doctors and patients, the well and the ill, large states and small states," are, by means of various fictions, treated as analogies of relationships between equals. But such analogies may not be adequate to deal with important dimensions of unequal relationships:

> A more realistic acceptance of the fact that we begin as helpless children, that at almost every point of our lives we deal with both the more and the less helpless, that equality of power and interdependency . . . is rare and hard to recognize when it does occur, might lead us to a more direct approach to questions concerning the design of institutions structuring these relationships between unequals (families, schools, hospitals, armies) and of the morality of our dealings with the more and the less powerful.[23]

This point of view could not only help us grope toward more satisfactory relationships with children, without "promoting" them to adults,[24] but could provide a better approach to inequality in general.

22. Alison Jaggar, *Feminist Politics and Human Nature* (Totowa, N.J.: Rowman & Allanheld, 1983), pp. 40–41.

23. Baier, "Need for More than Justice," pp. 52, 53.

24. Baier writes that relationships with unequals "have had to be shunted to the bottom of the agenda, and then dealt with by some sort of 'promotion' of the weaker so that an appearance of virtual equality is achieved . . . children are treated as adults-to-be . . . [etc.]" (ibid., pp. 52–53).

Overall, Baier holds that the basic assumptions of liberalism are not "a good minimal set, the only ones we need pressure *everyone* to obey," because "these rules do little to protect the young or the dying or the starving or any of the relatively powerless against neglect." Nor will they help us teach people to be actively concerned about the welfare of others.[25] More demanding versions of liberalism belie this generalization, but they are not the ones upon which the bulk of our current practices are based.

Moral theory realistically grounded in human needs would have to start with the premise that thwarting satisfying relationships harms, that promoting such relationships is a fundamental good, and that cooperation, not competitiveness, is "natural" and desirable. Instead of presupposing that we are independent and selfish, we would be assuming that interdependence and care for others were the norm. Thus conflict, not harmony, would be the novel form of behavior that needed explaining.[26]

Closely related themes are being pressed by communitarians, who believe that liberalism and the conception of the individual upon which it is based are fundamentally mistaken. They question the deontological emphasis of this tradition, arguing instead for attention to common ends. Implicit in their view is a less individualistic notion of personhood, one in which social relationships play a larger part. Communitarians argue that we are in part constituted by our roles and our communities, and are therefore bound in some ways by their assumptions and demands.[27] This general line of thought emphasizes not only our essential social interdependence but indeed the degree to which we as individuals are socially constituted.[28]

25. Ibid., p. 53.

26. Jaggar, *Feminist Politics*, p. 41.

27. Michael Sandel, "Introduction," in *Liberalism and Its Critics*, ed. Sandel, (New York: New York University Press, 1984), pp. 5–6. Some works defending such views are Michael Sandel, *Liberalism and the Limits of Justice* (Cambridge: Cambridge University Press, 1982); Alasdair MacIntyre, *After Virtue* (Notre Dame, Ind.: University of Notre Dame Press, 1981); Charles Taylor, *Hegel* (Cambridge: Cambridge University Press, 1975); Michael Walzer, *Spheres of Justice* (New York: Basic Books, 1983). Of course, there are significant differences among these writers. See, e.g., Marilyn Friedman, "Feminism and Modern Friendship: Dislocating the Community," *Ethics* 99 (January 1989): 275–90, for a critical view of some of Sandel's assumptions.

28. This issue cannot be dealt with fully here, although we have seen something of it in other sections. Suffice it to say that I think that sociologists, anthropologists, and so on have provided ample evidence to counter the sociobiological claims that we are essentially

What conclusions can be drawn from arguments of the sort that have been examined here? What is striking about these theories is their emphasis—despite their diversity and spread across the political spectrum—on the importance of greater cooperation and concern for others in moral and political thinking. In that sense, they supply what seems to me and to many others a badly needed corrective to the contemporary over emphasis on individual conceptions of the good at the expense of universal basic needs for food, shelter, education, and medical care.[29] The inescapable point is that social concerns must play a more central role in our moral thinking if we are to have a good society.

Another factor that must now play a greater role in our thinking is something not mentioned in the critiques I have described, but to which I have already alluded: the physical environment. In the past we could pursue our own conceptions of the good without threatening the survival of life on earth. This is no longer the case.[30] Consequently, no moral theory that fails to take our mutual interests here into account is defensible. What theories are ruled out by considerations of this sort? It seems to me that a strong case can be made for the inadequacy of both libertarianism and "thin" liberalisms that try to minimize limits on appropriate conceptions of the good.

---

biologically determined. A good general introduction to this problem is chap. 3 of Beryl Lieff Benderly, *The Myth of Two Minds* (New York: Doubleday, 1987).

Interestingly, John Stuart Mill, in some respects the quintessential liberal, was not unaware of the need to create bridges between individuals to form a community. In *Utilitarianism* he argued that "utility would enjoin, first, that laws and social arrangements should place the happiness, or . . . the interest, of every individual, as nearly as possible in harmony with the interest of the whole; and secondly, that education and opinion . . . should so use that power [over human character] as to establish in the mind of every individual an indissoluble association between his own happiness and the good of the whole" (p. 418). Thus we cannot imagine buying our own happiness at the expense of others, and the impulse to promote the general good becomes a matter of habit. This conception also provides protection against the fiendish desert-island cases people construct to undermine utilitarianism. His conception here, however, remains essentially atomistic in that concern for others as separate units is merely *added* to the conception of a separate individual.

29. I also think that these developments are at least in part a reaction to the fact that the old moral theories are not holding up very well as people attempt to apply them. For more on this issue, see the Appendix.

30. This is to say not that localized disasters did not occur but only that population growth and technology had not advanced to the point of undermining the ecological systems that make our life possible. For discussion of the kinds of limits we need to face, see Virginia Held, *Rights and Goods: Justifying Social Action* (New York: Free Press, 1984), chap. 13.

Contemporary libertarianism is a descendant of the old-style classical liberalism that preceded modern, democratic liberalism.[31] One of the chief and most forceful expositions of libertarianism may be found in Robert Nozick's *Anarchy, State, and Utopia*. In that work Nozick lays out his argument for a minimal state, any extension of which he holds to violate individual rights. To defend his position he contends that justice ought to be regarded as a historical principle, not what he calls an "end-state" one. A historical principle determines the justice of an outcome by the way it came about; an end-state principle judges the outcome by some independent idea of what the results of distribution should look like. In his view, justice requires no more than the following three rules:

1. A person who acquires a holding in accordance with the principle of justice in acquisition is entitled to that holding.
2. A person who acquires a holding in accordance with the principle of justice in transfer, from someone else entitled to the holding, is entitled to the holding.
3. No one is entitled to a holding except by (repeated) applications of 1 and 2.

If your property holdings are a result of the operation of these three rules, you are entitled to what you own. The misery of others creates no legal obligation on your part to help them, although you may do so privately out of charity if you wish.[32]

Nozick prefers this historical principle of justice because it allows society to function without continuous interference in people's lives. So-called end-state principles must periodically adjust states of affairs to make sure that the results of transactions do approximate the desired outcome. This adjustment entails taking things (usually

31. I am using George Sabine's terminology, considered standard, I believe, and found in *A History of Political Theory* (New York: Henry Holt, 1950). "Classical" liberalism is linked with laissez-faire economic doctrine and emphasizes the freedom to be let alone, so-called negative freedom. "Modern" or "democratic" liberalism developed from classical liberalism, building upon its perceived inadequacies, and takes a more complex view of freedom. Included in the notion are not only the political and civil liberties so valued by early liberals but a minimum standard of material and social welfare. The state is expected to take positive action to provide for both the liberty and the welfare of its citizens (p. 741).

32. Nozick, *Anarchy, State, and Utopia*, p. 151.

money, in the form of taxes) away from some and giving them to others. Nozick contends that such taxation amounts to slavery:

> Seizing the results of someone's labor is equivalent to seizing hours from him and directing him to carry on various activities. If people force you to do certain work, or unrewarded work, for a certain period of time, they decide what you are to do and what purposes your work is to serve apart from your decisions. This process whereby they take this decision from you makes them a part owner of you; it gives them a property right in you.[33]

Is some libertarian scheme of this sort feasible or desirable?[34] One major practical problem is that in "real life" it is unlikely that we would ever be able to wipe out all unfair gains and start from a position of equality. Nor, even with such a just beginning, does the prospect of enforcing only just transfers seem very manageable. In their absence, it is easy to imagine chaos and misery. Nineteenth-century England illustrates what can happen under those circumstances.[35] One might argue that the horrors of the Industrial Revolution arose from a complex set of historically conditioned circumstances that are unlikely to recur today. There is no reason to believe, however, that new forms of the same problems would not arise. To the extent that differences in wealth and power develop, they chip away at the real value of civil liberties, as well as undermine the social stability necessary for a good society. Furthermore, even if we as-

33. Ibid., p. 172. See also, e.g., Jeffrey Paul, ed., *Reading Nozick* (Totowa, N.J.: Rowman & Littlefield, 1981).

34. For further discussion of these and other problems, see, e.g., Paul, *Reading Nozick*.

35. George Sabine describes the flaws in classical laissez-faire liberalism in his discussion of the development of modern democratic liberalism. He argues that by the 1830s, classical liberalism's detrimental effects on the working classes were becoming so obvious that protective legislation became imperative. "In 1841 the report of a Royal Commission, appointed to investigate the coal-mining industry, shocked all England with its revelations of the brutality that existed in the mines: the employment of women and children, barbarously long hours of work, the absence of safety devices, and the prevalence of revolting conditions both sanitary and moral": *History of Political Theory*, p. 701. Social awareness of these conditions was reflected in contemporary fiction and nonfiction. By 1875 the quantity of labor legislation amounted to the abandonment of classical liberalism—not as a result of any unified social theory but rather as a "spontaneous defense" against the ravages of the Industrial Revolution. Sabine argues that although early liberalism was in principle a theory of the national common good, in reality it expressed the interests of the industrial class that was gaining power in the nineteenth century. But its consequences weakened adherence to it by those who had genuinely believed that it would promote the welfare of all (p. 702).

sume a just initial state and just transfers, it is easy to imagine vast disparities in wealth and power developing within a generation or two. A moral theory unresponsive to this outcome seems to me to be not much of a moral theory at all: humaneness or caring for others appears to be entirely optional. But do we really want a society governed by the principle that "no one should be forced by law to help others, not even to tell them the time of day if requested, and certainly not to give them a portion of one's weekly paycheck"?[36]

So this theory is vulnerable to a pair of simple yet powerful objections. First, it focuses almost exclusively on a single value—freedom—and only in one context: property rights. And it is one thing to assert the value of liberty, but quite another to assert it as the only value, or one that always overrides others.[37] Second, the libertarian conception of freedom is far too narrow: it assumes that freedom requires merely noninterference, instead of recognizing that it may require positive help. One might suppose the analysis of the concept of freedom to be value-neutral, having no significant political consequences. This supposition, however, is false for a society where freedom is considered the highest value, because if the satisfaction of a certain interest (one that might just as plausibly be defined as a positive freedom) is not defined as a form of freedom, it will be judged less pressing when it conflicts with a negative freedom. This is especially likely to happen when such interests must be satisfied before members of less powerful groups can exercise their negative freedoms. In short, as Virginia Held argues, "to be free, the man of property may need only to be free from interference, but the person without property or the means to acquire it needs more in order to be *free* than to be left alone with nothing." Held goes on to suggest that

> it may be helpful to think of freedom in terms of independence. . . . It is then clear that for human beings to be independent in a developed, industrial society, and for independence to extend to groups previously excluded from it such as the poor, minorities, and women, human

36. John Hospers, "What Libertarianism Is," *The Libertarian Alternative*, ed. Tibor Machan (Chicago: Nelson-Hall, 1974), p. 18.

37. For some problems with this aspect of Nozick's view, see esp. Thomas Nagel, "Libertarianism without Foundations," in Paul, *Reading Nozick*. See also Held, *Rights and Goods*, chap. 8, esp. pp. 131–36, for an excellent treatment of libertarianism and freedom.

> beings must be assured of much more than an absence of interference. They must be assured of access to the means to live: decent jobs, minimum incomes, medical care, housing they can afford, and child care.[38]

This point about negative and positive freedom also applies to the proponents of equal rights examined here who might well object that they are not, like Nozick, right-wing libertarians vulnerable to the charge of noxious preoccupation with property. But their view of freedom as primarily negative, and the primacy they accord to it, if generalized, gives rise to many of the same problems as right-wing libertarianism. The emphasis on negative freedom simply underestimates the harm people can do each other when they are left to their own devices, as well as how human potential is stunted if it is deprived of social resources for its development. As Paul Nash rightly notes, "the same freedom can operate differentially for different sets of people. For example, . . . freedom from restraint for employers can mean loss of freedom for employees, especially in dangerous occupations." Libertarian governments are prepared to act only on behalf of very limited aims, and although their action may be strong or even barbaric (as when workers are massacred to protect private property), they leave a very wide realm of human life unprotected by guarantees of help. In that sense they can be weak governments, and dictatorships have usually followed weak governments, not strong ones; weak governments create a popular demand for order, any kind of order. And, Nash reminds us, "a strong government can use its authority to intervene in the life of a nation to encourage variety and freedom as well as, or rather than, constraint and uniformity."[39] Thus states can be instruments of oppression or of well-being; if we know who benefits from a state's actions, we know a great deal about its nature. "Thin" liberalisms that emphasize the importance of leaving individuals free to pursue their own conception of the good life and recognize only minimal demands on us on behalf of others will be prone to the same problems.

Before going any further, we need to lay to rest the fear that the only alternative to a relatively "thin" liberalism is an unattractive "moralism" or "perfectionism." Richard Lindley, a proponent of teenage liberation, writes:

38. Held, *Rights and Goods*, p. 129.
39. Nash, *Authority and Freedom in Education*, pp. 68, 67.

> *Moralism*, as I define it, is the view that certain sorts of activity should be banned because they are immoral, even though they harm nobody, except on the grounds of their alleged immorality. *Perfectionism*, as I define it, is the view that certain ways of life or sorts of activity are so excellent that people ought to pursue them, and if resistant, should be compelled to pursue them, even though they benefit nobody, except on the grounds of their alleged excellence.[40]

There are clear differences between these approaches and the more demanding conception of morality I argue for here. Libertarianism and thin liberalisms attempt to maximize individual freedom. Their insight that people ought to be able, other things being equal, to pursue their own conceptions of the good life is valuable: it is desirable to preserve as large a realm of liberty as possible with respect to such matters as association, movement, and occupation. But we must also recognize certain hitherto ignored needs as legitimate social demands and institutionalize provision for them. For, as Bellah, Baier, and Jaggar argue, if liberty-oriented theories work at all, it is because they rely on an underground value system to meet the needs unrecognized by their precepts. It makes much more sense to look our needs straight in the eye and build provision for them into the social fabric. This is a far cry from the moralism described above. In short, there is a viable middle ground between conceptions of morality that place minimal demands on us and those that impose on us a conception of the good unrelated to visible welfare.

How does the foregoing relate to the question whether children should have equal rights? On the one hand, it raises questions about the moral underpinnings of children's liberation. On the other, it suggests that children's moral development needs more attention than it has hitherto received, and that the demands of such development should be taken into account as we ponder when adult rights should be recognized for children. Let us consider each of these question's in turn.

40. Lindley, "Teenagers and Other Children," p. 75. This position is a hostile but perhaps quite accurate characterization of Lord Patrick Devlin's position in *The Enforcement of Morals* (New York: Oxford University Press, 1965).

The Moral Underpinnings of Children's Liberation

Proponents of children's liberation are making a moral claim: justice requires that children be granted equal rights. Although they rarely offer very much information about either their general moral theory or how the claim and the theory are connected, one can infer from their arguments that freedom plays a preeminent role in the overall scheme of things. And, as I have already pointed out, this value tends to go hand in hand with the kind of individualism that has dominated analytic philosophy until quite recently. The case for children's liberation therefore falls clearly within the liberal camp.[41]

There is so much variety within that camp, however, that there is room for at least two opposing positions with respect to this question. My hypothesis here is that only some versions of libertarianism/thin liberalism are consistent with children's rights. Richer liberalisms will most likely preclude such rights.

Let us first look at the relationship between children's rights and libertarianism. Because of his prominence among libertarians (despite their differences), it would make sense to see what Nozick has to say about the matter. As it turns out, however, he fails to take a stand on the consequences of his approach for children. It is therefore rather difficult to be sure what the implications of his position might be. About all one could safely infer is that children cannot participate fully in society before they can understand and use the three principles of justice necessary for fair property holdings.[42] The age of emancipation would therefore depend on the exact form of those principles, something about which he leaves us remarkably ill informed. To be consistent, other libertarian theories would have to have analogous requirements.

Thus it seems that not even a quite unrestrictive libertarianism necessarily implies equal rights for children. It might still be true, however, that equal rights for children must be premised on some very weak version of libertarianism. Libertarianism holds that government should interfere only minimally with individual decisions

41. Shulamith Firestone does not seem to agree; but I suspect that her position is incoherent. See *The Dialectic of Sex* (New York: Bantam, 1970).

42. See Nozick, *Anarchy, State, and Utopia*, pp. 330–31, 150–53.

about how to live. Moral libertarianism holds that we, as individuals, should also interfere as little as possible in the decisions of others. One justification for this position arises from skepticism in regard to the ability to make judgments about better or worse ways of life: if it is difficult to evaluate such judgments, there can hardly be much of a case for coercing people's choices. The other major justification for this position arises from the overriding value placed on autonomous choices: even if people choose wrongly, there is nonetheless great value in letting them act on those choices. As I suggested earlier, I think the case for equal rights for children appeals to both of these lines of argument, despite the obvious tension between them. Let us therefore consider the implications of each in turn.

A skeptical libertarianism asserts that we cannot really evaluate ends: people have widely varying values, and reason cannot show that some are superior to others. Not only do we have a hard time knowing what is in a given individual's best interest, but our stock of moral knowledge is even smaller: we can, at most, require people to respect the equal freedom of others.

It is easy to see the close relationship between this kind of skeptical libertarianism and the skeptical version of the case for equal rights for children. If we know so little about ends, it would be irrational as well as unjust to demand more knowledge of children before we recognized their rights. And conversely, a liberation theory that proposes only a weak test such as the capacity for instrumental reasoning will be most consistent if it is tied to this kind of skeptical libertarianism. Saying that children should be able to move freely in the adult world when they can reason instrumentally makes the most sense when that is all adults are doing.

Given a nonskeptical moral theory that holds that some values are better than others and that this fact can be known, it would be difficult to make a case for instrumental reasoning capacity as the criterion for equal rights unless it could be shown that children developed good judgment only as a result of early freedom to act on poor judgment. Liberationists (somewhat inconsistently) do tend to argue to this effect, but, as I will show later, they also tend to underestimate the devastating consequences of this approach and ignore the merits of a program of gradually increasing freedom. If this attempt to reconcile a weak test for rights with a nonskeptical moral theory fails, then the most plausible moral basis for the skeptical version of children's liberation is a correspondingly skeptical libertarianism.

What about the nonskeptical libertarian position that argues for the value of freedom? It says that if freedom is the highest value, then consistency requires equal rights for children, too. This claim is true even if we know that they will make mistakes, mistakes that will hinder or sometimes preclude altogether their development into Kantian autonomous beings who are ruled by principle. This libertarian line is obviously vulnerable to the objection that such autonomy, not mere self-determination, is the better value. That is, in fact, the position of moderate liberals who think that there are grounds for limiting children in certain ways in order to ensure their later autonomy. More important for my purposes here, this conviction that short-run freedom is the overriding value ties children's liberation to a very extreme form of libertarianism even more tightly than did the skeptical argument. Such a libertarianism views freedom as the overriding moral and political value, reduces to an absolute minimum the grounds for interfering with individual choices, and is the antithesis of the more demanding moral theory for which I have argued.

My desire for such a demanding theory is not a mere aesthetic preference: as I have argued, there are excellent reasons for thinking that undemanding theories such as libertarianism just won't work, let alone provide adequate conditions for human flourishing. Hence if the only moral theory consistent with equal rights for children fails to do these things, the case for equal rights must fail, too.

Suppose, however, that the preceding argument has gone astray in some way and that, contrary to its contention that equal rights for children could consistently be backed only by a very stripped-down theory such as libertarianism, those rights are instead compatible with a moderate liberal position, one that recognizes greater limits on the right to pursue our own conception of the good. A morally adequate version of such a theory would still be incompatible with children's liberation for the following reason. I have argued that a morally adequate theory must take into account such facts as the necessity for cooperation with respect to both human needs and those of the earth. It would therefore have to provide for the prerequisites for such cooperation, including whatever is necessary for the development of prudent and moral persons. This kind of moderate liberalism could arise via a Rawlsian theory that let enough information about human development, social conditions, and the physical environment penetrate the veil of ignorance to produce principles of justice that either by themselves guarantee a period of protection for children or ensure the choice of subsidiary principles that do so.[43]

This work has already provided good grounds for thinking that these prerequisites are incompatible with equal rights for children, and more are forthcoming. So here is a general problem that will plague any attempt to find a moral home for child liberation. A theory that is consistent with equal rights for children will be defective with respect to the prerequisites for an adequate moral theory. A theory that meets these moral prerequisites, however, will rule out children's rights because the necessary information about human life on earth will include information about children that will make it clear that equal rights for them are untenable. This difficulty constitutes a major stumbling block for the view in question: it looks as if children's liberation is a moral orphan.

Perhaps it will be argued that this objection is illegitimate, coming as it does from someone who is arguing against the overriding significance of theory. I do think we need to concentrate more on practical moral problems and less on highly abstract and predominantly logical aspects of theories. And I think that if we were forced to choose, we would do better with a rough sort of theory that serves us well in general than with one that does a better job with certain kinds of desert-island cases at the expense of more homely ones. This is not to say, however, that broad issues of consistency of the sort discussed here should be ignored: it seems to me still imperative to ask how a given moral decision fits into the larger theoretical picture.

Justice Revisited

In this chapter I have argued that despite its apparently moral basis, the debate about equal rights for children has been for the

43. Thinking in terms of the original position and the veil of ignorance that keeps individuals from ensuring that the rules of justice benefit them isn't, of course, the only way to think about liberal political theory. Brian Barry suggests that Rawls needs this apparatus only so long as individuals are expected to behave in a self-interested way. If, however, those persons are instead motivated by a desire to reach agreement on reasonable terms, the veil of ignorance would become unnecessary. See Brian Barry, *Theories of Justice* (Berkeley: University of California Press, 1989), pp. 371–72.

most part blind to an essential element in human development. Tolerable—let alone good—life depends on the moral character of the members of society. The moral character of those individuals depends not only upon their possessing self-control but upon a caring that is reflected in action that promotes the interests of others. Furthermore, currently popular moral views tend to underestimate the extent to which we need to limit the pursuit of our own private projects in order to care for others in this way. I conclude that there is good reason to doubt whether a moral theory adequate in this respect would recommend equal rights for children.

What response might proponents of equal rights make to these claims? If they argued for the capacity for instrumental reasoning as the criterion for equal rights, they would be vulnerable to two objections. First, as I have argued, this criterion is weak and therefore overinclusive: it grants equal rights to children who could barely—if at all—manage their lives. Second, it, together with its accompanying high valuation of freedom, implies too thin a moral theory, one that cannot accommodate the kinds of social needs already discussed. To this latter criticism it is difficult to see any good response, although, as I have suggested, the points to be looked at in the rest of this work would help clinch the case. To the first criticism, they might respond that overinclusiveness is not a practical problem. Both Howard Cohen and Bob Franklin argue, in the context of voting, that there is nothing wrong with children having rights they do not exercise, as with the readiness to exercise them comes the competence to do so.[44] It would be fair to keep an open mind about this idea, although I think that the burden of proof should be on showing, on a case-by-case basis, that no serious harm is likely to come of any such proposed right.

Any less inclusive criterion, liberationists point out, would exclude, along with most children, some adults. Recognizing equal rights for adults (no matter how incompetent) but not for children (no matter how competent) would constitute serious injustice.

As I have been arguing, I have serious doubts about the ability of even most teens to live well independently. Although some may be unusually competent, they will still almost certainly be relatively

44. Cohen, *Equal Rights for Children*, chap. 8; and Franklin, *Rights of Children*, pp. 39–40.

lacking in the kind of background knowledge acquired only by experience and in the virtues and values that come of time, training, and education. Nonetheless, it would be difficult to prove that the most idiotic adult is more competent than the most mature teenager. However, I don't think that this is the claim upon which equal rights should, in any case, turn.

Nor should it turn upon the obviously true claim about the inadequacy of some adults. The reason is this. Even liberationists, after all, lament the mistakes and immorality of adults. It seems to me that instead of asserting children's right to be equally silly and weak, it would be at least as plausible to argue for the overriding importance of helping children develop the self-control and other enabling virtues necessary for living more satisfying and moral lives. And, as we have seen, there is good reason to suppose that helping children develop in desirable ways requires conditions incompatible with equal rights for them. We could create the conditions for helping them develop in desirable ways by adopting, instead of the weakest possible criterion for equal rights, a more stringent one that does exclude some adults. The consequence that they, too, would be deprived of equal rights could quite plausibly be avoided by the following considerations.

Proponents of children's rights argue that since children have certain capacities, just as adults do, they should be treated like adults.[45] If we assume, for the moment, the truth of the empirical claim about capacity, their argument draws strength from the fact that some adults do not use their capacities.[46] However, what if most adults do use their capacities whereas most children do not?[47] Why shouldn't we regard *this* difference as morally relevant?

The belief that it is such a morally relevant difference is strengthened by the following considerations. We are used to comparing pairs of individuals to see whether there are morally relevant differences between them, and in general this is an appropriate approach

45. This position assumes that children do in fact have all the relevant capacities, a question that remains to be shown. It also assumes that differences in degree (caused by varying amounts of learning about the world, for example) cannot be morally relevant. I think I have given some reason to doubt this claim.

46. Cohen, remember, argues that we also think it morally relevant that when adults do not use their capacities, their reasons are different from children's.

47. This distinction has a venerable history; see, e.g., Aristotle, *Nichomachean Ethics*, II, 5.

to judging moral claims. If a particular capacity or characteristic is considered the ground of a given right, then having that capacity or characteristic gives one a prima facie claim to this right. And if the right involves protection of a very important interest, it ought to be recognized even if that entails some inefficiency or inconvenience on the part of others, for we consider it wrong except in very unusual circumstances to sacrifice justice for efficiency.[48]

Now, the rights at issue here, while not fundamental (like the right to life), are nonetheless significant. Therefore, if a good number of children could be found with the relevant characteristics, a strong case could be made for finding ways to recognize the corresponding rights *for them.* If no reliable procedure for judging competence could be found, however, we would face a dilemma: should we recognize those rights for all children in spite of the harm that would undoubtedly come of recognizing them for those who are not ready? I am not sure how I would respond, although I do think that our overall bias should be to advance justice, even at considerable cost. I am relieved of the need to deal with this dilemma, however, because the criteria for having equal rights suggested by liberationists are inadequate, and therefore, despite the fact that many children could meet them, it does not follow that equal rights for children should be based upon them. The criteria I suggest instead are so much more demanding that no young children and only a very few mid- to late teens could meet them. In a case of this sort, it becomes important to look at the statistical differences in the characteristics of the relevant classes. Any individual we pick at random from one class may match a member of the other with respect to the qualities we are looking for. However, the distribution of certain

48. This approach to rights relies heavily on the theoretical structure laid out by John Stuart Mill in chap. 5 of *Utilitarianism.* Rights, according to Mill, "is a name for certain classes of moral rules which concern the essentials of human well-being more nearly, and are therefore of more absolute obligation than any other rules for the guidance of life." On Mill's mind was, among other things, the kind of security we can have only if members of society are prevented from oppressing others for their own convenience. Thus the most fundamental rights are those that can be overridden only in the most extreme circumstances, if ever. Rights representing lesser interests might occasionally have to give way, however, in the face of stronger conflicting rights that arise to prevent harm or confer great benefit. This theory thus both protects our most fundamental interests (under the rubric of "justice") and allows us to take account of the need to promote the general welfare. Applied stupidly or in bad faith, it will of course, like any other moral theory, as Mill himself pointed out, result in misery.

important characteristics varies widely between the two classes. Thus it may be that 99.5 percent of the members of the class of children are susceptible to foolish, headstrong behavior, whereas only 15 percent of the members of the class of adults are similarly inclined. And the existence of this difference in distribution means that a given right will lead to very different consequences for the two classes.[49]

We can most profitably understand this way of looking at the matter by distinguishing between law and morality. We know that law cannot attempt to cover adequately every case because of individual variations.[50] Instead, it deals in classes of cases, partly on the basis of statistical generalizations. This approach can lead to serious injustices in some cases, injustices courts attempt to rectify by qualifying the generalizations upon which they are based. But given the scope of law, some arbitrariness is expected and probably ineradicable because of the constraints posed by the need for clear rules and avoidance of serious harm. Sometimes individual tests are appropriate but they exact a price in efficiency or other values. In the moral realm, we expect to start with individual cases and are much less

49. We need to be sensitive here to the distinction between classes of persons whose capacities may be artificially depressed or altered by oppression and those who are not subject to such disabilities. Thus, for instance, the fact that the class of women, as a whole, probably scores less well on certain kinds of math tests shouldn't be grounds for prohibiting women from pursuing mathematics because there is good evidence that social pressures make it more difficult for women to excel at it. (Even if that were not true, it might still not follow that keeping women out of math would make sense, of course.) Liberationists tend to conflate these two cases, claiming that children do have the potential to behave more maturely. Although I agree with them that this is probably true in some limited ways, there is no evidence that their overall maturity could be brought up to the desired level. I look at this question in more detail in chap. 6 and 7.

We also need to be sensitive to the difference between cases in which what is at issue is the mere provision of an opportunity to show whether you can learn a given skill or meet a given standard and the provision of a liberty that assumes that a particular kind of development has already occurred. The former can often be provided to all at relatively little cost, so that there is no justification for limiting access to the opportunity even if we suspect that few individuals will qualify. The latter may, as here, have unacceptably high costs: perhaps, for example, some motorcyclists are such careful drivers that mandatory helmet wearing is an unnecessary constraint on their freedom; however, the overall costs of making helmets optional may be too high to tolerate.

50. See for some discussion Martin P. Golding, *Philosophy of Law* (Engelwood Heights, N.J.: Prentice-Hall, 1975); and Norman E. Bowie and Robert L. Simon, *The Individual and the Political Order*, 2d ed. (Engelwood Heights, N.J.: Prentice-Hall, 1986), chap. 7. See also Aristotle, *Nichomachean Ethics and Politics*.

tolerant of principles that appear to run roughshod over their particular features.[51]

Here we are thinking about both realms. It is necessary, therefore, to come up with a suitably general approach for the law, while trying to ensure its sensitivity to special cases. It would therefore be appropriate to argue for a legal distinction between children and adults, but one that could be overridden by special provision such as competence tests for unusually mature children to achieve legal majority, just as we now allow for emancipating minors. At the same time, it would in any case be important to urge parents of such children to recognize their maturity and treat them accordingly. It would be surprising if this were not often done already, as it is plausible to think that children's maturity is not completely unrelated to parental good sense.

Now if we are interested in fair and well-functioning societies, and if these characteristics are enhanced when more rather than fewer individuals exercise their capacities in certain ways, than we must accordingly emphasize *habits*, not capacities. And we ought to be interested in such societies. First, as I have suggested, circumstances have changed in such a way that civilization as we know it—and perhaps life itself—may not survive unless we change our ways quite drastically. We are threatened with several kinds of ecological catastrophe caused primarily by preoccupation with immediate advantage whatever the long-term cost. The responsibility for such practices and policies rests with those who instigate and permit them, as well as with those wealthy enough to be able to choose wiser paths. Citizens of the United States are, therefore, on both counts, more responsible than most.

Second, quite apart from these environmental problems, many people live short, miserable lives as a result of poverty, poverty that could be diminished or perhaps even eradicated were wealthier individuals to share their resources with them. Furthermore, a variety of other social problems, such as racism and sexism, haunt us and make life much worse than it has to be for oppressed groups.

51. This is not always true, of course. Consider the slippery-slope argument against active voluntary euthanasia, which discounts the interest of some in being killed allegedly to safeguard the interests of others in not being killed. This kind of example demonstrates the inconsistencies that creep into moral philosophy when people fail to take a comprehensive enough view.

Averting environmental disaster and addressing these urgent social problems will require of many of us substantially higher standards of behavior, with respect both to our mutual interests and to the welfare of others. Not only will some members of the current generation of adults have to change their attitudes, but those higher standards will have to be inculcated in children. It is reasonable to believe that a longer rather than a shorter period of preparation for adulthood is necessary (although obviously not sufficient) for the relevant kind of learning.

In chapter 1 I argued that judgments about interests demand a kind of knowledge that takes time to acquire. This fact holds for judgments about both one's own interests and those of others. Since judgments about others' interests are central to moral action, the considerations raised in this chapter reinforce the conclusions reached in the last.

Whether the character development necessary to subordinate one's own interests to those of others and to carry out those judgments would further delay the point at which it would be appropriate to grant young people equal rights would, I suspect, depend to some degree on the social environment, as well as on which theory of moral development is correct. So, for example, if some Kohlbergian account is true, then equal rights would, other things being equal, have to wait at least until the development of adult logic at about puberty. If, on the contrary, coherent moral impulses are present early on, and especially if society encourages their expression in natural and satisfying ways, then those rights could, in principle, be recognized earlier. In practice, however, since moral action depends not just on having an impulse to do the right thing but also on the ability to decide what the right thing is—something that may require substantial background knowledge and logic—equal rights might have to wait at least as long as if such moral impulses weren't present. Since American society does not, in any case, encourage the early development of concern for others, late rather than early development of mature moral behavior could be expected.

As I have argued, liberationists have a tendency to assume that the average child will quickly come to function at least as well as the average contemporary adult. Under current conditions, that would not be good enough. In any case, I do not believe that there is sufficient evidence for this view, and I think, in fact, that it would be far more plausible to suppose that the average liberated child would at best barely scrape by. It is surely unlikely that individuals in such desperate straits would be able to participate effectively in the fight for a better world. Having a larger rather than a smaller percentage of the population fall into this category might well make the difference between success or failure.

Given these considerations, would it be unfair to children to impose upon them a longer period of apprenticeship than the one proposed by liberationists? And, in particular, would it be unfair to expect them to develop higher levels of self-control, enabling virtues, and moral behavior than has so far been demanded of many of the rest of us?

I think it is true to say that continuing our present way of life means that our children will be lucky to inherit a livable world; even if they do, their children most likely won't. It is also unlikely that, if we go on as we are, we will be able to rectify the inequities that result in suffering and premature death for so many. In comparison with these things, it seems to me that impressing upon children a consistently higher standard constitutes by far the lesser evil. If this conclusion is thought to be dubious, then it is surely time to revise our notion of justice. Either justice cannot be the overriding moral value it has been taken to be or else we need a richer conception of justice, one more closely tied to the most fundamental values. This conclusion is predicated on the moral priority of a minimally decent life for all, but that ought to be uncontroversial.

The following lines of argument are open to those who would oppose this conclusion. First, one might doubt that the world is in such bad shape. Detailed justification of this claim would be out of place here; however, consideration of contemporary injustices as well as of such environmental problems as pollution and the greenhouse effect should suffice to strike outrage and fear in any reasonable heart. Second, one might doubt whether prudent and moral behavior has any power to improve the situation. Again, dealing with this problem in any comprehensive way would require us to go far beyond the scope of this work. It should suffice to say that such doubt must rest upon antihumanistic assumptions that are in any case incompatible with the present enterprise. Third, one might object to my view of the somewhat relative nature of justice.

It is important to get clear about what is at issue here. I am not claiming that it is possible to do without justice: our basic sense of fairness requires the kind of evenhandedness implicit in formal justice, of treating like cases alike. But deciding which cases are alike is not the straightforward task proponents of equal rights contend. I have been arguing that there are good reasons for rejecting a highly inclusive criterion for equal rights, and that the narrower alternative proposed instead does not, if it is adopted in conjunction with the statistical approach described here, constitute the injustice liberationists suppose. There is no compelling *internal* argument for either possible criterion; that is, there is nothing about the criteria themselves that forces us to choose either of them. Only by looking at the *context* in which they work can we begin to find reasons for choosing one rather than another. In other words, filling in the formal outline of justice in a particular way appropriately depends on *external* conditions. And if we protect our most important interests by designating them rights, to be protected by the strictures of justice, this is as it should be.

PART II

The Argument from Consequences

Chapter 3

HUMAN DEVELOPMENT

> . . . although I believe that the age of majority is set much too high for engaging in most of the activities now denied to children, I have no empirical basis for asserting that only children under some specific age (say, twelve years) ought to be paternalistically restricted from engaging in certain activities. One of my main points is that those who have set the age of majority at eighteen years have no such basis either.
>
> —Laurence D. Houlgate, "Children, Paternalism, and Rights to Liberty"

Remember that the argument for children's liberation falls into two basic parts. On the one hand, it is thought unjust to withhold equal rights from children. On the other, it is argued that the consequences of their having such rights would not be bad.

I have shown that the argument from justice is far more dubious than it at first seems. One version depends upon the choice of a very weak criterion as the candidate for a morally relevant difference between children and adults; the weak criterion leads to the judgment that there is no such difference between the two classes. But choosing a stronger criterion leads to the judgment that there is indeed a difference of that sort. I have argued that there are good reasons for adopting a more rather than a less demanding criterion, reasons that avoid the charge of inconsistency. Hence it is justifiable to deny the conclusive nature of the argument from justice.

Not only is the appeal to justice less than compelling, but, as I have hinted, among the grounds for doubting its worth are considerations that should lead us to see why it is plausible to suppose that if children have equal rights, they are less likely to develop enabling virtues and the self-control upon which they depend. If liberated children don't develop such virtues, they will live less satisfying lives and there seems little hope of a better world—or perhaps any human world at all. And there are indeed grounds for believing that liberated children are unlikely to develop these desirable traits. This matter should be of interest both to those who want to evaluate liberationist arguments and those who simply desire more information to help them settle on general guidelines for handling children.

Knowledge about child development is largely empirical, and we could be more secure about it if we had available to us an example of a society where children have equal rights; we could then see what happens and decide whether we like it or not. A surprising amount of useful information can be found, however, if we are willing to make some assumptions about what equal rights would entail and to venture beyond the territory usually frequented by philosophers.

My central assumption here is that if we are alert, we can gather evidence about what it would be like if children had equal rights. In general, the marker we are looking for is greater liberty for children, the kind that endows children with protection from treatment that overrides their desires for the sake of their interests. In practice, then, we seek examples of circumstances in which children make their own decisions, in the absence of or despite adult advice about what to do. Once we connect liberty with equal rights in this manner, historical experience, as well as psychological and sociological studies, can be seen to have substantial relevance to our concerns.

Historical Evidence

Annette Baier argues that moral philosophers need to root their thinking in history:

> Unless we know the fate of communities that tried to implant and live by the moral principles we consider, how can we have any empirically tested opinion about their soundness? . . . [This information] is not decisive, of course, for the validity of those principles for us now, but it does seem relevant data for the moral philosopher. Unless our moral reflections are historically informed, they will be mere speculation.[1]

1. Annette Baier, "Doing without Moral Theory?" in *Postures of the Mind* (Minneapolis: University of Minnesota Press, 1985).

Useful historical information comes to us via experiments in child-rearing founded on two closely related conceptions of human development. These experiments were based on ideas of Rousseau and Freud.

The notion that human development is internally driven and that our job is to encourage natural development with a minimum of interference is known as the "growth metaphor" in educational thought.[2] It is contrasted with the Lockean idea that we are constructed by experience.[3]

These characterizations of the way humans develop are extremes. That is, they represent opposite ends of a possible continuum. On the one hand, the growth metaphor suggests an organism whose development is entirely determined by internal factors; on the other, the Lockean notion of the *tabula rasa* presents us with the picture of an organism entirely at the mercy of outside events. Neither of these ideas is very plausible to begin with, and they embody the beginning stages of thought about how we develop. Nowadays most thoughtful people agree that both internal and external factors play important parts in our growth, although the extent to which one or the other is thought to predominate varies with intellectual fashion and politics.[4] The extreme versions, however, sometimes still have power to bewitch: consider how influential sociobiology, the latest incarnation of the growth metaphor, has been lately.[5]

The historical figure most commonly associated with the growth metaphor is Jean-Jacques Rousseau. Rousseau's treatise on educa-

2. Jane Roland Martin, *Reclaiming a Conversation* (New Haven: Yale University Press, 1985), p. 50.

3. Locke's general views about human mental functioning are to be found in his *Essay Concerning Human Understanding*, ed. A. C. Fraser (Oxford: Clarendon, 1894). The most extreme versions of the social construction thesis are just as erroneous as popular interpretations of Rousseau. See John Locke, *The Educational Writings*, ed. James L. Axtell (Cambridge: Cambridge University Press, 1968), and John W. Yolton, *John Locke and Education* (New York: Random House, 1971), esp. chap. 2.

4. Generally, those who wish to stress the inevitability of certain behavior patterns tend to attribute more weight to internal biological factors. This tendency depends on the mistaken assumption that it is always easier to alter environment than biology. But the complex interactions between biology and environment raise serious questions about this position.

5. Sociobiological explanations of human behavior have been somewhat less in evidence in the popular press lately, although they now seem entrenched in some areas of biology. For an excellent refutation of the theory's application to humans, see Philip Kitcher's *Vaulting Ambition: Sociobiology and the Quest for Human Nature* (Cambridge, Mass.: MIT Press, 1985).

tion, *Emile*, laid out a detailed plan of education for a boy, *Emile*; much less detailed were the radically different recommendations for his female counterpart, Sophie.[6] Theorists have concentrated on the recommendations for Emile, ignoring for the most part those for Sophie. This omission is significant because Emile's development is consequently taken as the model for *human* development.

Emile is to grow up alone with his own tutor, who affords him great freedom. His tutor's job is to supervise him, allowing natural consequences, not punishment, to teach him how to act.[7] Rousseau's prescriptions are generally considered to constitute a growth theory, although the total control required to make sure Emile learns his lessons undermines such an interpretation of his writing.[8] This fact is extremely significant for our ultimate evaluation of the validity of the growth metaphor, but what is of interest at this point is how his ideas were used.

In her book on the history of childrearing advice, Christina Hardyment describes the consequences of a late eighteenth-century British fling with Rousseau. The parents' interpretation of *Emile* was that the children were to do as they liked from ages two to twelve. They were to have natural surroundings and no academic training, and "all their actions had to spring from necessity rather than obedience." The children's freedom was of paramount importance. Again, this understanding of Rousseau's precepts may not reflect his ideas accurately, but it is of special interest to us because it resembles the environment that equal rights would provide.

What happened? Hardyment writes:

> Unfortunately, parents and educators rapidly became disillusioned by their experiments with nobly savage children. Richard Lovell Edgeworth's boy became so unmanageable that he was sent away to boarding school. David Williams described one little child of nature who, aged 13, slept on the floor, spoke "a jargon he had formed out of the several dialects of the family," could neither read nor write, and was

6. Jean-Jacques Rousseau, *Emile, or On Education*, trans. Allan Bloom (New York: Basic Books, 1979). For further interesting discussion of Rousseau's views on girls and boys, see Martin, *Reclaiming a Conversation*, pp. 39–45.

7. Rousseau, *Emile*, p. 35.

8. See Martin, *Reclaiming a Conversation*, pp. 50–51. For a discussion of this view of Rousseau, see Bruce A. Ryan, "Jean-Jacques Rousseau and Behavior Control: The Technology of a Romantic Behaviorist," *Behaviorism* 4 (Fall 1976): 245–56.

"a little emaciated figure, his countenance betraying marks of premature decay, or depraved passions; his teeth discolored, his hearing almost gone."[9]

It would be interesting to know more about the details of these children's upbringing, as well as their ultimate fate. By itself, this account isn't particularly compelling, although it might reasonably make one wary of glowing theoretical speculation about the probable good effects of free childrearing.

This conclusion is especially important when it is viewed in the full context of Rousseau's theory. Remember that his recommendations with respect to boys and girls were radically different. Although Emile is to be as free as possible (suggesting the growth metaphor), Sophie is not. She is to *learn* to play a nurturing, supporting role in life and to endure whatever injustices she is subjected to.[10] Particularly striking, in light of Rousseau's objection that it is "barbarous" to pile social constraints on top of the already onerous physical ones children face, is his recommendation that little girls be trained to interrupt whatever they are doing at a moment's notice.[11] The conclusion that the growth metaphor is inappropriate for Sophie

9. Christina Hardyment, *Dream Babies: Three Centuries of Good Advice on Child Care* (New York: Harper & Row, 1983), p. 19. This description does lead one to wonder what the child could have been up to that destroyed his hearing. In the case of a contemporary child, the answer would, on the contrary, be obvious! For another fascinating account of models of child development in the context of the history of ideas, see John Cleverly and D. C. Philips, *From Locke to Spock* (Melbourne: Melbourne University Press, 1976). They recount some of the most bitterly fought controversies, including environment vs. heredity, discipline vs. indulgence, and childhood innocence vs. original sin.

10. See *Emile*, chap. 5. Rousseau writes: "Girls ought to be vigilant and industrious. That is not all. They ought to be constrained very early. This misfortune, if it is one for them, is inseparable from their sex, and they are never delivered from it without suffering far more cruel misfortunes. All their lives they will be enslaved to the most continual and most severe of constraints—that of the proprieties. They must first be exercised in constraint, so that it never costs them anything to tame all their caprices in order to submit them to the wills of others. If they always wanted to work, one would sometimes have to force them to do nothing. . . . From this habitual constraint comes a docility which women need all their lives, since they never cease to be subjected either to a man or to the judgments of men and they are never permitted to put themselves above these judgments" (pp. 370–71).

11. He says: "Do not deprive them of gaiety, laughter, noise, and frolicsome games, but prevent them from getting their fill of one in order to run to another; do not allow for a single instant in their lives that they no longer know any restraint. Accustom them to being interrupted in the midst of their games and brought back to other cares without grumbling" (ibid., p. 370).

seems inescapable: his prescriptions for her fit much more comfortably in a Lockean learning model of human development.

This fact about Rousseau's views raises two issues for us. Most important here is that since he is really proposing two different paradigms of development, we cannot arbitrarily pick one and generalize on it: this would constitute an appeal to authority that was not only illegitimate but defective. It is defective because, as has already been suggested, Rousseau's views have been seriously misinterpreted and because one aspect is being taken for the whole. The other issue is that failing to notice Rousseau's bifurcated approach both results from and perpetuates blind reliance on our own similar approach to childrearing. As Baier and Alison Jaggar show us, our society, too, has a tendency to prescribe a universal model of development which is at best viable only when it is supported by a quite different and unrecognized complementary one for girls.[12]

Much fuller and even more suggestive information about the consequences of granting children a great deal of freedom is available to us from another, more recent period of experimentation. In the early years of this century, Vienna was gripped by excitement at the possibility of a new kind of education, a so-called psychoanalytical pedagogy. The promise of a new generation of creative and mentally stable individuals shimmered before the eyes of its proponents. Freud's ideas were central to this promising new approach to education.

The cardinal Freudian principle was that repression is the major cause of neurosis. As Sol Cohen explains, the solution to neurosis seemed obvious: "a freer, more lenient, indulgent, and permissive upbringing." More specifically, its advocates, warning against repression, believed that "so far as possible, one should leave the child alone, with as complete withholding of direct injurious influences as possible, and inhibit him as little as possible in his natural development."[13] This picture was completed by recommendations about early and complete sex education. These precepts are sufficiently like

12. See Baier, "Need for More than Justice," p. 50, and Jaggar, *Feminist Politics*, chap. 3.

13. Sol Cohen, "In the Name of the Prevention of Neurosis: The Search for Psychoanalytic Pedagogy in Europe, 1905–1938," in *Regulated Children, Liberated Children: Education in Psychoanalytical Perspective*, ed. Barbara Finkelstein (New York: Psychohistory Press, 1979), pp. 187–88, 190. Here Cohen quotes Otto Rank and Hans Sachs, in their 1916 *Significance of Psychoanalysis for the Mental Sciences*.

those that would guide the lives of children with adult rights to warrant a careful look at the attempts to carry them out.

By the 1920s a group of psychoanalysts, mostly women led by Anna Freud, had started in earnest to develop the new pedagogy. Anna Freud rightly argued that education starts the first day of a baby's life, not when it begins school. From that time, parents attempt to "civilize" babies, at the expense of their budding originality. So "civilizing" both crushes creativity and creates neurosis. The answer was to let children behave in ways hitherto defined as "naughty." The program was summed up as "progressive education," an education that was the "liberation of the instincts . . . a struggle against trauma . . . laissez-faire, with a minimum of intervention on the part of educators and parents."[14]

This movement culminated in a series of experiments. Among them were Siegfried Bernfeld's Kinderheim Baumgarten, Lili Roubiczek-Peller's Haus der Kinder, Anna Freud and Dorothy Burlingham's school, and Vera Schmidt's Moscow Children's Home and Psychological Laboratory. Most were short-lived, and appear to have been regarded even by their supporters as unsuccessful. By the late 1930s enthusiasm had waned. The major problem, Cohen reports, was "the growing weight of evidence that between principle and practice there was a huge lacuna, through which many a theory, and many a child, could fall."[15] The keystone of the theory was that sexual ignorance and repression create neurosis. But sexual liberation did not have the expected good results, as we will see shortly. Other hypotheses posited by the theory also failed to bear fruit.

14. Cohen, "In the Name of the Prevention of Neurosis," pp. 191–96. This is the view of Rudolph Ekstein, a proponent of "progressive education."

15. Ibid., pp. 197–201, 203. Cohen suggests that threatening political developments in Europe at this time, together with the specific political failure of the psychoanalytic pedagogists to make common cause with other educational liberals, may also have reduced the attraction of the theory.

> From this vantage point, the movement to create a psychoanalytic pedagogy was simply a new phase of a venerable movement that we can date back to Rousseau in the 18th century, and which was carried forward in the 19th century by Pestalozzi and Froebel. To Austrian and German teachers who had studied Rousseau, Pestalozzi, or Froebel, the emphasis in psychoanalytic pedagogy on the years of infancy, the critical role of parents, the merits of permissiveness, the educational value of play, the concept of "sublimation" and even infantile sexuality would not have been novel or bewildering. . . . Most of the child analysts repressed their previous awareness that some analytic concepts might have some connection with the history of educational ideas. They wanted to be "scientific" and original. (p. 203)

In 1945 Willi Hoffer described the practical principles of psychoanalytic pedagogy. At first educators concentrated on imparting information about sex to the children in their care; when this strategy had little effect, they moved on to providing an environment in which children could satisfy their instincts:

> The object was to minimize the frustration of instinctual demands, and to avoid castration fear and the condemnation of sexual activities. The child's right to enjoy his instincts was to be actively encouraged . . . if natural development were to proceed unhampered, gradual progress would follow automatically according to the stages described by Freud. Thumbsucking, pleasure in dirt, smearing, exhibitionism and scoptophilia, masturbation, and attempts at intercourse were expected to give way step by step to the normal processes of the latency period.[16]

Children were allowed nearly absolute freedom. Not only was sexual information willingly given, but masturbation was unrestricted. Children were allowed to see their parents' naked bodies. Expressions of jealousy, hate, and discontent were permitted. In general, "there was also a tendency to avoid any form of prohibition." All parental wishes were explained, and insight and affection were supposed to be the grounds of obedience: "authoritative demands were condemned as they were considered sadistic and likely to cause castration fear."[17]

Compare this approach with the one recommended for children by Howard Cohen. If children had equal rights, it would be wrong to do to them anything that would violate an adult's rights. Hence force is ruled out and the only remaining method of control is the promise of rewards: "the subject of the control must think it is 'worth it' to seek the rewards of the system." Since children are free to seek a different home, children who are unmoved by the reward system can, in theory, avoid even these trade-offs.[18] In short, children

16. Willi Hoffer, "Psychoanalytic Education," *Psychoanalytic Study of the Child* 1 (1945): 301.

17. Ibid. One wonders how these strictures were interpreted for girls.

18. Howard Cohen, *Equal Rights for Children*, p. 94. Cohen does recognize the de facto power of parents over dependent children with no alternatives, however. It seems to me that this almost inescapable point undermines the voluntary nature of the environment

enjoy a kind of freedom now available only to adults; no longer are they subject to the coercion of parents who expect obedience to their wishes.

The psychoanalytic educators found that the assumption that inner forces would direct the children through Freud's psychosexual stages was false. Children reared according to these principles did not develop into the unrepressed, creative, but otherwise normal individuals that had been foreseen. Although they were less inhibited, latency failed to moderate their distressingly infantile behavior. They showed relatively little interest in the world about them, preferring to daydream, were not toilet trained, and displayed volatile emotional activity. Hoffer writes that the expected school behavior did not materialize: the children showed no special creativity and could not concentrate. "They seemed egocentric; group demands affected them little. They were extremely intolerant of the demands of adults: timetables, mealtimes, table manners, routine hygienic measures, even if leniently handled, became sources of conflict. Their mental health could by no means be described in glowing terms. The children "showed an unexpected degree of irritability, a tendency to obsessions and depression, and certain peculiarities which during subsequent analytic treatment usually proved to be concealed anxiety."[19]

These noble experiments were thus chastening, and they put the burden of proof on liberationists to show why their approach would result in a better outcome. Moreoever, as with Rousseau, it turns out that the principles governing this research were misconceived

---

with which he is trying to provide children. In any case, his dichotomy between force and rewards fails to recognize the true nature of many parent-child interactions. This theme will be taken up later.

19. Hoffer, "Psychoanalytic Education," pp. 302–3. Sol Cohen also reports that Dorothy Burlingham noted similar developments in her "Problems Confronting the Psychoanalytic Educator," in her *Psychoanalytic Studies of the Sighted and the Blind* (New York: International Universities Press, 1972). He goes on to say that these permissively raised children were suffering from what Paul Federn describes as "pathological narcissism." They "become so spoiled through the easy achievement of a high degree of forepleasure, that they lose the capacity for real and complete achievement": Paul Federn, *Ego Psychology and the Psychoses* (New York: Basic Books, 1952), p. 346. In "Psychoanalysis and the Training of the Young Child," *Psychoanalytic Quarterly* 4 (1935): 20, Anna Freud elaborates: "The fact is that we do struggle with the child over his instinctual gratifications. We want him to have control over his sexual drives, for if they are constantly breaking through, there is danger that his development will be retarded or interrupted, that he will rest content with gratification instead of sublimating, with masturbation instead of learning, that he will confine his desire for knowledge to sexual matters instead of extending it to the whole wide world. This we want to prevent."

from the start. Sol Cohen attributes the main mistake to an overly simple understanding of Freud. He argues that there are two tendencies in Freud, one optimistic and liberating, the other more pessimistic and controlling. The psychoanalytic educators had picked out from his complex and partially contradictory theories only one strand, ignoring the considerations that motivated the darker Freud. This side of Freud was evident even in the early days, and by the 1920s and 1930s had become the dominant theme.[20]

In particular, Freud began to attribute the creation of neuroses more to the role and clash of instincts and less to the environment: anxiety, he held, is created by inescapable conflicts inherent in the process of growing up. Furthermore, Freud came to see innate aggression as a major problem and concluded that social controls on it were necessary to preserve civilization. By the end of World War I, pessimism dominated Freud's thinking, leading to a pronounced antiliberationist temper: freedom was no panacea. His later conception of conflicting internal aggressive drives led him to infer that the gratification of instincts does not lead to mental health. Cohen concludes that "Freud's revised formulations on aggression demolished one of the main pillars of the permissivist bias in psychoanalytic pedagogy." Child analysts hence retreated from the earlier simple equation of freedom with healthy development and concluded that parents and teachers must collaborate to limit expression of children's powerful drives. They hypothesized that aggression and sex

20. Cohen, "In the Name of the Prevention of Neurosis," pp. 185–86. In 1933, for example, Freud wrote:

> We realized that the difficulty of childhood lies in the fact that in a short span of time a child has to appropriate the results of a cultural evolution which stretches over thousands of years, including the acquisition of control over his instincts and adaptation to society—or at least the first beginnings of these two. He can only achieve a part of this modification through his own development; much must be imposed on him by education. . . .
>
> . . . Let us make ourselves clear as to what the first task of education is. The child must learn to control his instincts. It is impossible to give him liberty to carry out all his impulses without restriction. To do so would be a very instructive experiment for the child-psychologists; but life would be impossible for the parents and the children themselves would suffer grave damage, which would show itself partly at once and partly in later years. Accordingly, education must inhibit, forbid and suppress. . . . Thus education has to find its way between the Scylla of non-interference and the Charybdis of frustration. (Lecture XXXIV, "Explanations, Applications, and Orientations," in *New Introductory Lectures on Psychoanalysis* [1935], trans. and ed. James Strachey [New York: Norton, 1964], pp. 147, 149)

were in danger of overpowering children's weak egos and that outside pressure was needed to help repress those instincts.[21]

The final nail in the coffin of psychoanalytic pedagogy came with the concession that education cannot aim at avoiding neurosis: because of the complexity of the human personality, development necessarily involves the production of mental distress.[22] In short, letting children make their own decisions in the name of freedom and healthy development leaves them at the mercy of internal impulses that they need to learn to control. Although it might have been true that they could best learn such control by exercising freedom, the evidence suggests that outside help is needed. In retrospect, it seems clear that a major mistake in this approach was getting drawn into a classic case of false dilemma: Hoffer later pointed out that "the alternative to the old-fashioned neglect or denial of infantile sexuality is not to admit its existence and then leave the child alone with his various drives. This is merely another way of neglecting the immature organism."[23] More generally, it would seem plausible to explore middle roads between total freedom and total control.[24]

By the 1940s and 1950s, many of these pioneering child psychoanalysts were producing critiques of American education.[25] Sol Cohen writes that they attacked the lack of structure, authority, and limits associated with progressive education: it spoiled children and did so on the basis of its inaccurate ideas about Freud's theories. They were at pains to dissociate psychoanalysis from such principles. "They preferred to forget that there had been at one time, and not that long ago, a very intimate connection between psychoanalysis and permissive pedagogy." Cohen urges us not to forget this episode in the history of childrearing. He concludes that "Freud's later revisions of psychoanalytic pedagogy, no less than the history of the movement to create a psychoanalytic pedagogy, add

21. Cohen, "In the Name of the Prevention of Neurosis," pp. 205–7.

22. This thesis was propounded in two books: Anna Freud, *The Ego and the Mechanisms of Defense*, and Heinz Hartmann, *Ego Psychology and the Problem of Adaptation*, both published in New York by International Universities Press, the first in 1946, the second in 1958.

23. Hoffer, "Psychoanalytic Education," p. 303.

24. See, e.g., John B. Watson, *Psychology from the Standpoint of a Behaviorist* (Philadelphia: Lippincott, 1919).

25. Many of the initial proponents of psychoanalytic pedagogy had emigrated to the United States.

up to the most trenchant and devastating critique of permissiveness extant."[26] Certainly, if these reports are reliable and the conclusions drawn by the protagonists defensible, we must take them very seriously in the quest for understanding human development.

In both the periods of experimentation we have looked at, it seems clear that conditions of very great freedom for children failed to lead to the good consequences the growth metaphor would predict. This result suggests that the metaphor itself is mistaken. This conclusion is reinforced by the fact that neither Rousseau nor Freud provides any real theoretical support for such a view of human development. In both cases the educational programs were based on only partial or mistaken notions of their work.

Nevertheless, this approach to childrearing seems to be of perennial appeal to thoughtful individuals. A fresh generation of idealists arose in the 1960s; Marie Winn recounts the comments of a father of three:

> By the time the children were old enough to understand words, we began spelling out their freedom to them, the fact that they didn't *have* to do what we say just because we're bigger and stronger, that they were entitled to their own opinions and desires. But it really worked disastrously. . . . We realized pretty soon that giving them absolute freedom was not enough, that you had to make them understand that people's rights can infringe on each other. And we soon realized that such an understanding was much too complicated for them. They just weren't old enough to be able to restrain themselves on their own.[27]

These idealists, too, concluded that children need substantial direction, even if that same direction would seem authoritarian if it were aimed at adults.

This vignette, like that of the children of Rousseau, would not, by

26. Cohen, "In the Name of the Prevention of Neurosis," pp. 208, 210.

27. Marie Winn, *Children without Childhood* (New York: Pantheon, 1983), p. 195. The father, who now directs a human rights organization, elaborates further the tension between his "belief in children's rights and the daily realities of parenthood": "I'd say to them 'I want you to go outside now,' because I had work to do and I wanted them to go and play, but they'd say, 'We don't have to. You said you're not going to tell us what to do.' Or they'd come up and say, 'I want to sit on your lap now' and I'd say, 'You'll have to wait until I finish this job,' and they'd say, 'No, I want to sit in your lap and I'm *going* to whether you want me to or not!'"

itself, constitute a decisive case against the growth metaphor. In conjunction with the much fuller and better-documented case of psychoanalytic pedagogy, however, these two cases do raise serious questions about it and throw the burden of proof on its shoulders, especially because there appears to be a dearth of evidence in its favor. It is possible, of course, that some liberated children developed well. Given the impossibility of examining the rearing of every child, we must rely on relevant accounts. In my review of the literature, I found no accounts that support the liberationist position, and it seems to me highly improbable that they exist, for reasons to be discussed shortly. Even if there were a counterexample of a free child turning out well, it would not do, if most children need more limits, to base social policy on it. Overall social policy on this question, however, would not prevent parents who discern such potential in their children from providing them with many of the freedoms ordinarily enjoyed only by adults.

It is also true that some quite young children can be treated with something like the respect we normally reserve for adults. This state of affairs arises, I think, because of the happy coincidence of an intelligent, cooperative child and a good parent-child relationship. It would probably be safe to venture that part of any such good parent-child relationship is a parent's consistent willingness to explain and justify rules and demands. As we shall see shortly, refusal to recognize equal rights for children does not mean that children are to be slaves of their parents. Liberationists believe that a child's desire should never be overridden except when that of an adult would also be overridden. Rejecting this principle, however, does not compel one to embrace the view that explanation and justification are unimportant. On the contrary, given that my rejection of equal rights for children is based on the assumption that they need learning time, such a view would be, on any plausible educational theory, contradictory.

We might wonder about the success of other apparently liberationist environments, such as Montessori schools and Summerhill. Neither, however, emphasizes freedom as consistently as the earlier experiments. Montessori seems to fall in the tradition of the real Rousseau; these schools deliberately manipulate conditions in order to restrict choices and lead to consequences selected by the teachers. So although there is considerable emphasis on physical freedom, the overall environment includes substantial guidance and pressure.[28] A. S. Neill, the founder of Summerhill, disagreed with this aspect of Rousseau's manipulative approach, but he did believe that social consequences (not just "natural" ones) ought to affect children's decisions. Although he argued for complete freedom, he limited "license," defined as interfering with the aims of others.[29] Putting pressure on children not to interfere with the aims of others would constitute a limit not placed on liberated children unless they were to do so in a criminal way. Hence neither Montessori nor Summerhill can provide us with evidence about the kind of thoroughgoing freedom that would be associated with equal rights for young children.

The foregoing material casts serious doubt on the growth metaphor and programs based upon it. It also casts doubt on the probable success of consistent liberatory schemes in general, regardless of the assumptions about human nature upon which they are based. This information would, by itself, be reason for extreme caution about instituting any such program. Again, it seems to me that the burden of proof is upon proponents of equal rights to show why their proposals for letting children make their own decisions could be expected to yield better results. Other kinds of evidence could reinforce or undermine this conclusion, however. It would therefore be helpful to examine recent psychological work focusing on the effects of freedom for children.

Psychological Research

A large body of research has examined the effects of various kinds of treatment on children. Particularly revealing is the literature on permissiveness. "Permissiveness" has a broad array of meanings, including granting permission, tolerance, and allowing discretion.

28. See Suzanne L. Krogh, "Moral Beginnings: The Just Community in Montessori Pre-Schools," *Journal of Moral Education* 11 (October 1981): 41–46.

29. See Richard L. Hopkins, "Freedom and Education: The Philosophy of Summerhill," *Educational Theory* 26 (Spring 1976). Hopkins quotes Neill's response to a question about the difference between Montessori and Summerhill: "'A kid can say *fuck* in Summerhill, but not in a Montessori school.' As long as parents and teachers insist on forming a child's character, all the free activity in the world will not produce free people" (p. 207).

These are very broad categories—too broad, as researchers have found, to deal with the array of behavior that is of interest to us. Contemporary childrearing literature therefore distinguishes among types of permissiveness.[30] The most useful distinctions are provided by Diana Baumrind, who differentiates between "democratic" and "laissez-faire" styles. "Democratic" permissiveness consists of actively involving children in decision making and providing them with reasons for rules.[31] Differing opinions are aired and evaluated. Children's views are treated with respect, and prevail when they are judged sound. The "laissez-faire" style provides a sharp contrast. Baumrind describes the laissez-faire parent as one who

> attempts to behave in a nonevaluative, acceptant and affirmative manner toward the child's impulses, desires and actions. She consults with him about policy decisions and gives explanations for family rules. She makes few demands for household responsibility and orderly behavior. She presents herself to the child as a resource for him to use as he wishes, not as an ideal for him to emulate, nor as an active agent responsible for shaping or altering his ongoing or future behavior. She allows the child to regulate his own activities as much as possible, avoids the exercise of control, and does not insist that he obey externally defined standards. She attempts to use reason and manipulation, but not overt power, to accomplish her ends.[32]

30. The distinction represents progress in understanding the mixed results of early studies on permissiveness. For example, a classic study of development examined two dimensions of parental treatment of children: democracy and control. Children of democratic parents were planful, and fearless, good leaders, but aggressive and sometimes cruel in getting what they wanted from others. The writers nonetheless concluded that a democratic approach (which included a voice in family affairs and many choices about one's own activities) was the best, despite their opinion that this strategy might lead to resistance to the demands of adult society. They preferred the products of this method to those of both highly controlling parents (obedient, suggestible, fearful children lacking in tenacity) and undemocratic, controlling ones (obedient, suggestible, lacking in curiosity and creativity). Neither of the latter approaches led to quarrelsome, aggressive, cruel children. See A. L. Bladwin, J. Kalhorn, and E. H. Breese, *Psychological Monographs* 58, no. 3 (1945): 493–94. Eleanor Maccoby suggests several problems with this study, and implies that some of the results can be explained by the failure to distinguish different elements of permissiveness: *Social Development: Psychological Growth and the Parent-Child Relationship* (San Diego: Harcourt Brace Jovanovich, 1980), pp. 368–71.

31. Denise Kandel and Gerald S. Lesser, "Parent-Adolescent Relationships and Adolescent Independence in the U.S. and Denmark," in *Influences on Human Development*, ed. Urie Bronfenbrenner (Hinsdale, Ill.: Dryden, 1972), p. 637.

32. Diana Baumrind, "Some Thoughts about Childrearing," in Bronfenbrenner, *Influ-*

In other words, a laissez-faire permissive parent attempts to get children to do what she wants by manipulation or reason; when they fail, she lets them have their own way. In this respect, laissez-faire permissiveness mimics the situation in a liberated household where children make their own decisions without overt coercion from parents or teachers.

These two types of permissiveness have in common the practices of consulting about important decisions and explaining rules. In other respects, however, they differ radically. The democratic style, unlike the laissez-faire model, is not inconsistent with high demands, parental control of the child's impulses, and modeling by the parent. Laissez-faire permissiveness, on the contrary, attempts to persuade, but lets the child have its own way when persuasion fails. It is therefore studies of laissez-faire permissiveness, with its implicit growth model of human development, that are likely to generate the kind of knowledge we seek.

An early article by David Levy suggests that psychopathy, a psychiatric condition characterized by subnormal ability to control impulses, can be caused by extreme permissiveness. People with this problem always put their own desires before those of others.[33] In his 1964 review of the literature, Wesley Becker reports that studies generally support what he calls the common-sense idea that more uninhibited behavior is the result of permissiveness. He describes a 1931 study that found that "children of submissive (permissive) parents were more disobedient, irresponsible, disorderly in the class-

---

ences on Human Development, p. 402. The comparison with both Rousseau and the psychoanalytic pedagogical ideal should be obvious.

33. David M. Levy, "The Deprived and the Indulged Forms of Psychopathic Behavior," *American Journal of Orthopsychiatry* 21 (1951): 250–54, cited in Daniel G. Freedman, "The Origins of Social Behavior," in Bronfenbrenner, *Influences on Human Development*. Freedman describes his own interesting experiments on dogs, based on Levy's ideas. Although different breeds behaved in distinct ways, in general he discovered support for the hypothesis that permissiveness leads to weaker impulse control than firm discipline (p. 53). By the age of nine weeks, dogs subjected to alternate forms of discipline were very different: "The subsequent history of these two [permissively raised] pups was not a happy one. Although people were initially taken with them because of their uninhibited friskiness, they were passed from home to home as each owner found something else to complain about. They seemed to have become untrainable'" (p. 54).

room, lacking in sustained attention, lacking in regular workhabits, and more forward and expressive."[34]

The picture is complicated by another powerful factor: whether the family environment is warm or hostile overall. Even in warm households, permissiveness leads to the kind of undesirable traits described here; permissiveness combined with hostility appears to be especially harmful. Becker points out that this combination "maximizes aggressive, poorly-controlled behavior." Many studies show a significant relation between permissiveness (especially in hostile households) and delinquency. In "normal" boys, aggression is likewise associated with permissiveness, or with inconsistently permissive and controlling behavior.[35] N. Kent and D. R. Davis found that children of parents who used "unconcerned" discipline also had lower IQ and reading scores than those of demanding parents.[36]

Eleanor Maccoby underscores these kinds of findings. Comparing permissive and nonpermissive families, she finds that the highest rates of aggressive behavior occur among children whose permissive parents sometimes respond punitively to transgressions.[37] In her discussion of impulsive adolescents, histories of permissive treatment are frequent. These youngsters

> were less able to wait for things they wanted and demanded immediate gratification and gave little attention to consequences. Their expression of emotions was often explosive and unregulated. They had poor ability to maintain attention and commitment to tasks they undertook. Their behavior had a superficial, unorganized, flitting quality, and they changed their minds and their enthusiasms frequently.

Their backgrounds were often troubled by parents in conflict, especially with respect to childrearing ideas. These parents "did not take the time or trouble to transmit age-appropriate skills to the chil-

34. Wesley C. Becker, "Consequences of Different Kinds of Parental Discipline," in *Review of Child Development Research*, ed. Martin L. Hoffman and Lois Wladis Hoffman (New York: Russell Sage Foundation, 1964), p. 191. He also notes problems with the studies given the wide range of definitions of permissiveness.

35. Ibid., p. 193.

36. N. Kent and D. R. Davis, "Discipline in the Home and Intellectual Development," in Bronfenbrenner, *Influences on Human Development*, p. 438.

37. See Maccoby, *Social Development*, p. 135. These studies do not examine the children of overtly abusive families.

dren," rarely expected chores or other responsible behavior, and did not demand high achievement from them.[38]

Maccoby gives a comprehensive account of Baumrind's work, which is of central importance for us. In her first study, Baumrind found that parents of children who rated low on self-reliance and self-control were moderately nurturant, but "conspicuously low in exercising control."[39] Her more recent work generally supports these early findings. It describes three distinct models of parenting, authoritarian, authoritative, and permissive.[40] Among the findings were that children of permissive parents "conspicuously lacked social responsibility" and were unusually dependent. Permissive parenting caused boys (but not girls) to be angry and defiant.[41] A follow-up study of preschoolers found that at age eight or nine "the children who are self-confident and oriented toward achievement . . . do not usually have highly permissive parents. And at this age the children continue to show the positive effects (if one values agency, that is!) of their parents' authoritative behavior when the children were preschoolers. Furthermore, agency was enhanced if the parents continued to demand mature behavior and enforce rules firmly as the child entered school."[42] One particularly telling finding is that low de-

38. Ibid., p. 197. These studies presumably control for "normal" hyperactivity.

39. Diana Baumrind, "Child Care Practices Anteceding Three Patterns of Preschool Behavior," *Genetic Psychology Monographs* 75 (1967): 43–88, quoted in Maccoby, *Social Development*, p. 375.

40. Authoritarian parents "attempt to shape, control, and evaluate the behavior and attitudes of their children in accordance with an absolute set of standards; value obedience, respect for authority, work, tradition, and preservation of order; discourage verbal give and take." Authoritative parents, on the other hand, were

> likely to: attempt to direct the child in a rational, issue-oriented manner; encourage verbal give and take, explain the reasons behind demands and discipline but also use power when necessary; expect the child to conform to adult requirements but also to be independent and self-directing; recognize the rights of both adults and children; set standards and enforce them firmly. These parents did not regard themselves as infallible but also did not base decisions primarily on the child's desires. [Baumrind, "Some Thoughts about Childrearing," cited in Maccoby, *Social Development*, p. 376]

41. Diana Baumrind, "Current Patterns of Parental Authority," *Developmental Psychology Monographs*, 4, no. 1, pt. 2 (1971), cited in Maccoby, *Social Development*, p. 378.

42. Diana Baumrind, "Socialization Determinants of Personal Agency," paper presented at the biennial meetings of the Society for Research in Child Development, New Orleans, 1977; cited in Maccoby, *Social Development*, p. 378. Maccoby describes "agency" as "the tendency to take initiative, assume control of situations, and make ef-

mands for such mundane habits as politeness and help around the house is associated with high aggression, undercontrol of impulse, and immaturity.[43]

Maccoby points out that recent studies provide inconsistent results with respect to high levels of parental control. Her discussion suggests, however, that a major part of the problem is that widely varying definitions of control have been used, and it is plausible to believe that different kinds of control have different results. After all, when the same word is used to denote high but reasonable demands in a warm household and authoritarian parenting, there are bound to be differences in the outcomes.[44]

In general, the picture emerging here associates impulsiveness, irresponsibility, disorganization, aggression, and general immaturity with laissez-faire permissiveness. Conversely, democratic permissiveness that is characterized by some kinds of high control, coupled with rational explanation and warmth, is related to the opposite traits.[45] These studies are remarkably consistent, given the difficulties

---

forts to deal with the daily problems that arose." She sees two dimensions to the quality: (1) "social agency" involves active participation and leadership in group activity; (2) "cognitive agency" involves a clear sense of identity, striving to decide on and strive for standards, rising to meet intellectual challenges (and liking the process), and originality (p. 377). There is every reason to evaluate these qualities positively.

43. Maccoby, *Social Development*, p. 383. Maccoby points out the importance here of age-appropriate demands, however. In a permissive environment, it is sometimes difficult to know what such demands might be. It is clearly important to make sure that the child has the requisite skills, and skills, Maccoby emphasizes, are achieved by training. Children can be trained to avoid quarreling, tolerate frustration, and be helpful, as well as to acquire such mundane skills as tying shoelaces. She attributes these good consequences of high demands (especially a feeling of competence) to the learning required for meeting them: "The children of demanding parents acquire a wide range of skills on which they can subsequently draw for their own enterprises outside the parents' home. In other words, high parental demands that are appropriate to the child's age and are accompanied by training can provide a steppingstone to self-reliance" (ibid.).

44. The children of authoritarian parents, who demand high control by fiat rather than reasoning, lack empathy, have low self-esteem, only weakly internalize moral standards, lack spontaneity, affection, curiosity, and creativity, and do not establish good relationships with peers. This kind of parenting is also associated with aggressive children who are more likely to become juvenile delinquents. The traits that predominate appear to be related to the warmth of the household.

45. Thus Maccoby reports that the results of Baumrind's first study showed that "children who were happy, self-reliant, and able to meeting challenging situations directly . . . had parents who exercised a good deal of control over their children and demanded responsible, independent behavior from them but who also explained, listened, and provided emotional support" (*Social Development*, pp. 374–75). Her second study showed that children of authoritative parents "had independent and socially responsible children"

inherent in such work; there appears to be no solid evidence refuting them.

They are, of course, subject to the usual caveats about research on humans.[46] Nonetheless, such findings are highly suggestive. It would obviously be foolish to believe that they are the last word on the topic of childrearing styles, but it would be even more foolish to

---

(p. 377). The third showed that desirable kinds of agency (active, independent, original behavior) were "enhanced if the parents continued to demand mature behavior and enforce rules firmly as the child entered school" (p. 378). Consistent enforcement of demands and rules helps children to control aggression and coercion; high demands lead to low aggression and altruistic, competent behavior (pp. 381–83).

One of the most interesting research projects involved studying the family backgrounds of older student protesters. Jeanne H. Block, Norma Haan, and M. Brewster Smith, "Socialization Correlates of Student Activism," in Bronfenbrenner, *Influences on Human Development*, noted substantial differences in the upbringing of "activists" and "dissenters." "Activists" engage in more constructive social action and more protest action than the mean of the whole sample. They attempt to remedy suffering and injustice. They also believe that society does not live up to its ideals and protest to change the situation. "Dissenters" score above the mean on protest activities but below it on constructive social action. In short, they concentrate on negative demonstrations of their beliefs (p. 645).

Activists' parents are in some respects permissive: "They encourage the individuation and self-expression of the child, are more accepting of sexuality, and reject harsh punitive disciplinary methods." However, they demand independence, responsibility, and maturity from their children. They control aggression. These practices contrast with those of parents of dissenters: "dissenters' parents were described as making relatively minimal demands upon the child for independent mature behavior, being laissez-faire with respect to limits and discipline, being tolerant of self-assertiveness, and de-emphasizing self-control" (p. 655).

Thus the parents of the more admirable protesters exhibited exactly the characteristics found in other studies. It is interesting to note that this kind of research was undertaken at a time when many people were condemning protesters as "spoiled brats." They were indeed unpopular in many circles, partly because they were regarded as troublemakers by those content with the gap between rhetoric and practice in domestic and foreign policy. Seeing such discrepancies and trying to do something about them is surely something we want to foster in children; otherwise we will never have a more just society. But some individuals used violent and unjustifiable means to try to achieve their ends, and some were in the movement because it was exciting and fashionable. Much less favorable evaluation of them is appropriate. In particular, the distinction made by Block and her colleagues between constructive activists and mere dissenters is worth considering. We need people who work toward their goals in ways that go beyond mere protest.

46. Maccoby suggests the following: First, most of the studies deal only with early and middle childhood. Second, although the relationships are statistically significant, they are not especially strong: children are also affected by nonparental elements of their environment. Third, descriptions of patterns of behavior must necessarily simplify the many complex interactions in families. Fourth, different children may react differently to given practices; gender certainly appears to alter outcomes. Fifth, inferences about causality are not always certain. Influence may flow in both directions. Just as warm or hostile parents may elicit loving or aggressive reactions from children, compliant or defiant children elicit warm and democratic or hostile and authoritarian reactions from parents: *Social Development*, pp. 406–7.

ignore them: what empirical evidence we have points firmly against laissez-faire permissiveness if we value certain traits. Therefore, the burden of proof is upon those who argue for this kind of permissiveness to show either that the evidence is fatally flawed or that the traits are undesirable.

The recent psychological studies on laissez-faire permissiveness are of interest because they examine households where children are left quite free to make their own decisions, where parents are reluctant to override children's wishes except perhaps when they risk serious harm to themselves or others. This is the kind of home environment recommended by proponents of equal rights for children.

Given the vagaries of such empirical research, one might reasonably ask for additional theoretical explanations of these findings. Let us therefore consider such explanations and how they might fit into our understanding of the two contrasting models of human development.

The Growth Model versus Lockean Learning

In general, it is up to historians to provide accurate pictures of the past and up to research psychologists to provide valid, consistent studies of individual behavior. Thinking about theories that explain findings is an activity accessible to any educated person, however. And we must, if we are to make reasonable and democratic social decisions, attempt to sort out the fragments of information and claims that daily bombard us. So let us try to make sense of what we have just been seeing.

What kind of theory could help us order the bits of information so far described? Remember that we started out wondering about the consequences of letting children make many more of their own decisions. The growth metaphor implies that more such freedom leads to better results; the Lockean learning model is more cautious in its assessment of freedom. Laissez-faire permissiveness provides more freedom for children and hence its consequences are of special interest to us here as we try to decipher the principles of human development. Yet studies suggest strongly that laissez-faire permissiveness does not lead to desirable consequences, given the values many of us hold and which are necessary for social existence.[47] Why might this be so?

Diana Baumrind, whose work is so central to our interest here, examines two major assumptions implicit in the growth model of human development. One is that punishment is ineffective or harmful; another is that "unconditional love" is beneficial to children.[48] Neither turns out to be supported by current evidence.

Why not? How can we interpret those claims? Baumrind argues that properly applied punishment teaches children what their parents want and what will happen if it is not supplied. In short, it helps them control their own behavior.[49] Imposing such adult authority teaches children what is considered acceptable.[50] If we assume the demands are reasonable, this is an essential lesson, one that, as we saw, may not be learned when children are left free to express all their impulses, and a theme we will be seeing more of shortly. Baumrind equates what she calls "indulgent love"—love that does not require "of the child that he become good, or competent, or discipined"—with what she calls "unconditional love." Such love is "content with providing nourishment and understanding. It caters to the child and overlooks petulance and obnoxious behavior—at least it tries to."[51] What she is referring to might better be called "uncritical love," since it could otherwise be confused with the unconditional love that continues to love a child through thick and thin without abdicating responsibility to guide, teach, and, when necessary, criticize, pressure, or punish.

We saw that parents who try to provide their children with un-

47. I will argue for these claims in more detail later.

48. Baumrind, "Some Thoughts about Childrearing," p. 404. An interesting sidelight to this issue is the famous infant-food study cited by Dr. Benjamin Spock. John Sommerville points out that this study, showing that untrained children picked out balanced diets for themselves, was taken to show that "nature will never lead us astray." What people failed to notice was that only healthy foods were offered: *The Rise and Fall of Childhood* (Beverly Hills, Calif.: Sage, 1982), pp. 224–25. Would offering junk foods have changed the outcome? Any parent knows the answer!

49. Such punishment is not brutal, must be carried out if threatened, and must be reasonably prompt, though time must be allowed for the parent to make sure that the child knows why she is being punished, what proper behavior would consist of, and the reasons for the parent's preference: Baumrind, "Some Thoughts about Childrearing," p. 404.

50. Diana Baumrind, "Authoritarian vs. Authoritative Parental Control," in *Contemporary Issues in Adolescent Development*, ed. John Janeway Conger (New York: Harper & Row, 1975).

51. Baumrind, "Some Thoughts about Childrearing," p. 404.

critical love don't tend to be rewarded by loving, cooperative behavior. Why might the results of such treatment be so negative? Baumrind suggests that

> once the child enters the larger community, the parents are forced to restrict or deprive. Accustomed as the child is to immediate gratification, he suffers greater deprivation at such times than he would if he were accustomed to associating discipline with love. He does not accept nor can he tolerate unpleasant consequences when he acts against authority figures. Such a child, even when he is older, expects to receive, and is not prepared to give or to compromise.[52]

Baumrind points out that by loving unconditionally, the parent allows the child to behave egoistically at her own expense. I believe that what is hoped for is that the child will learn to emulate a parent's own selfless behavior, but what seems to be learned is that there is no penalty for selfishness. Studies show that when a child misbehaves in the presence of an adult, noninterference on the adult's part is taken as approval of the conduct, and increases its incidence.[53] The lesson here appears to be that once children develop the capacity for concern for others, they must be taught to demonstrate it. If they are not expected to do so, they assume that self-centered behavior is acceptable. Failure to provide negative feedback allows a child to escape the anxiety that ultimately should prevent antisocial behavior.[54] Consideration for others fails to become habitual.

The importance of learning in desirable maturation appears again and again in the literature. Maccoby, for instance, maintains that children have certain innate tendencies that facilitate social learning. She believes that they first attempt to adapt to the existence of others by getting what they can while avoiding punishment. Many then learn that they get along better by giving as well as getting. Finally some learn to operate in a principled way and demonstrate

52. Ibid., pp. 404–5.

53. Baumrind, "Authoritarian vs. Authoritative Parental Control," p. 137. In support of these claims Baumrind cites A. E. Siegal and L. G. Kahn, "Permissiveness, Permission, and Aggression: The Effects of Adult Presence or Absence on Aggression in Children's Play," *Child Development*, 30 (1959): 131–41.

54. See, for this point of view, Dorothy Rogers, *The Psychology of Adolescence* (Englewood Cliffs, N.J.: Prentice-Hall, 1977), p. 257.

genuine commitment to the well-being of others. She believes that several different learning processes are necessary to reach these stages:

> Children probably acquire empathic emotions through simple classical conditioning. They learn adaptive social behaviors partly by experiencing the consequences of their own actions and partly by observing the sequences of interaction engaged in by other people. Some aspects of social behavior are simply a matter of acquiring habits (saying "please" and "thank you," smiling and shaking hands upon being introduced). But as children grow older, their social behavior increasingly becomes a matter of planned sequences, organized in pursuit of long-term or short-term goals.

She argues that children need knowledge of acceptable social behavior as well as genuine social consciousness if they are to integrate their own actions with those of others: "Learning to understand other people's perspectives is important, but it is not enough. To become a socially mature person, the child must also share goals with others, and consider others' perspectives in order to arrive at cooperative plans for pursuing these mutual goals." She believes that parents can encourage this development by various means, including providing structure and consistently enforced reasonable demands.[55]

Furthermore, such learning enhances self-esteem. Self-esteem is the measure of feelings of one's own worth.[56] People with high self-esteem have confidence in their own perceptions and judgments, express them to others, and expect to succeed at new endeavors.[57] These traits are valuable because they allow one to value oneself and resist pressures for self-destructive and immoral behavior.[58] Hence high self-esteem would appear to be a prerequisite for enabling vir-

55. Maccoby, *Social Development*, pp. 407–10. See also recent work on empathy in young children, such as William Damon, *The Moral Child* (New York: Free Press, 1988), chap. 2. The existence of such a tendency is compatible with Maccoby's findings, I think, and it could be explained in evolutionary terms. Although early manifestation of such empathy would facilitate moral development, by itself it wouldn't guarantee moral behavior, as I argue here, because moral behavior has a significant cognitive component. For further discussion of the development of morality, see Jerome Kagan and Sharon Lamb, eds., *The Emergence of Morality in Young Children* (Chicago: University of Chicago Press, 1987).

56. Anton Frans de Man, "Autonomy-Control Variation in Child Rearing and Aspects of Personality in Young Adults" (dissertation, Rijksuniversitat, Leiden, 1982), p. 57.

57. Maccoby, *Social Development*, p. 272.

58. De Man, "Autonomy-Control Variation," p. 58.

tues and moral acts. S. Coopersmith found that high self-esteem in children is positively related to warm but firm, strict control.[59] He explains this result by arguing that such treatment leads children to develop self-discipline. These inner controls provide them with guidelines for successful interactions with others.[60] This hypothesis makes a lot of sense. I suspect that even permissive parents have a great deal of trouble suppressing their irritation at some behavior; a child is bound to be aware of such undercurrents. Children without inner controls will also have greater difficulties than usual in the outside world. Other children and adults will find them tiresome, will want to avoid them, and they will not be successful in school. These problems raise anxiety levels and engender a feeling of powerlessness. Even if children are not consciously aware of what is going on, they must sense that their parents do not care enough to help them deal with the world, and this feeling must further erode their security. Another consequence of treating children firmly is that it helps them distinguish themselves from others. Doing so is a prerequisite for recognizing the needs of others, which helps in turn to teach the difference between desire and reality.[61]

One aspect of firm control is consistently enforced high demands. Such demands appear to raise self-esteem by promoting hard work and achievement. If children are expected to achieve, and helped to do so by being encouraged to work hard and persist at tasks (rather than being allowed to think that they are just not smart enough), they come to have a sense of power and control. They also learn a way to get approval from others.[62]

59. S. Coopersmith, "Studies in Self-esteem," *Scientific American* 218, no. 2 (1968): 96–106.

60. Described in de Man, "Autonomy-Control Variation," pp. 58–59, and Maccoby, *Social Development*, p. 280.

61. Maccoby, *Social Development*, p. 280.

62. Ibid., pp. 286–90. Maccoby cites studies by R. Loeb, H. L. Bee, and C. S. Dweck in support of this position. Sarane Spence Boocock points out that very little contribution to common interests is expected of American children. She argues:

> Examination of the role of the child (role defined as a location in a social system with the rights and obligations attached to that position) indicates that it is unbalanced and becoming more so. Child development models which focus upon obtaining even finer knowledge about the special characteristics of each stage in the child's life and upon maximizing cognitive, emotional, and social development at each stage have a lot to say about children's rights but are virtually silent on the subject of obligations." She believes that this development is not positive: "cross-cultural work like the Whitings' suggest that children, like other social beings, can only be integrated

Learning control and skills, then, increases self-esteem and makes further good experiences more probable. Failure to learn decreases self-esteem and makes further bad experiences more probable. Learning is more likely if parents (or other adults close to the child) pay close attention to the child, and systematically attempt to teach him or her such skills and control. Loving but firm demands and restrictions (carefully explained and justified) appear to be most effective in such teaching.

These conclusions need considerable fleshing out, of course. It is one thing to understand the general principles enunciated here; it is quite another, as any parent or teacher knows, to apply them. It seems clear that many parents now let their children make too many of their own decisions, and their children would benefit from the closer attention and concern inherent in these recommendations.[63] It is also true, however, that many children—especially middle-class children—are subjected by their parents to very great pressure for academic and social success. There is no doubt that such pressure can be detrimental. Sometimes parents confuse high demands with a refusal ever to be satisfied by children's effort, leaving them with no sense of achievement. Sometimes, too, parents mistakenly push for achievement in areas in which a child has no interest or talent. Yet to deny the importance of reasonable levels of achievement in domains important to future development because of such misunderstandings would be, once again, to fall into the trap of seeing no middle ground between total control and total freedom.

This does not mean that deciding on the precise boundaries of the "reasonable" is an easy task; it is, in any case, one that will to some extent depend on the child, the circumstances, and the particular society. What we need to do is to isolate those characteristics that are essential for every child to develop in order to live a satisfying and moral life, then figure out how to achieve those goals. I have so

---

> into the larger society if they make some kind of contribution to it, and that their self-esteem depends upon their having obligations as well as rights. (Sarane Spence Boocock, "Children in Contemporary Society," in *Rethinking Childhood: Perspectives on Development and Society*, ed. Arlene Skolnick [Boston: Little, Brown, 1976], p. 343)

This claim about the link between self-esteem and obligation is plausible in light of the other information we have.

63. See Urie Bronfenbrenner, Preface, in *Two Worlds of Childhood: U.S. and U.S.S.R.* (New York: Pocket Books, 1973).

far argued for the centrality of self-control and certain enabling virtues based on that control, such as the appropriate use of reason, hard work, and tenaciousness in pursuit of excellence. These characteristics will most probably help children satisfy their own interests, but will also, in conjunction with caring for others, help them behave morally toward them. The best available evidence suggests that letting children make all their own decisions from the earliest possible age does not contribute toward these goals, and that, on the contrary, thwarting some of their desires ultimately helps them. This does not mean that children must live in the equivalent of a police state, where their every move is dictated by adults: this view is compatible with substantial freedom. Even quite young children can and probably should determine (within reasonable limits) such things as what to wear, how to spend their free time, and who their friends are; the scope of their choices should also expand with age. It seems clear, however, that certain other choices should not be permitted. So, for example, as a general rule it would be unwise to let a child refuse to go to school, skip her homework, or too regularly weasel out of household chores. A veto of such choices can and should be based on reason and delivered with warmth and even humor; the exact approach must, again, be tailored to the nature of the child and the particular situation.

In sum, the picture of human nature emerging here is seriously at odds with the growth model. Instead of envisaging children as essentially complete, needing only time and nourishment to develop, our picture conceives of children as unfinished beings who need a period of development and teaching to become admirable human beings. The experiments with laissez-faire permissiveness not only suggest that it is an ineffective childrearing method but also further underline the inadequacy of the growth model of human development that most plausibly supports it. It therefore makes sense for us on the basis of this evidence to proceed on the assumption that some apparently natural impulses must be controlled and more desirable traits consciously substituted for them: there is no particular reason to believe that these things will happen on their own.[64]

64. Martha Snyder, Ross Snyder, and Ross Snyder, Jr., argue this case strongly in *The Young Child as Person* (New York: Human Sciences Press, 1980). They argue that abandoning children to their own devices can create a jungle environment: "We cannot assume

There is much support of different kinds for the view that the self is constructed over time with generous help from the environment. One way of looking at the matter is provided by the child psychiatrist David Elkind, who holds that there are two ways of developing a self. What he calls "substitution" creates a "patchwork" self: feelings, thoughts, and beliefs are simply copied from others. No underlying principles or values unify the whole into a coherent world view. A clearly defined self requires such coherence and can be constructed only by what he calls "differentiation and integration." This process involves conscious evaluation of acts and states of affairs to create a consistent set of beliefs. Only such internalized principles enable one to do what one thinks best even in the face of temptation to do otherwise.[65] It would be plausible to believe that without systematic adult direction, our pluralistic, laissez-faire society is quite apt to lead to the proliferation of patchwork personalities. But individuals with such personalities are unlikely to flourish or help create a livable world. All the studies so far discussed are based on the assumption that environment influences perception, judgment, and inclination in fundamental ways. That assumption is widely accepted and is borne out both by such studies and by a vast array of other evidence, evidence that forces itself upon even the most desultory observer every day. In the course of a chat about his future education, for instance, the young son of a colleague of mine as-

that children can discover what is important for them in a vacuum, where adults hold themselves aloof. Nor can children choose what they have not experienced . . ." (p. 78). They attribute some instances of this way of dealing with children to laziness. I suspect they are right, although there is also reason to believe that many liberal proponents of this approach believe that it is genuinely best for children. In any case, the Snyders attribute what they call the "exploitive-opportunistic" mode of operation to permissiveness. An individual with such a conscience sees the world only in terms of his own wants: "What is needed is taken, what is desired is used irresponsibly. The rights and opportunities of others are disregarded. Stealing, bullying, arrogance, defiance of legitimate authority, refusal to acknowledge responsibility or enter into commitment, and a self-deceiving sense of persecution are manifestations of such a conscience." They argue that permissiveness encourages these traits by allowing children freedom even when it means hurting others or breaking commitments and not carrying out responsibilities. Protecting children from the natural consequences of their behavior (not part of Rousseau's agenda, by the way, but sometimes assumed to be necessary by proponents of permissiveness) teaches children to be irresponsible, for painful results are diverted by an adult who intervenes and always gives them "another chance" (pp. 81–84).

65. David Elkind, *All Grown Up and No Place to Go: Teenagers in Crisis* (Reading, Mass.: Addison-Wesley, 1984), pp. 15–17.

serted: "But boys can't go to college!" Such is life on the campus of a women's college.

Given the foregoing evidence together with the assumption about environmental influence, there is every reason to think that children need considerable shaping. Parental control is one source of such shaping. Another, more indirect, comes about as a result of exposure to desirable models. Urie Bronfenbrenner argues that we discover who we are and what we can become—our identity, in short—by being with a variety of people: "It is primarily through exposure and interaction with adults and children of different ages that a child acquires new interests and skills and learns the meaning of tolerance, cooperation, and compassion."[66] The people we are with must demonstrate these qualities, however. Our society now fails to provide youngsters with such experiences, and substitutes for them a dazzling array of conflicting messages. Lack of parental control and a paucity of meaningful adult models help explain why children are having such trouble learning to behave in prudent and moral ways.

This problem of good adult models has recently become especially acute. Many children now live in a world segregated in critical ways not only from adults but even from older children. We seem to be moving, even in the absence of full and explicit legal equality, toward a world with more freedom for children. Observation of this new world provides us with useful insights about the question now facing us.

Separate Worlds

To understand what is happening, we need first to take a brief look at the roots of this separate world. Historians concur that we are facing a new phenomenon in human history. How has it come about? A confluence of social, economic, and political trends appears to be responsible. John Sommerville suggests that economic pressures of the Industrial Revolution were a major factor.[67] Shul-

66. Urie Bronfenbrenner, "The Roots of Alienation," in his *Influences on Human Development*, p. 664.

67. Sommerville, *Rise and Fall of Childhood*, pp. 179–82. Sommerville also attributes some impetus to Victorian anxiety about children's sexual awakening. A bargain was struck: "adults would try not to consider teenagers as children (despite their continuing dependence) if they would concentrate on their intellectual and emotional problems and

amith Firestone emphasizes the rise of the modern nuclear family in the nineteenth century: "with the increase and exaggeration of children's dependence, woman's bondage to motherhood was also extended to its limits. . . . Their oppressions began to reinforce one another. To the mystique of the glories of childbirth, the grandeur of the 'natural' female creativity, was now added a new mystique about the glories of childhood itself and the 'creativity' of child*rearing*."[68] Influences of this kind help explain the creation of one kind of segregation, one that has been developing for at least a century. In it children have been protected from the adult world, but have also received special attention from adults. The price of postponing adult responsibility has been a delay of adult freedom; the justification was children's need for a special period of learning. It is from this period that children inherit their special protective rights, at the expense of liberating ones.[69]

What is very new is the development of a separate, *unprotected* world. It is separate in that it is quite isolated from respected adults; it is unprotected in that children are expected to manage many adult freedoms on their own, whether legally sanctioned or not. A variety of disparate factors appear to be accelerating this trend. Among them are the increasing number of women working outside the home and the failure of society to replace their child-care function adequately. Some people are just too busy to spend enough time with their children.[70] Another problem is ignorance. Some people underestimate how much teaching children need. Anybody who has watched children carefully can attest to the fact that they soak up their surroundings like sponges.[71] This ability usually enables them to survive even in the absence of much teaching; but there are many

---

not try to act too grownup. In the meantime, adolescents would be given their own clubs, magazines, books, fashions, and hobbies to keep them happy" (pp. 205–6).

68. Firestone, *Dialectic of Sex*, p. 91.

69. Proponents of children's liberation argue that the trade-off was not optimal, of course.

70. See Bronfenbrenner, *Two Worlds of Childhood*. His assessment of the amount of time and attention Russian and American parents give their children is eye-opening.

71. Caroline Whitbeck raises the critically important matter of the extent to which knowledge about children has been excluded from the body of "scholarly knowledge." She attributes this situation—quite rightly, I think—to the fact that women, with their store of experience about children, have been excluded until recently from academic pursuits: "The Moral Implications of Regarding Women as People: New Perspectives on Pregnancy and Personhood, in *Abortion and the Status of the Fetus*, ed. William B. Bondeson, H. Tristram Engelhardt, Jr., Stuart Spicker, and Daniel Winship (Dordrecht: Reidel, 1983).

important things a child may not pick up if they are not explicitly taught. They range from toothbrushing and handwashing to sensible attitudes about money and sex.

Sometimes, too, people are unsure about what they know, both in the practical realm and with respect to values. Values appear to be especially problematic as rapid change seems to undermine self-confidence about handling a new world. This doubt can be especially unsettling when we are faced with articulate and apparently secure children—children who might stop loving us if we insisted on having things our own way.[72]

For a long time schools abandoned "character education," and attempts to address value questions still cause bitter debate. Even "values clarification," a program that simply attempts to help children be more aware of their values, has created fierce political battles.[73] Despite growing theoretical interest in moral education, some schools have only recently begun to institute programs intended to instill basic values, and there is reason to think that parental character education is spotty at best.[74] It is apparent in any case that skepticism about values is very widespread. As teachers of philosophy are all too aware, many college students have an immovable belief that values are merely "personal opinions" and are, as such, all equally justifiable.[75]

72. See Blustein, *Parents and Children*, pp. 4–5. Dr. Spock elaborates on these themes in "Some Things I've Learned," in Gross and Gross, *Children's Rights Movement*. He believes that some parents feel insecure telling their kids what they think, "because they wonder whether it's old-fashioned and out of date to do so." Parents also "are afraid that if they're too firm they'll make their children hate them, or their children won't love them as much as they would like them to" (p. 273).

73. We are apparently not alone here. Rita Liljestrom reports that many parents in Sweden feel that staff at daycare centers have no right to "influence" children: "The Public Child, the Commercial Child, and Our Child," in *The Child and Other Cultural Inventions*, ed. Frank S. Kessel and Alexander W. Siegal (New York: Praeger, 1981), p. 142. Values clarification, although apparently innocuous, gets caught between the accusations of those who think it teaches relativism and those who think it conveys hidden moral messages incompatible with their own beliefs.

74. Although there is great interest in theoretical aspects of moral education, there doesn't seem to be any corresponding wealth of coherent, long-lasting implementation; the political vulnerability of such programs is probably a major factor here. For some discussion, see Bruce Cook, "A Moral Education Curriculum for Quebec Primary School Children," *International Journal of Social Education* 3 (Fall 1988): 78–85; Douglas Kirby, "The Effects of School Sex Education Programs: A Review of the Literature," *Journal of School Health* 50 (December 1980): 559–63; and James S. Leming, "Curricular Effectiveness in Moral/Values Education: A Review of Research," *Journal of Moral Education* 10 (May 1981): 147–64. It also seems reasonable to infer the inadequacy of much parental moral education, for the kinds of reasons we have been seeing.

75. Perhaps this is our penance for long attraction to relativism and subjectivism.

Another critically important factor in the new children's world is changing values. Bronfenbrenner attributes part of the breakdown in what he believes is "*the process of making human beings human*" to children's lack of opportunity to internalize and act on parental and community values inculcated during their early years.[76] No doubt this problem explains some difficulties teenagers are having, but I fear that the problem goes a good deal deeper than this. There is evidence of such significant changes in adult values and practices such that some of those formerly embraced are at risk of not being communicated at all. One such change involves the extension of libertarian assumptions to the family.

A Yankelovich study of the American family found that 43 percent of parents ("new breed") prefer self-fulfillment and "duty to self" above worldly success and duty to others—including their own children. Their attitude is: "I want to be free, so why shouldn't you children be free? We will not sacrifice for you because we have our own life to lead. But when you are grown, you owe us nothing." Accompanying this view is a hands-off policy with respect to both communicating values and the kinds of activities necessary to inculcate them.[77] Among the possible sources of this philosophy of liberation are an assortment of conflicting principles and beliefs, such as adherence to a growth model of human development, pluralism of values, the prizing of freedom, selfishness, and quite possibly media encouragement of the creation of a vulnerable new class of consumers.[78] The explanation for these ideas becomes relatively unimportant, however, once they get translated into the policy of letting children choose their own values and pursuits so far as possible.

Regardless of its source, then, this new world is here. What is it like? Its central feature is the absence of respected adults. Their absence subjects children to a multitude of powerful, contradictory pressures. Patrick Welsh, a high school English teacher, reports that "in 1960, parents and teachers were the leading influence on thirteen- to nineteen-year-olds. By 1980, teachers had slipped to fourth

76. Bronfenbrenner, "Roots of Alienation," p. 664.

77. Reported in Packard, *Our Endangered Children*, p. 8.

78. I have not seen any extended discussion of this last point, but I suspect it could be significant. "Liberated" children armed with money and without significant parental supervision create whole new markets; this consideration can hardly be ignored in a capitalist economy. Certainly the commercial world is not unaware of this fact.

place, behind peers, parents, and media (television, radio, and records)."[79] So instead of modeling themselves on these responsible adults, many teenagers are relying on peers and the popular culture. Yet parents and teachers represent the responsible adult world to teens. The resulting vacuum alters the contours of their world appreciably.

A good many parents have, for whatever reason, abdicated their authority.[80] The children of such "new breed" parents are noticeably different from those of "traditional" ones. "New breed" children get much less pressure—"less pressure from their parents to excel in school, to be popular or to be outstanding in other ways among their peers."[81] They tend to become peer- rather than adult-oriented. Unsurprisingly, peer-orientedness is increasing. Writing in the 1970s, Bronfenbrenner found that children of every age were more dependent on their peers than they had been a decade earlier.[82]

What are peer-oriented children like? It turns out that "they present negative images of themselves vis-à-vis the adult world of values, both in behaviors in which they engage and the values and attitudes they express." They do worse in school. They hurt others more and feel less guilty about having done so.[83] They have quite negative views of themselves and their friends: they are pessimistic about the future, rate lower in responsibility and leadership than adult-oriented youngsters, and lie and skip school more often. They also are more prone to engage in such illegal behavior as drug use, delinquency, and violence.[84] A study of 8,553 students at 102 New York State schools shows that "high school students who report they have a low affiliation with their family are *five* times more likely to get caught up in the drug or heavy drinking scene than high school stu-

79. Patrick Welsh, *Tales Out of School* (New York: Viking, 1986), p. 6.

80. The children are not generally lured away from their parents' influence by more attractive spheres: they do not want to spent time with parents or teachers, but are not particularly enthusiastic about being with their friends, either: John Condry and Michael L. Siman, "Characteristics of Peer- and Adult-Oriented Children," *Journal of Marriage and the Family* 36 (August 1974): 552.

81. Packard, *Our Endangered Children*, p. 27.

82. Bronfenbrenner, "Roots of Alienation," p. 660. Bronfenbrenner also discovered that children were more peer-oriented when one or both parents were often absent. Children of such households described their parents as both less warm and more relaxed about discipline.

83. Condry and Siman, "Characteristics," p. 551.

84. Bronfenbrenner, "Roots of Alienation," p. 660, 662.

dents who report having a close affiliation with their family."[85] They lack self-esteem; other children and teachers share their low evaluation of themselves.[86] Their parents' preferences with respect to their engaging in socially constructive, neutral, or antisocial behavior have virtually no impact on these children's acts.[87] The similarity of these descriptions to the consequences of David Elkind's patchwork personalities is striking.[88] In any case, these findings are consistent with Welsh's experience of children's vulnerability to what he sees as a "seductive" youth culture, equipped "with its own music, drugs, precocious sexual mores and values."[89]

The notion of a youth culture is not new. Awareness of the developing subculture of youth arose in the 1930s and the concept was christened in the 1940s by Talcott Parsons. Its values are opposed to those required by the adult world: consumption is preferred to work, hedonism to routine and responsibility.[90] There is some debate in the sociological literature about its importance and the source of the values it promotes, but there seems to be no doubt of its contemporary influence on many youngsters.[91] Technological toys and new adolescent freedom render it especially attractive now. Unfortunately, neither the youth culture nor the influences in society it reflects are in the business of looking out for children's long-term interests or for those of society as a whole.

Children also see a great deal that could lead them to lose respect for adults. Hypocrisy and downright dishonesty on the part of public officials are routine grist for media mills. Exposing such behavior is essential for democracy, but a persistent diet of scandalous revelations may suggest to children that it is so pervasive as to undermine any reason for integrity on their part. Children may also see dubious

85. Packard, *Our Endangered Children*, p. 72.
86. Condry and Siman, "Characteristics," p. 551.
87. Siman, reported in Bronfenbrenner, "Roots of Alienation," p. 661.
88. Elkind, *All Grown Up and No Place to Go*, pp. 15–17.
89. Welsh, *Tales Out of School*, p. 6.
90. Michael Brake, *Comparative Youth Culture* (London: Routledge & Kegan Paul, 1985), pp. 39–40.
91. See, e.g., John Janeway Conger, "A World They Never Knew: The Family and Social Change," in *Contemporary Issues in Adolescent Development*, ed. Conger (New York: Harper & Row, 1975). There is debate about whether youth culture is an independent source of anti-bourgeois values or simply a reflection of one strand of our pluralistic culture. The latter hypothesis is certainly tenable, given the orientation and influence of the media.

behavior on the part of their parents or other close adults—heavy drinking, tax cheating, wild behavior following divorce, or other manifestations of "new breed" parenting.[92]

In its general outlines, then, the picture before us is this: Many children have a great deal of freedom, little guidance from adults, and an environment studded with tempting diversions. A growth model of human development would predict that children will thrive in such a world, and develop into creative, self-possessed, and morally responsible human beings. A learning model, in contrast, would predict that children will have great difficulty maturing and that those difficulties will often continue on into adult life. A glance at the problems faced by those currently rearing children, or at the immature behavior of many young adults, should be enough to suggest which model seems to fit most closely the preponderance of facts.[93]

How might a Lockean learning model explain these difficulties? I have argued that a plausible conception of desirable maturity presupposes sufficient self-control to practice enlightened self-interest as well as to subordinate some of one's lesser interests to the stronger ones of others. Associated with this control are a kind of thoughtfulness about choices that is acquired only by learning, effort, and practice. Only thus do we come to take responsibility for our actions. Such responsibility helps us manage freedom in beneficial ways; without it freedom can easily lead to self-destructive and immoral behavior. When increased freedom is tied to demonstrations of responsibility, children's desire for independence motivates them to endure the delayed gratification inherent in learning responsibility. When freedom is offered early and with no strings attached, why should they make the effort to learn self-discipline and thought-

92. E.g., ibid.; Winn, *Children without Childhood*, chap. 2. There seems to be general agreement that parents exert less control over their children after divorce; as divorce is now very common, the baseline of permissiveness against which controlling parents are judged is surely raised. See, e.g., Bronfenbrenner, "The Parent/Child Relationship and Our Changing Society," in *Parents, Children, and Change*, ed. L. Eugene Arnold (Lexington, Mass.: Lexington Books, 1985), p. 52. It should also be noted that a study of childrearing practices among ten national groups found American parents to be by far the most permissive: Wallace E. Lambert, Josiane F. Hamers, and Nancy Frasure-Smith, *Child-Rearing Values: A Cross-National Study* (New York: Praeger, 1979), p. 346.

93. This is not to say that all lapses in self-discipline, responsibility, or moral behavior are a result of internal factors: a harsh and unsupportive environment clearly contributes substantially to such behavior. But the individual element is clearly also highly significant.

fulness? If you already *have* freedom, then growing up means only the addition of burdensome responsibility. Hence when freedom is taken for granted, children are less likely to shoulder the kind of responsibility we appropriately associate with adulthood and which, I have argued, is essential for a just and flourishing society. Even if they do, watching their friends' happy-go-lucky lives will tend to erode their own commitment to the kind of development for which I have been pressing. In short, separating freedom and responsibility could hardly discourage more effectively the kind of learning necessary for a smooth emotional transition between the roles of child and adult.

What, if anything, might proponents of the growth metaphor reply to all this? They might, on the one hand, concede that liberated children *are* likely to be immature, but that the compelling call of justice requires us to undertake—if possible—social measures that will compensate for that immaturity. On the other hand, they might assert that the only true test of liberation would be liberation itself.

Given the inadequacy of the appeal to justice, the first position has little to recommend it; in chapter 6, however, I examine an intriguing attempt to sustain it. The second position is simply implausible. It would have to claim that the unfortunate consequences of freedom detailed in this chapter result from the fact that children are provided with only part of the conditions for successful growth. Responsible behavior would emerge if they had the same responsibility as adults to choose their living arrangements, support themselves, and meet all the other demands of the free life. While this position has some appeal, it seems to me that the material presented in this chapter puts a major burden of proof on those who would defend it.

To the extent that this viewpoint is based on a growth model of human development that would, in the absence of adult pressure, most plausibly bend children in the right direction, it turns out to lack both theoretical and experimental justification. If nothing else, its promise of an internally directed "right" outcome could be achieved only with the help of a benevolent deity or evolution. Given the lack of evidence for the former, we are left with the latter. It would be most surprising, however, if the demands of reproductive fitness were to coincide with our conception of desirable development.[94]

94. Evolution, in any case, gives us no particular reason to think that it operates exclusively (or even mainly) by hard-wiring behavior patterns into animals. See John Tyler

Conversely, the hypothesis that children have lots of learning to do before they can handle adult freedoms has considerable experiental support as well as theoretical credibility. The historical evidence described here is both believable and supported by a large body of contemporary psychological research and sociological observations. All three can be knitted together via a relatively commonsensical theory into a coherent whole.

Overall, it seems safe to say that children's liberation is looking a bit green about the gills. The appeal to justice is unconvincing, as is the attempt to place it in a general moral context. Moreoever, all the evidence so far suggests that the optimism about consequences evinced by proponents of equal rights is unwarranted. The next two chapters will reinforce this position as well as suggest other reasons equal rights wouldn't be a good idea.

Bonner, *The Evolution of Culture in Animals* (Princeton: Princeton University Press, 1980).

Chapter 4

LIBERATED CHILDREN

So we should not be surprised when the mother throws her child out at three years old. She has breast-fed it, with some ill humor, and cared for it in some manner for three whole years, and now it is ready to make its own way. . . .

At the age of three a series of *rites de passage* begins. In this environment a child has no chance of survival on his own until he is about thirteen years old, so children divide themselves into two age levels and form age bands. The junior band consists of children between the ages of three and seven, the senior band caters for the eight- to twelve-year-olds. I know of one girl who stayed in until she was nearly fourteen, but she offered certain enticements in return. Normally, thirteen is the maximum. . . .

—Colin Turnbull, *The Mountain People*

We have just been seeing that there is good reason to suppose that children need systematic teaching if they are to acquire desirable traits. Such teaching involves treating them in ways that we quite rightly think inappropriate for adults; it would therefore be a bad idea to leave them alone to run their own lives. This means that special institutions dedicated to providing the necessary teaching and support are required.

Traditionally, much of this teaching has been provided by children's biological parents. The shortcomings of this approach are obvious and regularly provoke alternative proposals for communal systems of childrearing.[1] These proposals are interesting and some

1. For discussion of some of the issues, see, e.g., Melford I. Spiro, *Gender and Culture* (New York: Schocken, 1979), chap. 1.

version of them might well constitute an improvement over the current system of biologically based families.

I have two reasons for avoiding the details of this controversy. One is that communal childrearing is unlikely to become a live option in the foreseeable future. Although the intent of this work is not to provide a compendium of advice about children, I hope that it can supply some practical guidelines about how they should be dealt with. Therefore it makes sense to consider conditions something like those that actually obtain. The other reason is that my main concern here is to look at children's—and society's—needs. Most of the details about how to meet them must be left for another day.[2] Hence I shall be focusing on the family.

What would it be like living with children with adult rights? Although libertarian proponents of equal rights for children might downplay the importance of this question, it is nonetheless of critical importance for consequentialists, who hold that pressing for change without a vision of what it would entail would be unwise.[3] We have just been looking at reasons why the rosiest predictions of liberationists are unlikely to be realized: the growth model that pushes for the fullest freedom for children has nothing to recommend it and the social sciences present us with a surprisingly consistent picture of the undesirable consequences of letting young children set their own agendas the way adults do. This picture is somewhat abstract, however; let us therefore attempt to clarify it, bring it down to earth, and extend it.

Before doing so, we must get clear about just what is at issue. I have so far been using the terms "equal rights," "adult rights," "the same rights as adults," and "children's liberation" interchangeably. One might argue that, because of their different implications, such looseness is inappropriate. "Children's liberation," for example, might reasonably be taken to denote quite another set of rights than those now recognized for adults. "Adult rights" might refer to the

2. As I have been arguing, our goal here must take account of the interests of several sometimes conflicting constituencies—children, parents, and society at large.

3. Some liberationists, such as Howard Cohen and Richard Lindley, argue at least in part on consequentialist grounds; however, they hold that the consequences of liberation are better than the consequences of our current protectionist policies. For articulation of the position that such speculation about outcomes is important, see Annette Baier, "Doing without Moral Theory?" in her *Postures of the Mind* (Minneapolis: University of Minnesota Press, 1985).

rights now recognized for adults, or perhaps, more hopefully, to the rights adults *ought* to have. Finally, "equal rights" need not imply "the same rights as adults," just as equal rights for women need not imply that they should have only the rights now recognized for men: equal rights are compatible with a core set of rights that are the same for everybody, together with another set of peripheral rights that vary according to morally relevant differences among classes of individuals. Thus equal rights for women are compatible with special rights that pertain to pregnancy and lactation.

Some liberationists, who at first appear to be pushing children's access to the rights now enjoyed by adults, turn out in the end to be arguing for something quite different. John Harris, for instance, endorses a limited version of equal rights for children. He denies that equal rights would mean that children "would be emancipated, not forced to go to school, permitted to vote and to work, etc., and that all else would remain the same."[4] Instead, we would recognize their special needs, which doesn't imply that they aren't being treated as equals. To the extent that such special treatment entails restrictions to which adults are not subjected, however, this approach can hardly be distinguished from protectionism, which also wants to treat children differently according to their special needs. Thus his idea that we might limit children's work opportunities more than those for adults would be inconsistent with his initial argument for equal rights.

So there appear to be two logically distinguishable positions here. One recognizes for a given class of children essentially the same rights as adults. The other recognizes for it different rights based on the particular characteristics of its members, rights that may entail restrictions to which other classes are not subject. What characteristics count as differences depend partly on social context. So for every society there is one liberationist position but many possible protectionisms. To the extent that liberationists (such as Harris) shrink from the implications of equal rights as I describe them, they are in fact recommending some version of protectionism, and their arguments, ostensibly against protectionism in general, only tell (at most) against some particular form of it.

Given this distinction, I propose to use the term "equal rights"

4. Harris, "Political Status of Children," p. 50.

much the way it is used with respect to women and men. That is, we recognize for them a large array of rights in common, with a few special rights based on morally relevant differences—rights that, for the most part, provide special help or opportunities.[5] So "equal rights for children" will refer to a situation in which children have access to all the rights that are now recognized as fundamental for adults, with a few special rights based on need. Such a special right could be a right to facilities in public buildings to accommodate their shortness.

Special rights, however, would not include protective rights that limit children in ways in which adults are not limited. In other words, they would no longer be able to take for granted any protective age-related benefits they now have a right to expect from society. Among these, as we have seen, are the right to live with and be supported by parents, free schooling, and so forth.

This is an extreme view of liberation. It is tempting to reject it on those grounds alone, given that we might instead call for nonprotective rights that provide children with support, schooling, and so forth without the limits implied by protectionism. One might argue, for example, that children could go to school if they wanted, but they wouldn't be required to do so, and they wouldn't necessarily be required to work, either.[6] Now it is possible that moral expectations would by themselves encourage virtually all children to occupy themselves in some constructive way, by which I mean either learning or socially useful labor. But I think that some skepticism about this claim would be warranted here. And if my doubts were borne out, not only would this outcome undermine any psychological or moral connection between freedom, support, and responsibility but it would presuppose a world where there is no need for productive work. Or, if not, by what right are children but not adults offered these choices? The liberationist argument holds that children

5. Notice that women's "rights" have not always been and are still not entirely of this benign and helpful nature. For a thorough account of the battle over "protective" rights, see Leslie Feldman Goldstein, *The Constitutional rights of Women* (New York: Longman, 1988).

6. John Holt says: "I do not say . . . that these rights and duties should be tied into one package, that if a young person wants to assume any of them he must assume them all. He should be able to pick and choose": "Liberate Children," in Aiken and LaFollette, *Whose Child?* p. 85. He does go on to point out that some rights are "in the nature of things tied to others," even though others are a matter of convention, etc. But there is nothing here to suggest that certain rights ought morally to be linked to others.

shouldn't be less free than adults; if they are to be more free, additional argument is needed. Such argument could appeal to some special necessity for children, but not adults, to be free of obligation. As we have seen, however, there doesn't appear to be any empirical support for this thesis: quite the contrary. Arguments to this effect are, in any case, in danger of resorting to the very distinctions between children and adults that liberationists are at pains to deny. In short, liberationist proposals tend to suffer from a certain inconsistency.

Other problems with equal rights for children emerge as we take a closer look at how they would actually function in the key areas of family, education, and work. These areas are linked in at least two ways. On the one hand, if children are truly to have the same rights as adults, contemporary protective rights will no longer keep them in any particular living situation. Nor are adults subject to the kinds of laws that currently restrict children's work and require them to spend time in school. So even if there were no internal logical links between these (and other) rights, we would have to confront their reality. But there are such links. If children are to have the freedom to live where and how they please, as even relatively fainthearted liberationists such as Harris assert, they must also be able to support themselves, since no-strings support for them can't consistently be defended by liberationists without further implausible argument. If children must support themselves, then they cannot be required to go to school: they must, like adults, be free to spend their time working instead.

Getting clear about these issues is of the greatest importance; only by taking seriously the most consistent version of liberationism can we do so, even if only the bravest actually hold such a position. And only by doing so can we address Howard Cohen's claim that "in the course of protecting children we have stunted the fullness of our relationship with them and slighted them as people."[7] If it is argued that protectionist rights in fact oppress rather than help (as they have historically been intended to do), then it is important to see whether this claim is true or not; the best way to do so is to explore the full implications of equal rights for children by trying to understand what all our lives would be like if children had them. More-

7. Cohen, *Equal Rights for Children*, pp. 7–8.

over, if, as most of us no doubt suspect, those lives would be worse, it is important to see in what ways this is the case. Only thus will we be able to begin to build up a positive picture of what children need in the way of rights.[8]

Family Matters

What problems can we discern, as we peer with a philosophical eye into the homes of liberated children? One might distinguish "macro" problems about responsibility and "micro" problems involving the dynamics of interactions of family members. The two are tightly intertwined.

Understanding the principles motivating the move toward equality should help us see what is at issue here with respect to the big picture. Recognizing adult rights for children implies a liberal view of human relations. Applied to the family, this means that, in Bruce Hafen's words, "the family is increasingly seen not as a unit, but as a collection of individuals." Hence "one now sees the two traditions of individualism and family life on a collision course."[9]

The underlying premise of the liberated family is that the individuals it comprises will stay together only as long as they are getting something out of the arrangement.[10] Thus each family is a voluntary association that is constantly reassessed. Family members are equal in all important respects, and it follows that children's wishes ought to count as much as those of the adults.

In theory, then, children would be legally free to leave the family, but so, as liberationists omit to mention, would parents! Dissatisfied children could take off on their own; dissatisfied parents could equally easily abandon their children. Lest this seem an unrealistic worry, we must remember how many fathers already abandon their children, and that it is not unknown for mothers to do so also, either by running away or by adoption. Given what we have seen of children's needs, and what we will see of what awaits them in society at large, it seems to me that this state of affairs needs to be avoided at

8. To do so we will in the end adopt something rather like Harris's equal consideration, which allows us to treat different cases differently on the basis of the morally relevant differences between them ("Political Status of Children," pp. 54–55).

9. Bruce C. Hafen, "Puberty, Privacy, and Protection: The Risks of Children's 'Rights,'" *American Bar Association Journal* 63 (October 1977): 1383.

10. Sommerville, *Rise and Fall of Childhood*, p. 218.

almost any cost. Liberationists could deny this implication by arguing that parents would have a duty to provide their children with a home, even if children had no duty to live in it. But this response, although convenient, seems to me inconsistent with the liberal premises upon which the liberationist argument is based. Another response is to propose radical social change to accommodate independent children's needs. Some of these proposals, such as stronger labor legislation, simply amount to a more consistently applied protectionism, and libertarian proponents of equal rights would have to object in principle to such changes. From my point of view, while the kinds of changes liberationists suggest tend to be desirable in themselves and would make the world less hostile to both children and adults, they address neither children's special need for basic learning nor the question about just who is to provide the social resources being doled out, and why. So on the face of it, the prospect for liberated families is already unpromising.

What about the relationships within intact liberated families? Liberationists hold that the central moral dilemmas within the family turn on the fact of dependence. When individuals are dependent, they tend to be powerless; they cannot exert what we would regard as the normal and fair amount of control over their lives. One particularly upsetting aspect of this state of affairs is that conflicts of interest are not usually resolved in their favor.[11]

Women, despite some recent improvements in their position, are often still dependent; they are therefore at risk of unfair treatment in marriage. There is no doubt that children's even greater dependence also results in much unhappiness on their part. Some such misery is clearly a consequence of unjust treatment: they can be physically and mentally abused and their basic needs ignored.[12] Some of their discontent, however, is a consequence of control that, because of the differences between them and women, is not unjust.

Given this framework, we need to consider how issues of control and conflicts of interest would arise and be resolved if children had equal rights. Let us examine each of these questions in turn.

11. In this discussion I assume a family based on the marriage (or a marriage-like relationship) of man and a woman. A few of the problems discussed might not apply to single-parent households or to relationships between couples of the same sex, but most would. For the sake of simplicity, however, I limit consideration to the first situation.

12. See, e.g., Franklin, *Rights of Children*.

At present, children are for the most part dependent on their parents, although certain factors in contemporary life provide some children with sources of power with which to counteract the resulting dependence. A good deal of power, however, still generally rests with parents.

If children had equal rights, some of this power would remain in parents' hands; their attitudes would determine to a considerable extent how it would be wielded. "New breed" parents would be assisted in their approach by the liberation program. They would get social approval for their relaxed handling of children, and they would not be held responsible when their children got in trouble. If, on the contrary, parents believed in shaping their children, and if they had a good relationship with them, then their home life might not be too different from that enjoyed by similar families today. These parents' power would in many cases be noticeably attenuated by social changes, however, even when legal rights were not at issue. The more children expected to run their own lives, the more difficult it would be for parents to persuade them to practice appropriate self-control; and since, as children grow older, more and more interactions must be based on persuasion rather than power, the baseline of expectation about compliance with parental preferences would drop.

At the same time, as I have suggested, it is clear that children are not automatically freed by legal changes: power relationships reflect other social and economic facts as well. Harris suggests that the law "extend to children . . . the right, only recently established for spouses . . . to common ownership of the family home" as one way to manage "competing and incompatible rights to free choice of life-style." This arrangement, he believes, would give every family member a stake in the home, and he sees no reason to fear that "this would mark the end of family life or lead to a state of perpetual family litigation."[13] This may seem like such a silly idea that it is not worth analyzing, but such analysis helps illustrate morally relevant differences between women and children and shows why proposals that advance the liberationist program may be ill founded.[14]

13. Harris, "Political Status of Children," p. 53.

14. The middle-class (or even upper-middle-class) point of view is obvious here, as it operates on the assumption that the family owns a home in the first place—a state of

If children had a right to an equal say in the family, then giving them this kind of economic power would help ensure that they could actually exercise their right. If such power carried with it the same responsibility for upkeep and repair that inexorably follows for adults, having it could, in addition, be a maturing experience. But, as we have seen, there are good reasons for doubting whether children should have an equal say, as well as reasons for thinking that the salutary emphasis on responsibility wouldn't occur.

Foreseeing some resistance to children's partial ownership of the family home, Harris contends that

> a host of similar disasters were all predicated upon the recognition of equal status for women within marriage, the family and the home. But there is little evidence that more radical equality for women has made marriage, and family life impossible. . . . We should perhaps be encouraged by the fact that the same list of disasters and warnings about dire consequences for life as we know it was raised as an objection to the emancipation of women and to all subsequent extensions of equal rights to them as is now produced to defend the continued control of children.[15]

What could be said about this suggestion? First, it may be false that equal rights for women is not disruptive to existing institutions: on the contrary, it would be strange if those institutions were not disrupted, for they are predicated on women's cooperation and free labor. On the one hand, antifeminists already blame most social problems on the progress already achieved by women.[16] Although their accusations may arise more from nostalgia for traditional power relationships and fear of competition than fact, it is undoubtedly true that improvements in the status of women have disrupted family and society. Such disruption, coming from such factors as easier divorce, reproductive choice, and more equal participation in the work force, is the price of justice for women.

---

affairs increasingly unlikely for a majority of the American population and for the British one Harris is talking to. What does this say about equal rights for poor children?

15. Harris, "Political Status of Children," p. 53.

16. See, e.g., Elizabeth Douvan, "The Age of Narcissism, 1963–1982," in *American Childhood: A Research Guide and Historical Handbook*, ed. Joseph M. Hawes and N. Ray Hiner (Westport, Conn.: Greenwood, 1985), p. 17: "The conservatives blame the feminists for the destruction of the family and the moral collapse that underlies it."

It should also be pointed out, on the other hand, that we have yet to feel the full effects of women's equality. Despite failure to pass the Equal Rights Amendment, legal emancipation is well under way. Yet women are still not participating in all areas of life on an equal basis with men. If they ever do, the boat is likely to be rocked even more vigorously.

The appropriate response to the problems created by more just arrangements is social accommodation to the new needs.[17] Thus in the case of women, accommodation requires society to find alternative ways of doing the jobs women used to do without pay and to help those trapped by transition. Blaming women for the loss of benefits once provided by their subordination would be like blaming blacks for a slump in the cotton industry after emancipation.

Social disruption caused by instituting equal rights for children would require the same response if their current status were truly unjust. As we have seen, however, there is no reason to think that protectionism per se oppresses children. Contrasting their case with that of women highlights still further the difference in their situations.

First, even if women do not bring cash into the household by working outside the home, they contribute essential labor to it. Most children do not; many families still adhere to a vision of childhood that precludes productive labor. Indeed, children are exceedingly expensive: in 1980 it was estimated to cost between $100,000 and $140,000 to raise a child.[18] No doubt the figures are substantially higher now. Is this economic factor morally relevant? Although we

17. The moral demand for such accommodation is all the more pressing when the relevant social changes are not solely the result of increased justice, as in the case of less discrimination in the workplace. Women's massive presence in the workplace, for instance, is probably caused mainly by such developments as the decreased buying power of the average wage, increasing freedom (on both sides) to divorce, and the unwillingness of society to hold men equally responsible for their offspring.

18. Viviana A. Zelizer, *Pricing the Priceless Child* (New York: Basic Books, 1985), p. 3. Zelizer notes the contrast between two radically opposed attitudes toward children: "The birth of a child in eighteenth-century rural America was welcomed as the arrival of a future laborer and as security for parents later in life. The economic value of children for agricultural families has been well documented by anthropologists. In many cultures, between the ages of five and seven, children assume a variety of work responsibilities—caring for younger children, helping with household work, or tending animals." This notion eroded until by "the 1930s, lower-class children joined their middle-class counterparts in a new nonproductive world of childhood, a world in which the sanctity and emotional value of a child made child labor taboo" (pp. 5–6).

would not want to posit any direct relationship between financial contribution and authority, there is an important connection here that will be explored in more detail later.

A further difference between women and children is that children are born into families, whereas women (at least in principle) voluntarily form them on the basis of love and compatible world views. This fact should foster negotiation and compromise. Although we would hope that bonds of affection between parents and children would do the same, the situation is much more volatile because of the psychological differences between women and children: women are mature individuals who are not in need of the kind of teaching that is appropriate for children.

Such reasons should be enough to suggest grounds for viewing the family as a voluntary association between a woman and a man (and promoting the conditions that make this conception realistic), but not between parents and children; we will be seeing others. Thus uncritical acceptance of arrangements intended to equalize children's power in the family must be ruled out; it does not follow, however, that no increase in children's power is desirable, only that we must take care that power supports justifiable aims.

How would liberation affect parent-child relationships? Cohen maintains that recognizing equal rights for children doesn't mean that parents won't be able to control them; "it is only to say that they may not control them in ways which they could not use on other adults without violating their rights."[19] As we saw earlier, he construes this constraint as ruling out force and requiring parents to rely on conditional rewards.

Even if, for the sake of argument, we go along with this dualistic view of control, it is not clear that equating any use of force with illegal assault is a good idea. If sensible childrearing methods are being used, one would expect physical punishment to give way quite early to psychological means of control. Nonetheless, a key question is whether small children can be adequately taught without occasional recourse to physical restraint or punishment. Such physical control may be uniquely useful in training young children to avoid traffic and other life-threatening hazards. No doubt rewards for

19. Cohen, *Equal Rights for Children*, p. 94.

good behavior and psychological control are preferable to physical control, but it is still possible that the latter may be a necessary adjunct to simple explanations about other kinds of prohibited behavior, especially before language is a reliable form of communication.[20] If physical punishment is sometimes the most effective means of teaching children, then this aspect of liberation is not in their interest. Whether there is a serious problem here remains to be shown; Sweden's prohibition of physical punishment should provide valuable evidence. If it turned out that on the whole children do better without physical punishment, prohibiting it could be justified by showing that its use invites abuse; there is no need for equal rights.

In any case, the relationship between children and adults is much more complicated than Cohen's position would suggest. First of all, punishment can be either physical or psychological. Second, many interactions between children and adults involve simple authority, and neither punishment nor reward is at issue.

If children had equal rights, it is true that physical punishment would be ruled out. It is not illegal to practice psychological punishment on adults, however, so it would not be outlawed for children. Given the prevalence of psychological punishment, this point diminishes the force of Cohen's argument. To salvage it he needs to recast his distinction between physical force and conditional rewards into a distinction between physical and psychological methods of control. The apparent advantage of equal rights for children would then be reduced, as parents might not have to alter their methods of control very much, unless psychological punishment were made illegal—hardly a possibility.

More damaging to the liberationist case would be acknowledgment that most parent-child interaction involves simple authority. By "simple authority" I mean a parent telling a child what to do,

20. Advocacy of physical punishment assumes that it is effective. Baumrind argues that it is so ("Some Thoughts about Childrearing," p. 404). Ross D. Parke adds that "the operation of punishment, however, is a complex process and its effects are quite varied and highly dependent on such parameters as timing, intensity, consistency, the affectional and/or status relationship between the agent and recipient of punishment, and the kind of cognitive structuring accompanying the punishing stimulus": "Some Effects of Punishment on Children's Behavior," in Bronfenbrenner, *Influences on Human Development*, p. 393.

without recourse to either threat of punishment or promise of reward. And it is the success of this method that is most telling against the case for equal rights.

Adults don't take kindly to this kind of interaction, for it presupposes some inequality. We consider it tolerable only in learning situations or emergencies. Even so, picture the shaky equilibrium established in some of these situations—in learning how to drive, for instance. Emergencies are another story: anybody who has the presence of mind to take charge tends to be followed. But we routinely direct children, especially young children, in this way; we could, in fact, hardly get them through the day otherwise. As they grow older, they quite appropriately start asking for reasons—reasons that should usually, of course, be forthcoming. In my experience, however, even quite rebellious teenagers continue to accept a good deal of this kind of direction.

What are we to make of this fact? On the one hand, it reinforces the idea that children are different from adults. A plausible explanation of their acquiescence is that they cannot learn everything they need all at once and so are "programmed" to take much more direction than adults. Liberationists might retort that children's acquiescence just shows how beaten down they are: like happy slaves, they don't even know when they are being oppressed. To answer this objection, it is necessary to appeal to experience, both that of being told what to do as a child and that of telling children what to do. Although most of us no doubt still burn with resentment at a few orders we regarded as authoritarian, one would expect much more retrospective anger (on the part of those not mistreated by ordinary standards) if the yoke of childhood were truly so heavy. It appears that the slave hypothesis has nothing but coherence with the liberationist thesis to recommend it.[21]

Granted, such down-to-earth details are considered subjective and are quickly rejected by many scholars. That such rejection is appropriate (or even consistent) is dubious. It is at least in part a consequence of the paucity of women scholars who could bring their experience with children into the realm of accepted scholarly wisdom, as well as a consequence of the humanities' hostility to the messy particulars of daily life. We cannot resolve some questions because

21. Happy slaves are, in any case, probably more myth than reality.

the relevant evidence just cannot get through the gates. Even more abstract and "scholarly" studies of the sort described in chapter 2, which strongly suggest how treatment inappropriate for adults appears to lead to good results in children and vice versa, may not pass muster. Yet we will never be able to resolve these questions once and for all without evidence of these kinds.

The failure to attend to such actual parent-child relationships seems to me to be a serious weakness in the liberationist position. It also tends to lead to the simplistic equation of unequal power with oppression.

David Elkind questions the popular conception of parental authority:

> Exerting parental authority doesn't mean that we can't play ball with our children or joke with them or have fun with them. Being a parent doesn't mean being an ogre or a relentless disciplinarian. Rather it means asserting ourselves as adults who have more experience, knowledge, and skill than our offspring. Children and teenagers are young and inexperienced. They very much need and want guidance and instruction from us.[22]

The crux here is the distinction between power and authority. It is surely difficult to conceive of any situation—even one involving children—where ordering others about (on pain of punishment), just because you feel like it and without any moral aim in mind, could be justified. Such wielding of "naked" power, however, is not at all what telling children what to do (one form of parental authority) is about. Authority is based on acknowledged superiority with respect to some trait relevant to the task at hand, and is directed toward some goal the child would judge desirable were he or she fully informed and rational. As I argued earlier, adults often (although not always) are in a position to exercise authority over their children. If children are to flourish, society needs to create an atmosphere in which it is understood that parents are reliable and knowledgeable unless they demonstrate otherwise by dishonesty, abuse, or some other serious betrayal.[23] As liberationists stress, we obviously need ways to rescue children from parents who abuse their power; in par-

22. Elkind, *All Grown Up*, p. 205.
23. Further elucidation of these concepts is obviously necessary.

ticular, as children get older they need safe havens to discuss problems they are having with their parents, places where they can get a perspective on their own desires. Undermining parental authority in general to achieve these ends seems to me to be throwing out bath and baby.

If children had equal rights, they would be sent a strong message that adults' greater experience is not a crucial difference between children and adults. Young children would presumably be relatively unaffected by that message, although their parents might be still less willing than at present to provide the kind of structure toward which the studies discussed in chapter 2 point. Under these circumstances, we might reasonably expect teenagers to experience more difficulties growing up, and awareness of their new rights would most likely still more increase resistance to parental attempts to instill self-control, enabling virtues, and moral behavior. Less fundamental but still valuable traits such as neatness and organization, or love of learning, would quite likely go by the boards as parents struggled just to pass on the basics without being pasted with unpleasant labels. Only those children with especially determined and energetic parents would get the training and support necessary to take the harder path. So even if the legal changes inherent in equal rights for children might not directly affect family relationships, they could, at the very least, be expected to accelerate the kind of troubling trends already examined.

In jeopardy, in fact, is the teaching role of families. Now, as I have suggested, what is important is that the teaching get done, not who does it. Equal rights would, I believe, undermine that role without offering anything but the school of hard knocks to replace it. Substantially gone would be social support for parental transmission of self-control, enabling virtues, and moral values, for as John Sommerville points out, "under pure egalitarian theory, few propositions are more reprehensible than those authorizing some to control or even to influence significantly the value choices of others."[24] What follows from this theory is that we ought not to be influencing children, let alone using authority to tell them what to do, even for their own good. It would therefore seem to be just as wrong to pressure them

24. Sommerville, *Rise and Fall*, p. 218.

to develop good study habits as to push them into drug dealing, just as wrong to raise them to help cripples as to turn them into racists.[25]

Now the power to shape children carries with it awesome responsibility, and we know that it is sometimes used in unreasonable ways. Cohen, attempting to rebut the idea that equal rights would much alter parental power, admits that equal rights wouldn't even protect children from religious indoctrination.[26] I suspect he is right. Parents who are determined to inculcate specific religious or political beliefs usually realize that success depends on an early and emotionally laden start. Young children are likely to take such teaching for granted and hence won't rebel. Older children may do so, but their only recourse may be to leave home. In this case, there would be no benefit to liberation, since for many children independent life would not be a realistic option. Moreover, children do not need equal rights to be rescued from bad homes.

The central issue here is *who* decides that a given family is bad for a child. Liberation puts the decision in children's hands. And although we might agree that some children need an escape hatch, it does not follow that they are usually the best judges as to when this is the case. As we have just seen, they could well be satisfied with circumstances that are not in their best interest; conversely, they may rebel against those that are.

Cohen begs us to consider the case of Jenny, a twelve-year-old who wants to exchange her rather strict home for a friend's more easygoing one: "The parents have done nothing which could legally be described as child abuse or neglect, . . . they have genuine concern for the child's development, . . . and they are rather strict disciplinarians."[27] Cohen judges that it would be paternalistic for them to prohibit Jenny's moving in with a friend because of the implication that they know better than she what is good for her. Who are we, asks Cohen, to say what she needs? But what if she hasn't yet learned the importance of honesty or responsibility, and just wants to get away from her parents' attempts to help her to do so? What

25. I will be discussing the issue of influencing children in more detail shortly. For now it suffices to say that the teaching necessary for children's maturation requires some kinds of influence, both within the family and outside it.

26. Cohen, *Equal Rights for Children*, p. 95.

27. Ibid., p. 66.

if, in fact, there is ample reason to believe that without her parents' warm but appropriately firm discipline she will fail to learn self-control and moral behavior? Letting children leave home under these circumstances amounts to saying that they should be free to escape the hard labor required for maturation.[28]

The extent to which this comes to pass will depend on a variety of factors. In general, individuals willing to abandon the family (whether children or adults) against the wishes of the rest would potentially have disproportionate decision-making power. Who this is likely to be depends a good deal on what awaits defectors. If children are the truly equal members of society envisioned by radical liberationists, then they will have to be financially self-sufficient. Purely economic factors would therefore have substantial bearing on what happens. The most likely scenario is that equal rights for children would be implemented in a world organized more or less like the current one. Thus middle-class white teenagers would most often be in a position to leave, although the unskilled jobs available to them combined with the high cost of living would be a serious deterrent. As now, many would no doubt be recruited into miserable lives of crime or prostitution. Independent life would therefore not constitute an attractive or desirable option for most children.

Before going any further, we should note an additional factor, one likely to have ever more impact on parent-child relationships: divorce. Divorce still further increases the potential for discord and manipulation of both children and adults. Not only may parents have a genuine desire for a relationship with their children of a sort that is possible only when they and the children live together, but some will regard it as a triumph against their estranged spouse to get a child to choose to live with them. It is far from clear that such wars are in the best interest of children. Children are quite likely to be attracted and won over by such weapons as relaxation of discipline, relief from responsibility, and material comfort. These enticements favor the wealthier parent and further undermine attempts to raise responsible, self-disciplined individuals. Bad childrearing, like coinage, drives out good. Conversely, children can manipulate parents by threatening to defect to the other if they do not get their own

28. Again, this is not to say that there are no circumstances in which it would be desirable to help a child find another home.

way. Cases of this sort indicate that social factors not immediately connected with equal rights might affect the way they worked in unforeseen ways.

Anybody who has tried to raise children in a situation in which their leaving home is a credible threat knows how corrosive it is. Such a threat can have the beneficial effect of making you seriously evaluate your policies, but it is just as likely to lead to manipulation and emotional blackmail. Good and responsible parents find themselves constantly weighing the effects of discipline against the unhappiness it causes: If I don't make a stink about *this* lie, am I ruining my kid's character? And if I do, will she insist on going to live with her mother, who lets these things go? The dilemma is similar to that faced by untenured professors trying to decide how demanding to be, given that negative student evaluations may be used to deny them their jobs. Children, on the other hand, are constantly teased by the thought that they don't have to take what is being dished out. This state of affairs leads, at best, to an uneasy truce in which a parent's walking on eggs undermines children's best interests.

Even where leaving is not a credible threat, the assumptions underlying equal rights for children can undermine needed learning. As I pointed out earlier, some parent-child relationships are good: the child internalizes expectations early and behaves ever more responsibly with only the lightest touch of authority on a parent's part; such a child can be treated almost like an adult, even in the absence of equal rights. Democratic permissiveness that emphasizes explanation and justification of rules is, it seems to me, quite likely to play a big role in encouraging such a happy situation. It doesn't follow that reducing control to an adult level from the start will create such an "easy" child, though. Quite the contrary: remember Baumrind's results. Given how greatly children's personalities differ, it is possible that democratic permissiveness won't necessarily create this kind of relationship, even if it should always be tried. Some children, after all, fail to internalize even the most basic rules and require constant pressure to meet even minimal standards of progress toward maturity. If even democratic permissiveness may sometimes provide them with too much "moral" support for their failure to mature at a normal pace, how much more difficulty is laissez-faire permissiveness likely to create? None of these considerations should be taken to show that more control is always better than less, or that protectionists must in every instance prefer control to freedom, but only that control may sometimes be necessary and appropriate, especially for young children.[29]

Suppose, for instance, that a child routinely refuses to help around the house, or does a hopeless job. At present, although this is a difficult situation, determined parents have the upper hand because they can point to the importance of developing habits of cleanliness, cooperation, and so forth. Without social support, however, even such basic parental values may have little authority.

Consequently, it seems to me that liberation for preteens might too often thwart the kind of learning that it is essential to promote, while failing to protect them from manipulation and indoctrination. It would place new emphasis on the importance of childhood as a time of life to be enjoyed at the expense of preparation for adult life. These ends are not always in conflict, and it is clearly appropriate to attend to both. But submerging the one so completely in the other is unwise.

So, in reality, the limited practical power of children's liberation to effect fundamental social change together with the power it would newly place in children's hands would probably undercut whatever maturation could have been expected from their assumption of more adult roles. In other words, to the extent that children gain power in the family, they will be able to avoid painful experiences that teach responsibility. In sum, the undesirable trend toward recognizing liberty without corresponding responsibility would be accelerated.

It hardly needs saying that once children become teenagers, tinder piles multiply: skipping school, homework, curfew, sex, drugs, dress, loud music, and simple courtesy often become battlegrounds. Conflict seems almost a foregone conclusion. The difficulty with the liberation point of view is that conflict has a tendency to become conflated with conflict of interest.[30] A conflict of interest occurs when two individuals have legitimate interests that cannot both be satisfied. I have suggested that morality calls upon us to satisfy the

29. For studies and speculation about the timing of control, see de Man, "Autonomy-Control Variation."

30. To some extent, this is true also for younger children. Once children reach the age of ten or so, however, many become more aware of their surroundings and more articulate about their wishes; the possibility of leaving home also becomes more (though still not very) realistic.

stronger interest. I think it is probably also generally recognized that special relationships, such as parent-child relationships, can involve commitments on the part of parents to subordinate more of their own interests than would otherwise be required. As any thoughtful parent knows, translating this theory into practice is no easy task; we find ourselves asking time and time again: Is *this* something I owe my child?

Liberationists rightly point out that protectionism has a way of covering up possible conflicts of interest between children and adults. The underlying suggestion is that there is an analogy with the case of women, whose interests, until recently, were thought to be adequately protected by laws that left their affairs in the hands of men. The answer, for women, was to give them the power to protect their own interests. But women are adults who can handle their own affairs; given children's immaturity, there is little reason to think that the same approach would benefit them.

We know that some of children's interests ought to have priority for parents; getting parents to behave accordingly is essential for children's well-being. Any decent society must have a backup system for children whose parents are not meeting their basic needs. Contemporary Western societies have mostly relied on the state for this protection, although, as liberationists rightly emphasize, the record of that alternative is to some degree a sorry one. As I argued earlier, however, it is far from clear that liberating children is the answer to this problem.

Equal rights promise children the power to ensure that their basic needs are met without direct reliance on the good graces of other adults. What they deliver, instead, is a weapon that in the short run helps children get their own way, whether the conflict in question is one of interests or not. It might be reasonable to accept this result if the bad consequences of children's running their own lives were outweighed by the guarantees for their important interests. I think that by the end of this work it will be absolutely clear that this is not the case and is not likely to become so in the foreseeable future.

Some disagreements between parents and children involve true conflicts of interest. For example, a parent with a demanding work schedule needs some free time, which might have to come at the expense of a child's desire for the parent's attendance at a school function. In general, as I have suggested, the stronger interest ought to prevail here, although it isn't always easy to see which it is.

Other conflicts don't necessarily involve serious interests at all, only tastes. Teenagers tend to have a penchant for loud rock music, which lots of adults detest. Rights aren't really an issue here (even if some of us would like to declare silence a right): these are surely matters to be dealt with by negotiation and compromise. One would hope that even liberated children (not to mention adults!) would see that enjoyable family life depends on some give-and-take here. Sometimes a technological fix works: probably many an undeclared war has been ended by earphones.

Some conflicts, however—and this point is central to my case—are asymmetrical. They involve a teen's claim that a serious interest is involved, a claim that a parent denies. Now sometimes parents wrongly deny that a given desire involves an interest. For instance, parents may insist that children prepare for an occupation—medicine, say—in which they have neither aptitude nor interest, or refuse help in preparing for one, such as acting, for which they have real talent. Parents may also refuse to pay for an abortion that is clearly in a girl's interest. Some such cases are serious violations of children's rights and we need to find alternative ways to provide for children's needs. It is claimed that equal rights would do so, but unless vast social changes accompany them, this seems unlikely; a much more fruitful approach would, I think, be additional protective rights for them. For example, we could subsidize education more fully.[31] And we could provide abortions (and other reproductive services) to teenagers free of charge.[32]

What about the opposite case, in which children are in fact mistaken about their interests? The kind of case that stands out in the strongest relief is the one of teenagers who assert a right to do as they please, just like an adult. A problem can arise either because their immaturity is likely to create problems for themselves or for others which an adult would avoid or because, given their age and situation, the consequences overall would be worse. Most actual cases probably involve a combination of these features.

Why should parents have anything to say about teens' school-

31. This strategy by itself is clearly insufficient to open up all occupations to those who could engage in them successfully: income and education of parents affects children's capacities in fundamental ways that only now are coming to be recognized. But it's a step in the right direction.

32. Again, justice requires society to provide a minimum level of health care to all; but this approach would, by itself, meet an especially urgent need.

work, drinking, or sex life? Why should they care how they dress or do their hair? Why indeed? I agree that after a certain age children should be able to suit themselves as to appearance, although I claim the same right they do to hoot at what strikes me as bizarre. With this independence, however, should also go responsibility for the relevant expenditures.

Would that the other issues were so easy to resolve! Our legal system generally operates on the assumption that competent adults should be free to do as they like unless they commit illegal acts.[33] Yet when people we care about behave in self-destructive ways, we nevertheless try to persuade them to change their behavior. As children grow older, the same general approach seems most justifiable. They are often dependent on us in ways that other adults are not, however, and this dependence provides a lever. Given the special traps that await immature individuals, it seems appropriate to use the power inherent in that lever. Children's liberation would lessen parents' ability to apply such pressure: when notions about the illegitimacy of any interference in another's goals is in the air, informal levers become less effective. As I have suggested, liberation would supply some of the means for independence without necessarily supplying the major social changes that might help ensure a minimally acceptable outcome.

What about schooling, for example? What if a teen refuses to take school seriously or wants to drop out? The consequences will depend in part on outside circumstances; some would be able to do these things with impunity, for their situation permits them to make up work or return to school without any major penalty. But many children would not be in such fortunate circumstances and they would quite likely find themselves trapped for life in low-paying, dead-end jobs; they would also be deprived of whatever cultural enrichment further schooling might provide. These probable consequences of a poor school record are well known, but they are unlikely to be taken seriously by adolescents who want to drop out. Parents and other adults can help by painting graphic pictures of the consequences; they can also require a child to work if she drops out, giving her a taste of reality before getting too far behind in school.

33. For detailed discussion of this issue, see Joel Feinberg, *Harm to Others: The Moral Limits of the Criminal Law* (Oxford: Oxford University Press, 1984).

To be sure, by the teenage years, parents must exercise most of their authority by stating acceptable alternatives and sticking to them, even if that means throwing a child out of the house. In a sense, then, we are no longer talking about the kind of parental control liberationists object to, but more subtle pressures generally compatible with their stand except insofar as they think teens have a right to financial support no matter what their behavior.

Teens might also insist that drinking or doing drugs should be their own choice, just as it is for adults. But the reverberations both for themselves and for those about them suggest the desirability of pressing them to limit such activities in a way that might not be appropriate for adults.

The same is true for sex. Taboos on early sexual activity are breaking down: according to *Newsweek* "a recent [1987] Harris poll of U.S. teenagers indicated that more than half have had intercourse by the time they are seventeen." But only a third used contraception regularly; a third admitted to never using it, despite its availability. Consider the story of Vantra and her boyfriend, both sixteen. She used contraception only sporadically until recently, but after two months on the pill, her boy friend asked her to quit using it: "He wants a child. And I don't know, in a way I want one, and in a way it's just too early for one." But she did quit, despite the fact that they have sex at least twice a week.[34] Sadly, many people attribute the increase in sexual intercourse to peer pressure and our sexualized culture, not to affection or even desire.[35]

The consequences are no less serious or real, whatever their causes. Sexually transmitted diseases are epidemic, and one might reasonably expect to see an increasing number of AIDS victims in this age group, especially among poor minorities.[36] One could hardly call this consequence either trivial or self-regarding.

Another result of irresponsible sexual activity is substantial teenage motherhood. Yet the consequences of early childbearing are ex-

34. *Newsweek*, February 16, 1987, pp. 56, 61.

35. Elkind, *All Grown Up*; Welsh, *Tales Out of School*.

36. In fact, black women account for 52% of women with AIDS, well above their representation in the population at large; black heterosexuals start having sex earlier than their white counterparts, and are less likely to know about or use contraception. See Mindy Thompson Fullilove, Robert E. Fullilove, Katharine Haynes, and Shirley Gross, "Black Women and AIDS Prevention: A View toward Understanding the Gender Rules," *Journal of Sex Research* 27 (February 1990): 47–64.

tremely damaging.[37] Pregnancy doubles the risk that a girl will drop out of school; most such girls never return, regardless of their financial situation or ethnic background. Once the child is born, the girl is unlikely to be in a position to earn more than welfare would offer her and she has the responsibility of a child to boot. But if she chooses to go on welfare, her sense of agency and independence is seriously damaged. If she marries instead, she is not only unlikely to finish her schooling but also faces a significantly higher probability of divorce than a woman who waits until her twenties to marry.[38] Thus girls who engage in unprotected sex and who elect to keep their babies are at serious risk of a worse life than they could otherwise have expected.

But the damage does not stop there. The plight of their children is painful. Neither parent may take responsibility: they may be ignored by their fathers and handed to some female relative by their mothers. For the child, this may be a blessing in disguise, as the most irresponsible teens are those least likely to possess the qualities required for good childrearing.[39] As these babies get older, however, they show the effects of their unfavorable environment. Children of teen mothers score worse on ability tests, get worse grades, and expect less in the way of education than children of older women. They also get less education, marry earlier, and divorce more often.[40]

Surely these are undesirable consequences. The causes, again, appear to be twofold. On the one hand, teenagers are more likely to be

37. For an extended discussion of the issues, see Cheryl D. Hayes, ed., *Risking the Future: Adolescent Sexuality, Pregnancy, and Childbearing*, vol. 1 (Washington, D.C.: National Academy of Sciences, National Research Council, 1987).

38. *Newsweek*, February 16, 1987, p. 61.

39. Welsh, *Tales Out of School*, provides a frightening glimpse of contemporary teenage attitudes, especially in the black community. He reports that in 1982 a quarter of all black babies were born to teenagers, and quotes a school nurse at a large high school in Alexandria, Va.: "When I first began this job, I was a bleeding heart. . . . But the numbers just kept growing because no one said it is shameful to bring another human being into the world without caring for it. . . . When they're pregnant it's like being a star. Then they often shelve it with a mother or aunt." The fathers are often even more irresponsible. A teacher at the school says, "They hang around for a while, visit the kid, but soon drop out. There's seldom any long-term involvement. . . . Several times I've heard seventeen-year-old fathers in my English class boast that they were good parents because they visit their children once a week and give the mother 'Pampers' money." Many poor young black males seem to have had no fathering themselves, and no conception of the role: "The consequences of sex are not important," they maintain. Black girls tell Welsh that "most boys deny parenthood" (pp. 51–52).

40. Elkind, *All Grown Up*, p. 133.

impulsive about sexual activity than are adults and more vulnerable to social pressure to keep their babies; on the other, they are at a stage in their development where more can go wrong with their lives.[41] Recognizing equal rights for them fails to take these facts into account. Only the assumption that both of these factors would be remedied by equal rights could reasonably shore up that appeal. But, as we have seen, there appear to be no real grounds for believing such an assumption: quite the contrary.

So although the initial activity appeared to be of the self-regarding sort that could appropriately be the subject of a right ("I have a right to do what I want with my own body and life!"), the consequences belie this position: it is not in a girl's interest to deflect parents' pressure for responsible sex. Hence some disagreements about sex don't involve conflicts of interest of the sort that calls for society to protect a child's right to behave as she pleases.

This position is reinforced by the fact that some such kinds of irresponsibility may well boomerang on parents themselves. Who spends a lifetime helping instead of being helped by a son or daughter whose lack of employment skills was caused by failure to take school seriously? What about parents who must pick up the pieces of their children's drug-shattered lives? What about those mothers who wind up taking care of their daughters *and* their offspring? Do we want to reduce parents' power to protect themselves from these kinds of foreseeable consequences of irresponsible behavior on their children's part? There has been some discussion of what children owe their parents but it has tended to focus on the source of children's duty (based on enlightened self-interest) to obey their parents while they live at home or on what they owe them once they are gone.[42]

In general, it seems to me that although parents' interests must often take a back seat to the duties created by children's needs during the years of active parenting, there is a limit to what should be

41. According to a Harris Poll, the most sexually active teenagers are those most at risk in other respects. They are disadvantaged in terms of education and overall life prospects and know little about sexuality and contraception. See Clara S. Haignere, "Planned Parenthood Harris Poll Findings: Teens' Sexuality Knowledge and Beliefs," paper presented at the Annual Children's Defense Fund National Conference, Washington, D.C., March 11–13, 1987.

42. See, e.g., Blustein, "Children and Family Interests," and Jane English, "What Do Grown Children Owe Their Parents?" both in O'Neill and Ruddick, *Having Children*.

expected of them afterward. The answer that parents can simply ignore their offspring's needs does not satisfy: it overlooks the bonds of love and caring we hope are inherent in such relationships. There is something radically wrong with this picture of family, and indeed of the society of which it is a part.

Let us now turn to two other facets of the question of equal rights, compulsory schooling and work.

Chapter 5

SCHOOLING AND WORK

> Initiation into a band is as rough as the *rite de passage* by which you are moved out of it. Entering a band, you are the youngest, have the least to offer, and have the least physical resistance. You are no asset to the band, and are therefore not much more welcome than you were at home. But at least you will be in the band for four or five years, so it is known that if you survive you will eventually be of some use. Within the band each child seeks another close to him in age, for defense against the older children. These become "friends." There are usually only between half a dozen and a dozen children in a band, so each child is limited to one or two friends. These friendships are temporary, however, and inevitably there comes a time, the time of transition, when each turns on the one that up to then has been the closest to him; that is the *rite de passage*, the destruction of that fragile bond called friendship. When this has happened to you three or four times you are ready for the world, knowing friendship for the joke it is.
>
> —Colin Turnbull, *The Mountain People*

Proponents of children's liberation believe that any difference in treatment between children and adults must be justified by reference to some morally relevant difference between the members of the two classes. Aharon Aviram argues that writers on education and society at large have taken such differences for granted and have therefore failed to provide the necessary justification for subjecting children to compulsory schooling.[1]

1. Aharon Aviram, "The Justification of Compulsory Education: The Still Neglected Moral Duty," *Journal of Philosophy of Education* 20 (Summer 1986): 51–58. Among the prima facie (but not real) exceptions he cites the following: Ivan Illich, *Deschooling Society* (London: Penguin, 1973); R. S. Peters, "The Justification of Education," in *The Phi-*

Aviram does not deny the possibility that compulsory schooling of some sort could be justifiable; he merely argues that no one has seriously tried to justify the current system, mainly because of assumptions about children's nature that appear to render the task unnecessary. He argues that society has relied on John Stuart Mill's unjustified views about children's incompetence. Aviram rightly argues that the principles of liberal democracy require us to recognize the necessity for defending compulsory schooling. My arguments so far respond to this demand by suggesting that the differences between children and adults warrant different treatment. In particular, I have been arguing that children need systematic teaching so that they may acquire desirable traits; I have also argued that they need parents to do this teaching. But parents need help: they usually can't teach children everything they need to know.

One reason is that life is so complicated that parents can only rarely know everything their children need to learn; most wouldn't have the time to teach them anyway. Furthermore, by recognizing parents' right to rear their children, society chooses a system that gives children (at best) an unequal start in life and (at worst) risks parental abuse. Some such abuse is so serious that children should be taken out of their parents' hands. Many other children continue to be at various kinds of disadvantage from their parents' way of life, however. Poverty, for example, is generally a major source of disadvantage for children; also, some households fail to transmit the kind of self-control and moral concern for others necessary for children's and society's well-being. Universal, compulsory schooling is one way of adding to and reinforcing the useful learning children get at home; for some children it may be the only source of such learning. Such schooling constitutes a reasonable compromise between leaving children's welfare entirely in the hands of their parents and attempting to place it in the hands of other social institutions.

Despite the fact that school can and sometimes does help children to overcome social handicaps, it has been argued that they would be

---

losophy of Education (Oxford: Oxford University Press, 1973), and *Ethics and Education* (London: Allen & Unwin, 1980); P. Hirst, *Knowledge and the Curriculum* (London: Routledge & Kegan Paul, 1974); J. P. White, *Towards Compulsory Curriculum* (London: Routledge & Kegan Paul, 1973); and L. I. Kimmerman, "Compulsory Education: A Moral Critique," in *Ethics and Educational Policy*, ed. K. A. Strike (Boston: Routledge & Kegan Paul, 1978).

better off if it were not compulsory. Liberationists must, if they are to be consistent, argue for the abolition of compulsory schooling. As we have seen, the right to live where you please implies a right to work; the right to work implies a right to dispose of your time as you choose. Consequently, individuals with a right to choose where they live cannot be required to go to school. In any case, no one requires adults to go to school unless they too are dependent on the state.

This argument would, if sound, justify ending such schooling, although proponents of equal rights also tend to try to strengthen their position by pointing out its overall bad consequences.[2] The issues raised by these questions are many and complicated. I shall seek here only to consider what can be said in favor of compulsory education, without trying to justify the particular forms adopted by any given society.[3]

What would happen if children were not required by the state to go to school? It seems to me that the following claims are plausible. First, some children would get little, if any, schooling, and schooling would more than ever depend on parental interest and income. Second, the public school system might collapse. Third, private schools might well proliferate even if the public schools carried on. Let us consider each of these possibilities in turn.

Some parents, either because they are poor, do not value education, or do not care about their children's future, would want their children to work as soon as they were able; some children might prefer to work and refuse schooling, just as some already undermine their schooling because they work too much. As I suggested earlier, given the current correlation between schooling and income, lack of schooling would probably trap most of these children in unsatisfying jobs.

It is true that some children are now so unhappy in school that they might nonetheless be better off, even in those jobs. Perhaps, if school could not be made more interesting and profitable, letting them go would be a reasonable alternative. I am not so skeptical as some about improving the schools, however, and in any case I would be troubled by the prospect of children stuck for a lifetime in such jobs on the basis of their immature decisions, especially since at

2. See, e.g., Lindley, "Teenagers and Other Children."

3. A form could be justified only by painstaking analysis of a wide variety of issues that will vary according to circumstance.

present that would simply perpetuate the existing class hierarchy, with women and male minorities at the bottom of the occupational heap.[4]

I also believe that parental income and support would become even more than now the decisive factor in occupational decisions unless society itself were to provide direct help to children who wanted more schooling. It would be ironic if equal rights were to become a mechanism by which economic and social inequality were still further entrenched in American life. That this should occur because of factors beyond the control of the rising generation, or even on the basis of their own immature decisions, should give pause to those who would otherwise favor purely voluntary schooling. Not only is this result undesirable in itself, but it would have seriously negative implications for the future of democracy.[5]

Because of their optimistic assumptions about how children will fare if they are liberated, proponents of equal rights tend to discount the possibility of increased inequality in society as a whole resulting from implementation of those rights. If that optimism is unfounded, as I think I am showing it to be, that prospect should, by itself, sabotage the case for liberation. Greater equality is, after all, the keystone of that case; if treating children more like adults leads to less equality, then the case gets hard to justify even on its own grounds. The damage to democracy would not be limited to this growing gap between rich and poor, however: good democratic decisions depend on an educated citizenry with the kind of self-control and values for which I have been arguing. Given the critically important ecological and political decisions facing us over the next decade, this issue is crucial.

Radical critiques of the educational system point out that the *exist-*

4. One might wonder *who* will do these undesirable jobs, since there is no reason to think that everybody will be able to have safe, interesting, and adequately paid jobs in the foreseeable future. At present it is the children of poor and working-class families who are most likely to wind up in them, and I am arguing that equal rights will most likely simply perpetuate this situation. Ideally, nobody should be doing such jobs for very long, and I would hope that in the long run they could either be eliminated by automation or spread throughout the population by some rotation system. Furthermore, society ought to balance intrinsic unpleasantness by other appeals, such as high pay. These approaches are obviously utopian at present. Perhaps the most that can be hoped for now is that merit, rather than class, play a larger role in deciding who shall escape them.

5. Amy Gutmann, for example, ultimately derives all our decisions about education from the need to sustain democracy: *Democratic Education* (Princeton: Princeton University Press, 1987).

ing system already merely legitimates and promotes contemporary inequality in the United States: instead of paving the way for equality, it solidifies the nonmeritocratic hierarchy implicit in our society.[6]

There is a good deal of evidence to support the view that schooling contributes less to social mobility than many have thought and that it has an especially stigmatizing effect on those outside the mainstream. In response to these claims it is important not to throw the baby out with the bathwater, however. First, it's hard to see how weakening schools or letting some children avoid schooling would improve this picture. Second, it is fairly clear how to begin remedying this state of affairs: states must develop school funding arrangements that allocate resources more equitably among schools.[7] To the predictable conservative skepticism that this move would change the situation very much, one might reasonably ask why, then, rich districts spend so much. And if money is so irrelevant, what is the objection to transferring some from the rich to the poor? In short, compulsory schooling is a necessary but not sufficient condition of a better society. That it is not sufficient is no reason to abolish it. The kind of social changes—social changes that liberationists recommend and require—that would be necessary to help children deal with the adult world without education would, if aimed instead at the schools, improve them so much that this criticism would no longer apply. Given the potential value of education, what could then justify giving up on schooling?

The decline (if not collapse) of the public school system, coupled with expansion of private schools, would almost certainly accentu-

6. See, e.g., S. Bowles and H. Gintis, *Schooling in Capitalist America* (London: Routledge & Kegan Paul, 1976), and Richard Rothstein, "Down the Up Staircase," in *And Jill Came Tumbling After*, ed. Judith Stacey et al. (New York: Dell, 1974).

7. Funding schools through property taxes means that the resources available on a per capita basis can vary tremendously. According to the U.S. Department of Education, Office of Educational Research and Improvement, *Digest of Education Statistics, 1989*, 25th ed., NCES 89-643 (Washington, D.C.: U.S. Government Printing Office, 1989), Table 146, p. 156, Mississippi spent $2,350 per child on education, whereas New Jersey spent $5,953 and Alaska spent $8,010. Some of this variation is due to differences in the cost of living, but the figures also conceal substantial differences within states. The inadequacy of the resources of poor neighborhoods tends to lead to underfunded schools that can't prepare children well. It's easy to see how a vicious circle is established from which the poor and minorities have difficulty extricating themselves. The obvious inequity here is finally being recognized by some courts. In Abbott v. Burke, 575 A.2d 359 (N.J. Sup. Ct. 1990), for example, Judge Robert Wilentz held both that poor districts had to be assured funding equal to rich ones and that the level of spending had to be sufficient to compensate for the disadvantages of their students.

ate inequality and other undesirable trends.[8] A universal, compulsory public school system can, in principle, guarantee children's exposure not only to the academic material essential for adult life but, even more important for our concerns here, to the kind of guidance with respect to self-control and the values necessary for optimum development of individuals and maintaining a just, caring society. Parents cannot be counted upon to offer good teaching, and even when they do, reinforcement from other social institutions is needed.[9]

I have been arguing that children need help learning both self-control and morality. In particular, we have seen that there is some reason to believe that children do not learn how to show intelligent concern for others unless they are systematically and deliberately taught. From very early on, children begin to have experiences that encourage them to be self-centered or solicitous of others. Much ought to have been learned by the time they start school, but school can certainly reinforce desirable learning or counteract the undesirable.

An interesting measure of this function is provided by a 1959 study of membership in the American Civil Liberties Union. This organization is a watchdog for civil liberties in the United States; as such it should be of special interest to those who value freedom. Twenty-five percent of its members were teachers; 66 percent listed their last level of schooling as postgraduate university work, 24 percent listed it as college, 7 percent listed it as high school, and 2 percent listed it as grade school.[10] Obviously, these figures differ

8. It is plausible that ending compulsory schooling would simply accelerate the trend for those who can afford it to send their children to private schools, perceived to be superior. I suspect that schooling could be made voluntary only if political support for the schools were still weaker than it is now; repeal of the attendance laws and the resultant drop in enrollments, together with the loss of the promise of equality, would most probably provide sufficient grounds for a taxpayers' revolt.

9. The necessity for consistency is one of Bronfenbrenner's central points: other societies send coherent value messages, whereas we send many contradictory ones. The result is confusion, which contributes to the failure to transmit basic values. See Urie Bronfenbrenner, "The Parent/Child Relationship and Our Changing Society," in *Parents, Children, and Change*, ed. L. Eugene Arnold (Lexington, Mass.: Lexington Books, 1985).

10. This study is reported in Nash, *Authority and Freedom in Education*, p. 77. In general Nash makes a powerful argument for the necessity of schooling. This research, by itself, doesn't make the case, but it is suggestive. In a different society, of course, moral education might conceivably occur in the absence of schooling, but what we need to consider is the likely effect under contemporary circumstances.

vastly from the distribution of education in the population at large. It is clear that we cannot assume that additional years of schooling necessarily promote concern for equality or human welfare, given the voting patterns in presidential elections.[11] They do, however, provide an opportunity for learning that supports these values.[12]

Schooling also provides, as I will argue shortly, a crucially important and possibly unique opportunity for children to learn about those who are different from themselves. Only this kind of learning will help eradicate prejudice about such differences as race, sex, and class. Although unjustifiable inequality and discrimination are not based solely on such prejudice, it significantly contributes to the misery of those who are its target. Not only do they suffer from dimin-

11. In the 1989 election, for example, increased income was consistently associated with progressively higher percentages of conservative votes (*New York Times*, November 10, 1988, B6). This pattern of voting is an ongoing phenomenon; see Warren E. Miller and Santa Traugott, *American National Election Studies Data Sourcebook, 1952–1986* (Cambridge: Harvard University Press, 1989), Table 6.5, p. 316. Income is correlated with years of schooling. In the United States it now seems that those who are better off are tending more and more to vote in what they see as their own self-interest, to the detriment of concern for the welfare of those less well off. This trend suggests that people are unconvinced of the importance of concern for others. The present work shows why.

12. Much of the average American's conviction about democratic principle may be superficial. Studies repeatedly show that many citizens fail to recognize or assent to such uncontroversial documents as the Bill of Rights. When Nash asked students about the Bill of Rights, he found unanimous approval for none of its amendments, and two were rejected by a majority. These were the provision in the Sixth for confronting one's accuser and the Tenth Amendment's reservation of rights to the people. As a result of this experience, and of another study of students at nine teachers' colleges, Nash concluded that "they pay lip service to the liberties that they have been taught verbally from elementary school through college, but when faced with specific issues they often take a stand that is more authoritarian than libertarian": *Authority and Freedom in Education*, p. 89. This study, conducted during the McCarthy era, showed that although most of the students said they believed in freedom of speech and thought, they would nonetheless be in favor of censoring speakers in schools and banning textbooks that criticized religious organizations. Furthermore, "a large majority would deport or silence those who do not believe in our form of government": Fay L. Corey, *Values of Future Teachers: A Study of Attitudes toward Contemporary Issues* (New York: Teachers College Press, 1955), p. 46, cited in ibid. Instead of standing up for their rights, they were accommodating pressures to avoid controversial stands and "questionable" groups and individuals. Despite the upheavals of the 1960s, there is little reason to believe that things would be very different now. Lloyd Duck describes a frightening little study: When students circulated part of the preamble to the Declaration of Independence among 252 residents of an Air Force base in Germany, only 16% recognized it; only 27% signed it; and 14% said they agreed with its ideas but wouldn't sign it. Some called the document "a lot of trash." Others thought it advocated revolution or unwarranted changes by "little people"; didn't give enough to the majority class; was too radical, was "pretty" but not workable, or was communistic. The results of this study were placed in the *Congressional Record*. See Lloyd Duck, *Teaching with Charisma* (Boston: Alleyn & Bacon, 1981), pp. 13–15.

ished freedom—a fact that undermines arguments based on freedom on their own grounds—but other values (such as fairness) would, in many cases, override the appeal to freedom. Progress on these fronts is slow and fragile: the price of equality, like that of liberty, is probably eternal vigilance. Schools don't necessarily promote equality (or any other value) but they can be more efficient vehicles for such promotion than any other institution.

Universal, compulsory education is our best bet for making sure that everybody is exposed to the perspectives, knowledge, skills, and strategies necessary for dealing with values. Ideally, the public education system would do such a good job that there would be no market or need for private schools or home teaching. These options now sometimes provide better education than the public system, although if they are laxly regulated, they also create loopholes through which some children can slip. The important point is that all children must be decently educated, both for their own sakes and for that of society.[13] Compulsory education is therefore a necessity, even though there is some leeway in what form it shall take. Only compulsory education can ensure that none will be deprived of the unique advantages of the learning it provides, and only compulsory education can ensure society of the kind of citizens it needs to create a fairer, more humane world.[14]

Problems with the Notion of the Moral Role of the School

Some critics see the specter of indoctrination in any attempt to teach the kinds of values I have been talking about. There is considerable disagreement about the definition of indoctrination.[15] These

13. Only education promises to help us avoid the central moral problem of democracy: unjust or imprudent decisions by the majority.

14. This is not to say that it is being very successful at it now; but there is little reason to believe that ending compulsory schooling would improve the situation, *pace* Ivan Illich.

15. Most of the disagreement turns upon whether the critical factor is the teacher's intent, the subject matter taught, or the method of its teaching. For further discussion, see R. S. Laura, "To Educate or to Indoctrinate: That Is Still the Question," *Educational Philosophy and Theory* 20 (1988): 63–69; Ben Spiecker, "Indoctrination, Intellectual Virtues, and Rational Emotions," *Journal of the Philosophy of Education* 21 (Winter 1987): 261–66; Alven Michael Neiman, "Indoctrination and Rationality," *Philosophy of Education: Proceedings* 43 (1987): 241–45; and Tasos Kazepides, "Indoctrination, Doctrines,

debates need not concern us here; I adopt John Chambers's conception of indoctrination as the "intentional implantation of equivocal or debatable content in the hope that no matter what counter-evidence is produced the . . . students will continue to hold the content as true and never see it as equivocal or false."[16] One of the virtues of this definition is the ease with which it helps us distinguish between indoctrination and education, which involves imparting material together with an accurate account of its warrants.

Popular opinion sometimes equates any influencing of others, especially vulnerable others such as children, with indoctrination or brainwashing. Even quite thoughtful people sometimes talk as if there is something sacred about individuals' values so that it is wrong to attempt to persuade people to alter them. But respect for individuals is compatible with attempting to influence them. Our respect for others is measured by the methods we use.

At issue, I think, are unarticulated (and usually unacknowledged) ideas about the importance of individual choice and opinion. It seems that what is taken to be vital about such beliefs is that they are *ours*. Underlying this view is some concept of "pure," uninfluenced choice.

When we stop to consider this notion, however, it makes no sense at all. It seems to be closely related to the natural law concept of "the natural" as what would happen in the absence of human action, and no less meaningless in the context of human society.[17] Beliefs thought to be of biological origin might be considered paradigm cases of uninfluenced belief. They would, of course, be uninfluenced by human sources but would be totally influenced by "nature." Whether humans have such beliefs is questionable; even if we did, however, their worth would remain to be shown.

If there is no coherent notion of uninfluenced belief, those who see influencing as an act of disrespect toward persons must in any case retreat to some distinction about the acceptability of influences from

---

and the Foundations of Rationality," *Philosophy of Education: Proceedings* 43 (1987): 229–40.

16. John Chambers, *The Achievement of Education* (New York: Harper & Row, 1983), p. 35. We might spend considerable space examining whether this is the most precise and desirable definition of "indoctrination," but Chambers's will do for our purposes here.

17. See Christine Pierce, "Natural Law Language and Women," in *Sex Equality*, ed. Jane English (Englewood Cliffs, N.J.: Prentice-Hall, 1977).

different components of the environment. One possible distinction could be made between "natural" pressures and social ones; another, between intended and unintended influences.[18] Insofar as we can make meaningful distinctions of these kinds, what significance ought they to have? Could either bear the moral weight implied by those who hold that we should refrain from intentional influencing, that arguing, teaching, training are always suspect? Might such distinctions be the legacy of the Rousseau who wrote "never present to his undiscriminating will anything but physical obstacles or punishments which stem from the actions themselves"? His justification was that "the weakness of the first age enchains children in so many ways that it is barbarous to add to this subjection a further subjection—that of our caprices—by taking from them a freedom so limited, which they are so little capable of abusing and the deprivation of which is of so little utility to them and to us"[19] We have already seen how selectively Rousseau applies this principle, but why, in any case, is it barbarous to explicitly impose restrictions on children? Is it really better to manipulate them so they do not understand the limits imposed on them? What could be more dishonest or undermine more thoroughly children's understanding of the requirements of social life?

Instead of relying on muddled principles of this sort, we need forthright discussion of what we want children to learn and how to help them do it. Thus we must address the question whether they learn to make better judgments if left entirely to their own devices or whether they should be exposed to teaching about important matters.

Contemporary Western cultures, as Patrick Welsh and others have pointed out, are a free-for-all of competing ideas. Children need opportunities to discuss them and to hear what grownups think. Welsh adds that

18. The difficulties involved in any but the roughest distinctions of this kind should be obvious, given the extensive alterations humans make to the environment and the vastly differing understanding and motivation of people.

19. Rousseau, *Emile*, pp. 85, 88–89. Rousseau's position here is especially debatable when we consider the distinction he made between the education of boys and girls. Boys are to be limited only by (the tutor's manipulation of) nature; girls are to be taught to interrupt their play at a moment's notice. These differences lead to and are reflected by their later role in society: men are to be free and independent citizens, women—it would not be an exaggeration to assert—their slaves. It is slaves who do the dirty work necessary to keep society running smoothly.

> these kids need more, not less, from schools. In a world of information overload, they need more help in separating the important and significant from the trivial and merely entertaining. We needed information from the schools. Kids . . . need to learn how to filter, interpret, and understand the flood of information. In a society in which divorce is commonplace and the youth culture puts a premium on precocious sex, heavy drinking and drug use, children need more emotional support and guidance than ever. In a time in our history when much is given but little is asked, they need real challenges against which they can shape their character, values, and minds.[20]

No less important, despite the apparently limitless array of ideas and positions presented to Americans, the parameters of debate about some kinds of issues are in fact far narrower than they seem, as a trip to another country will quickly demonstrate. So not only do children need guidance for threading their way among available choices, they need help in discerning the hidden boundaries of our discourse.

If children are left as much as possible on their own to make choices, it is possible but not likely that they will successfully pick their way through the maelstrom and emerge the stronger. But we cannot count on a satisfactory outcome. Nor is there any good reason to believe that only this process respects their individuality.

What is to be said in favor of the thesis that children should be left to figure things out by themselves? Howard Cohen argues that

> there is, finally, something to be said for learning from experience. It does not just strike us one day that the advice of others can be helpful and worth following. The more usual story is that sometimes we ignore it and wish we had not, and sometimes we follow it and are glad we did. Slowly, and through practice, we come to develop the capacities which free us of the need to do so in some aspects of our lives. . . . A sure route to the maturity of the faculties Mill valued so highly is the monitored aid in actually exercising one's rights.[21]

This is a puzzling passage. The importance of learning from experience is underlined, but so is the reality of gradually developing ca-

20. Welsh, *Tales Out of School*, p. 15.
21. Cohen, *Equal Rights for Children*, p. 73.

pacities and the value of "monitored aid" in exercising one's rights. Cohen seems to be suggesting that we can learn much that we need to know if we are left alone to try our wings. And he is also suggesting that we gradually and only with help learn the judgment necessary to do so successfully. But these two states of affairs are in contradiction. This comment therefore doesn't really provide support for Cohen's position that children should be completely free to make their own mistakes. A much more plausible conclusion would be that children need supervised practice in making decisions, starting with relatively small matters and moving on gradually to more significant ones.

No one denies the value of learning from experience. What is in question is whether, as liberationists propose, children benefit from complete freedom or whether a more gradual introduction to life's choices would help children make wiser decisions. No doubt, some parents now restrict their children too much, so that they experience frustration as they are growing up, and are unprepared for the choices they face as adults. Conversely, some "new breed" parents let children make virtually all their own decisions, with the kinds of results we have seen. Surely a middle road that provides children with progressively more responsibility before they are expected to deal with the structurelessness of the adult world would be superior to either of these approaches. This middle road would more reliably build up children's knowledge and confidence while minimizing the risk of serious and irreversible damage to them.

Our society is pervaded by insistent messages aimed at furthering the interests of those who promote them; they do not necessarily further the common good—often quite the contrary. Peers may persuade kids to try drugs to assuage their own guilty conscience or turn a profit. Tobacco and alcohol companies want people to smoke and drink more despite the documented ill effects of these practices. The electronic media want you glued to their offerings, regardless of whether you would be better off reading, playing games, talking, or exercising. More generally, businesses want to create the desire for goods that most people don't really need and can ill afford. And so forth. Instead of imposing impractical and authoritarian bureaucratic restrictions, couldn't we educate kids to recognize these voices for what they are? Is this not precisely what liberals argue for?

Consider just one example. Magazines and television abound in devilishly clever ads that commit obvious logical fallacies. Should we supinely yield the field to them, or should we fight back by teaching every child to see what is wrong?

This question makes it clear once more that influencing per se is not the villain here: what matters is aim, method, and content. Teaching children how to test claims will do a great deal more for their welfare than abandoning them, unfortified by information and skills, to hard experience. There is time enough for experience to do what it can, if the teaching doesn't take. Why, however, should we not first try to help children learn to choose among competing ideas? Why ignore two thousand years of accumulated human wisdom?

It should hardly need saying that it is, in any case, impossible to avoid influencing children, since by attempting to avoid influencing them, one is thereby teaching them that such influencing is wrong. But this is influencing them. The idea that we can withdraw from influencing is ultimately incoherent. Thus the notion that there might be some overriding and special value in children's own uninfluenced beliefs turns out to evaporate in confusion.

What kind of influence is acceptable, then? I have been arguing that we, as a society, ought to be helping children learn self-control, enabling virtues, and moral concern. Are worries about the possibility of mistakes or concern about defensible pluralism of values justified here?

It is true that certainty often eludes us: an obvious concern about teaching values is that we may be mistaken in our reasoning about either means or ends. We may be lazy or shortsighted, indulge in wishful thinking, underestimate the existence or importance of individual differences, or inadequately understand the world. Mistakes are inevitable, and the possibility of their existence should be recognized by periodic democratic discussion and rethinking of problems.

It was this potential for mistakes, among other things, that led John Stuart Mill to his position that grownups should not be subject to coercion except to prevent harm to others. He wrote: "It would be absurd to pretend that people ought to live as if nothing whatever had been known in the world before they came into it; as if experience had as yet done nothing towards showing that one mode of existence, or of conduct, is preferable to another."[22] But he con-

22. Mill, *On Liberty*, p. 533.

cluded that it is up to each adult to evaluate such claims, according to his or her own personality and circumstances. The views of others are their own conclusions, conclusions that may be poorly reasoned or may not be relevant to our situation.

In addition, Mill saw positive benefit in encouraging people to develop their own interpretation of human experience: "He who lets the world, or his own portion of it, choose his plan of life for him, has no need of any other faculty than the ape-like one of imitation. He who chooses his plan for himself, employs all his faculties."[23] This procedure is one from which he excludes children, judging it inappropriate for those below the age of reason. Liberationists, of course, urge upon us the idea that (at least) adolescents have reached that age. The fact that their dreams are different from those of adults does not mean that those dreams are worse or that we have a right to prevent their realization. Against this position, I have argued that some such dreams, if realized, would be especially harmful both to them and to society as a whole. Implicit in this conclusion, as I have argued, is the judgment that some goals *are* worse and can be shown to be so and that temporary restraint can be beneficial overall.

Parents and teachers need to be willing to examine such matters repeatedly to ensure that judgments truly reflect experience and careful thinking. Only thus can we attempt to guard against the kinds of mistakes that would render the liberationist position somewhat plausible. But there shouldn't be any real difficulty with the kinds of judgments I have been proposing. It is hardly arguable that children's failing to learn self-control, dropping out of school, having a baby, or doing drugs is desirable: these things undeniably increase the probability of outcomes nobody wants. Does it really make sense to object that we adults might be mistaken about these judgments when they conflict with what teens want?[24]

23. Ibid., p. 534.

24. Persuading them of these truths may be especially difficult, of course, when such behavior is widespread and apparently advantageous, at least in the short run. David Bakan describes the social conditions that foster such behavior in "Adolescence in America: From Ideal to Social Fact," in Skolnick, *Rethinking Childhood.* He emphasizes the role of "the promise"—"that if a young person does all the things he is 'supposed to do' during his adolescence, he will then realize success, status, income, power, and so forth in his adulthood"—in preventing such behavior. When society fails to live up to its end of the bargain, as it does for so many poor and minority youth, hedonism seems to make

This duty on the part of adults is still stronger with respect to fundamental moral issues. How can we go wrong in arguing for the importance of developing real concern for the welfare of others? We know that paradigm cases of lying, cheating, stealing, irresponsible sex, rape, and murder demonstrate contempt for that welfare. Judgments about these cases are uncontroversial and no consistent, viable moral system could condone them. I am not claiming that there is no legitimate disagreement about moral issues; it is clear, however, that certain attitudes and practices are essential for a decent society. On what grounds do we therefore refrain from discussing these values with children and expecting them to comply with our expectations? Again, are there really grounds for fearing mistakes about such judgments?

Mistakes are more likely with respect to the specific judgments about an individual child's future because of the necessity for knowing *this* child's interests. Not only does this fact suggest the need for greater humility in making judgments of that kind, but it argues for a much stronger duty for individual adults to pay close attention to children for whom they are responsible. I argued earlier that such vigilance is necessary for effectively teaching fundamental virtues and values; it is also essential for being in a position to give good advice about less general matters. These demands imply a considerably higher standard of parenting than is now considered adequate.[25]

To the extent that my position depends upon such a standard of parenting, it might seem to be vulnerable to the same objection I have on occasion leveled against proponents of equal rights—that it requires utopian social changes. It is true that for a sizable number of people a higher standard of parenting would constitute a major change. Moreoever, making it possible for some parents to engage in such parenting by providing for paid leaves and so forth would require substantial changes in the workplace. These changes would still, on the whole, be less radical (and therefore more likely to be made) than those necessary for the success of children's liberation.

---

more sense than restraint (pp. 244–45). It can be argued, however, that unfair as society's failure is, individuals are still more likely to be able to construct a better life for themselves if they do not do what appears to be in their short-term interest here.

25. I refer only to parents here, although this concern extends to teachers. Parents and teachers must work closely together because of their perspectives and resources. My sense is that teachers can often contribute in objectivity what they lack in time. It is such considerations that have led some thinkers to propose licensing of parents. See Hugh LaFollette, "Licensing Parents," *Philosophy and Public Affairs* 9 (Winter 1980): 182–97.

Improvements in education could, by themselves, make a considerable difference in parenting. Others, together with the preconditions for implementing them such as programs to help parents make time for their children, would require allocating social resources somewhat differently. This is a far cry from the fundamental structural change amounting to the creation of a full welfare state that would be necessary for children's liberation.

Given the foregoing, it seems to me that the worry about mistakes here is overblown. Emphasizing critical thinking in both family and school, however, should serve to allay any remaining fears about mistakes or indoctrination.[26]

What I have in mind when I speak of "critical thinking" is the kind of material that is now routinely taught in college in informal logic or critical thinking courses, and that even now is being encouraged in well-taught courses in other fields. The goal is to help individuals reason constructively. This task involves, among other things, stressing the importance of justifying beliefs and teaching about what counts as justification. In the course of such studies, children would be introduced to deductive and inductive fallacies. Such teaching would also have to discuss ways of evaluating reasoning about values. Such teaching doesn't necessarily imply a single, clear standard for every knowledge claim, but rather a variety of strategies and tests that would enable one to judge the relative reliability of claims. It does imply that every significant claim to knowledge would be accompanied by discussion of the warrants for its belief. Thoroughgoing education, in this sense, would mean infusing philosophy throughout virtually the entire curriculum.[27]

Helping children become sophisticated judges of ideas would be bound to create fierce opposition, as some popular religious and political beliefs cannot pass even very elementary tests. Some fathers and mothers, in particular, would argue that their parental autonomy was being violated.

26. It is here that we see the crucial necessity for both parental authority and schooling: the best hope for ensuring that children acquire these skills is to give them two shots at it. More would be better. There is a considerable literature on this issue; for a sampling of excellent work see M. A. B. Degenhardt, "The 'Ethics of Belief' and Education in Science and Morals," *Journal of Moral Education* 15 (May 1986): 109–18; and George Sher and William Bennett, "Moral Education and Indoctrination," *Journal of Philosophy* 79 (1982): 665–77.

27. For a discussion of what such a curriculum might look like, see Matthew Lipman, *Philosophy Goes to School* (Philadelphia: Temple University Press, 1988).

I concur with liberationists that children's interest in becoming more rational beings should override any exercise of parental autonomy that attempts to protect them from exposure to discussion of basic standards of reasoning. But our positions diverge in that I think children not only have a right to learn such material, regardless of their parents' protests, but have a duty to learn it, even at the cost of some loss of liberty. That duty arises not only from children's interest but from the interest of society in having more rather than less rational members.

Locating the exact boundaries of parental autonomy, children's rights, and society's needs is a difficult task that still awaits us. Court cases involving parents who wish to limit their children's education are deeply troubling: they raise fundamental questions not only about the right of members of a culture to choose their own way of life—even at the expense of their children's freedom—but about desirable kinds of societies.[28] Fortunately, my position does not require that the more general theoretical questions here be fully resolved. Critical thinking is something that should be introduced the first day of school and continued until the last: high-quality compulsory education (no matter what its precise form) would therefore guarantee children's exposure to it.[29] Although critical thinking would encourage children to question tradition, it needn't be solely destructive. To the extent that a tradition perpetuates a satisfying way of life, it would be found valuable. No tradition is likely to meet the needs of every child, however, and this approach to education would help open other doors for such children.

Although it would be helpful for such learning to be reinforced in children's homes, in practice there is no way of ensuring this support short of extremely intrusive measures. So society must rely on the schools to do the bulk of such teaching. Acquiescence to opposing values and spheres of influence may not teach the necessary material most efficiently, but it is probably the only politically feasible approach in a pluralistic society.[30]

28. See Wisconsin v. Yoder et al., 406 U.S. 205 (1972). For an interesting discussion of some aspects of this problem, see William Ruddick, "Parents and Life Prospects," in O'Neill and Ruddick, *Having Children*.

29. For further discussion of this issue, see Gutmann, *Democratic Education*, esp. chap. 1.

30. For discussion of parental rights, see Peter Hobson, "Some Reflections on Parents'

This proposal for emphasizing critical thinking is not incompatible with the view that we need to be teaching enabling virtues and care for others early on, as they are fundamental values that can pass the test of critical scrutiny. As children grow older, both these and other values can be exhaustively discussed.

Unless the educational establishment stands up to the predictable outcry against a hard-hitting emphasis on critical thinking, most of the goals I have been discussing are in serious jeopardy. Children will not be helped to judge the values they are being taught, they will not be able to recognize misleading or dangerous claims, and they will not be able to contribute to revamping human practices in ways that will help us surmount the mortal threats now confronting us.[31] This demand for emphasizing critical thinking might seem utopian, but unless we can rise to the challenge, it is beginning to seem doubtful that there will in any case be much of a world in which to enjoy equal rights. We must therefore create a social climate that makes it just as embarrassing to hold an ungrounded position as to walk naked on Park Avenue.[32]

Rights in the Upbringing of Their Children," and David Bridges, "Non-Paternalistic Arguments in Support of Parents' Rights," both in *Journal of Philosophy of Education* 18, no. 1 (1984): 63–74 and 55–61 respectively.

31. It is important not to underestimate what it takes to acquire the analytic skills argued for here. Paul Nash argues that people need help in learning "to read, listen to, and use their own language with understanding. They must be taught to distinguish between truth and propaganda, to judge the value of what they read and hear, to express themselves in speech and writing in such a way that their true intention emerges": *Authority and Freedom*, p. 86. The political dimension of these analytic skills is particularly important. As George Orwell said, "political language is designed to make lies sound truthful and murder respectable, and to give an appearance of solidity to pure wind": "Politics and the English Language," in Orwell, *A Collection of Essays* (New York: Doubleday, 1954), p. 177. There seem to be no grounds for thinking that anything has changed since he said it. As philosophy teachers are aware, students come to our basic courses woefully unprepared in these areas; many others never even take a philosophy course.

32. This open plan of education has some additional dangers. Most theses cannot be furnished with inescapable proofs. Therefore inexperienced or weak reasoners, or those who fail to understand the importance of the distinction between weak and strong induction, may fail to be convinced by them. Morality, in particular, might then be in some danger of succumbing to relativism, unless we can find a way to instill deep and unswerving concern for the welfare of others firmly in children's hierarchy of values. There is no doubt that teaching critical thinking sometimes handicaps adults vis-à-vis children, especially older ones, in a disturbing way: anyone who has ever argued with a determined teen knows that at times nothing short of a mathematical proof will do. Yet much of what an adult knows boils down to observation and experience. Unless children are taught to

It seems clear, then, that it is not only impossible but pointless and, indeed, harmful for adults to act as though they were preserving children's autonomy by not teaching the kinds of knowledge, skills, and values we have been discussing. If we fail to teach children, what they pick up is an uncertain conglomeration of conflicting ideas. As they are virtually unarmed with principles for evaluating or choosing, they are not likely to adopt a well-thought-out set of principles. Helping children develop self-control, enabling virtues, and care for others, while at the same time teaching them the rudiments of critical thinking, would go far toward helping them cope with the world without destroying their capacity to reason about more debatable matters.[33]

It is hard to see how this desirable development could take place without the conscious and systematic input of dedicated adults. For neither values nor critical thinking can be learned without extended reflection and discussion; adults must also present children with appropriate models. We, as a society, must impress upon adults the importance of their teaching roles with respect to these things. At the same time, we have got to trust that, despite possible conflicts of interest, such adults are more likely to have children's basic interests at heart than do other possible sources of influence on them.[34] Undermining respect for parent and school leaves children at sea, with the illusion that their limited experience provides as good a basis for judgment as that of most adults. Many children already believe that it does, and the dismaying consequences are well known to those

---

appreciate the somewhat elusive nature of this evidence, discussion argument will often fail to convince. One part of the solution is, as I suggested earlier, to stop undermining children's tendency to rely on parental authority, without thereby investing parents with papal infallibility. The other is for philosophers to continue working on beating out a clear path between anarchy and dogma! A related problem is that clever children, taught critical thinking skills early, might, if dishonest, find their power to befuddle others magnified. Our best defense here is universal stress on the value of reasoning, coupled with forceful emphasis on the importance of honesty in human relationships. Despite these difficulties, it seems safe to predict that the benefits of forthright social pressure in favor of pervasive critical inquiry about both means and ends would outweigh the disadvantages.

33. For interesting arguments about the connection between moral teaching and reasoning, see Sher and Bennett, "Moral Education and Indoctrination." One particularly powerful argument raises the point that moral teaching counteracts tendencies that would, in its absence, interfere with moral reasoning (pp. 670–72).

34. Again, none of this is to say that we should fail to foresee and provide for the breakdown of parental adequacy. Children need certain kinds of protection they are not now getting. It is important to try to provide it for them without at the same time giving them false ideas about their own maturity.

who must deal with children and young adults. This situation is in nobody's interest.

To return to the context of the school: none of this is to deny that there are incompetent or indoctrinatory teachers. It does not follow that indoctrination is universal, deliberate, or inseparable from state-supported education.[35] I have been arguing that we cannot avoid teaching certain values, that it is necessary, and that public schools can morally do so. It would be much more difficult to try to ensure that all children were taught desirable values if formal public schooling were no longer compulsory.

The Importance of Public Schools

It is clear that without compulsory education some children would get little or no schooling; they would therefore be deprived of the school's contribution to the kind of essential learning for which I have been arguing. And if, as I suspect would happen, private schools were to supplant in part or entirely the public school system, it would be much harder to ensure each child's exposure to them unless those schools were very tightly regulated.[36]

Now perhaps they *would* be so regulated. They are not regulated

35. This denial is in direct opposition to Tibor Machan's argument that state schools necessarily and illegally indoctrinate. Machan believes that the First Amendment requires public schools to refrain from any commitment to specific values. He recognizes that such commitment is unavoidable, since education cannot be divorced from values, but concludes that we should not have public schools. Although "explicit indoctrination is eschewed" in them, "the implicit favoring of certain views of life, morality, religion, politics, law, sexual behavior, etc. is evidenced throughout public education": "The Schools Ain't What They Used to Be and Never Was," in *The Libertarian Alternative*, ed. Tibor Machan (Chicago: Nelson-Hall, 1977), pp. 256–57. This leads to hypocrisy, which in turn leads to resentment. Machan is right that values cannot be expunged from education. But the rest of this argument is mistaken. The relevant segment of the First Amendment reads: "Congress shall make no law respecting an establishment of religion, or prohibiting the free exercise thereof; or abridging the freedom of speech, or of the press . . . " It is hard to see how this imperative precludes discussion of values in public schools. Machan *is* right about the consequences of this state of affairs: values have often been driven underground, but they do not disappear. To the extent that they are assumed and not examined, the effect *has been* indoctrinatory. Where Machan goes wrong is in claiming that there is a necessary connection between state-supported, compulsory education and indoctrination. Neither the First Amendment nor tax support prevents rigorous examination of fundamental values. If we are concerned about indoctrination, it makes sense to challenge schools to do more of this kind of teaching and support them against the attacks of those who would eliminate such inquiry or the schools themselves.

36. It is plausible to think that schools would continue to exist since many, if not most, parents would doubtless prevail upon their children to continue with school even if the state did not require them to do so.

in these ways now, however, and there is no particular reason to think that such regulation would be instituted at the same time as equal rights for children. This conclusion is supported by the fact that the emphasis on freedom that motivates liberation is unlikely to favor stricter controls on schooling.

Tibor Machan believes that the turn to private schooling would be desirable at least in part because of the greater say it gives parents over their children's education.[37] Proponents of equal rights for children could hardly embrace this outcome, however, as they wish to put power in children's hands, not adults'. I think Machan's prediction about parental power is true, however, and it is cause for concern.

Parents may believe a variety of unsubstantiated or dubious claims about children's nature. They may also adopt without critical inquiry whatever is fashionable in the way of popular wisdom about development or education. Thus before the advent of a spate of "gifted and talented" programs a few years ago, the notion of special treatment for those who learn at different rates was anathema.[38] In the teeth of common sense and without a shred of solid evidence, children who were ready and able to learn earlier and faster than their chronological peers were denied the opportunity to do so. Deprived of challenging experiences that might have kindled their thirst for learning, they were instead stupefied by a boredom that often had long-lasting bad effects.[39]

It is plausible that parents' beliefs (if sufficiently popular) would lead to the founding of schools that catered to them, no matter what they were. Reliance on private education would therefore in effect place children's education entirely in their parents' hands. Proponents of children's rights argue that it is children who should deter-

37. At present, he says, "parents are forced to comply with the State's conception of what is right for their children, not regardful primarily of the individual characteristics, talents, needs, aspirations, interests, qualifications, etc. of any given child." Thus the state can ignore parents' opinions about such matters as when schooling should begin and what kind of material should be taught: "Schools Ain't What They Used to Be," pp. 251, 256. These claims are not universally true, however, nor would they necessarily be true of any public school system.

38. The history of attitudes toward bright kids is instructive; see, e.g., Gertrude H. Hildreth, *Introduction to the Gifted* (New York: McGraw-Hill, 1966), or Gary A. Davis and Sylvia B. Rimm, *Education of the Gifted*, 2d ed. (Englewood Cliffs, N.J.: Prentice-Hall, 1989).

39. See my unpublished paper "Educating the Gifted."

mine their educational experiences, not second parties, whether state or parents. But in practice, taking educational policy out of the hands of the state does place it in that of parents. Small children will be schooled according to their parents' beliefs, and this early education will in many cases determine their subsequent attitudes.

Suppose, however, that some parents are persuaded by the argument that reading is no longer necessary in contemporary society because of the all-pervasiveness of the electronic media. Are we prepared to let their children attend schools that follow this notion? Or suppose, not entirely unrealistically, that parents buy the idea that girls have inferior mathematical ability. Are we prepared to let them send their girls to finishing schools that fail to encourage their intellectual development in this area? Such freedom for parents has serious implications for girls and for society, if Lucy Sells's argument that failure to pursue mathematics at the high school level creates a permanent handicap in the scramble for positions of power is sound.[40]

One of the most serious manifestations of this problem would arise with respect to religion. Parents may believe that as a matter of religious freedom they have a right to raise their children in their own faith, even when their "faith" conflicts with widely accepted and defensible secular beliefs.[41] Probably we can agree that parents should be able to acquaint their children with such beliefs at home. If by having their children attend private schools, however, parents can reinforce those beliefs and shield them from critical evaluation, the children are being indoctrinated in an unacceptable way.[42]

A still more fundamental problem arises in the realm of political and social beliefs. It emerges as resistance to genuine inquiry into political theory (concerning such basic issues as capitalism, democracy, communism and feminism), as well as into emotionally wrenching

40. Lucy Sells, "The Mathematics Filter and the Education of Women and Minorities," in *Women and the Mathematical Mystique*, ed. Lynn H. Fox, Linda Brody, and Dianne Tobin (Baltimore: Johns Hopkins University Press, 1980). The same problem would arise for minorities if parents swallowed the myth of Caucasians' superiority in math.

41. For more on religious education see T. McLaughlin, "Parental Rights and the Religious Upbringing of Children," *Journal of Philosophy of Education* 18, no. 1 (1984): 75–83; W. D. Hudson, "Is Religious Education Possible?" in *New Essays in the Philosophy of Education*, ed. Glenn Langford and D. J. O'Connor (London: Routledge & Kegan Paul, 1973).

42. See Alan Peshkin, *God's Choice: The Total World of a Fundamentalist Christian School* (Chicago: University of Chicago Press, 1986), for a frightening example of this problem.

issues such as sex. Racism provides us with a relatively uncontroversial demonstration of this problem. We know that some Americans are racist, and they want their children to share their derogatory attitudes about the members of other ethnic groups. Should we be prepared to let them sequester their children in schools made in this image?

That people who fear freewheeling critical inquiry are ready to restrict their children's experience (not to mention that of other people's children) is demonstrated by the proliferation of sectarian private schools and the campaigns for censorship in public ones. The witch hunt against "secular humanists" and attempts to remove books, courses, and teachers with "offensive" views do little to engender confidence in a purely private education system. A network of private schools would create new choices, some undoubtedly worthwhile. Others would undeniably tend to narrow rather than enlarge their pupils' vision.

A superficial understanding of this alternative may focus on the increased choices available for those parents who would prefer private schooling but who must now, for financial reasons, send their children to public schools. But greater freedom for some children would be bought at the price of less or no freedom for others. And greater freedom for parents might well mean less for children: being sent to an indoctrinatory private school may please a parent but blindfold the child.[43]

Diversity may be good, but it does not follow that more diversity is always better.[44] Radically divergent world views may tear a society apart by undermining areas of agreement necessary for peace and cooperation. In some respects, the United States is already one of the most heterogeneous societies now existing. Such heterogeneity can be sustained only so long as there is broad agreement on basic principles in regard to human equality, tolerance, and limits on violence. When members of a society fail to agree about such fundamental

43. We already face this problem to some extent, although state regulations should in principle allay the problem. That they do not now does not mean that we could not do better in the future. But if the libertarian program is realized, such regulation would probably go down the drain along with compulsory schooling. Consider, among other cases, Wisconsin v. Yoder, 406 U.S. 205 (1972).

44. Our bias in favor of ever-expanding diversity is presumably not unrelated to the intellectual traditions recounted by Arthur Lovejoy in *The Great Chain of Being* (Cambridge: Harvard University Press, 1936).

matters, communities disintegrate: witness the warring factions in Northern Ireland and in Lebanon.[45]

In short, compulsory public schooling can provide a defense against narrowly sectarian education that both constricts children's future possibilities and erodes tolerance and understanding of others.[46] These are not "neutral" aims, as their opponents are the first to point out, but they are the preconditions of any decent society.[47] That the public schools are not now fully successful at these tasks fails to justify dismantling the system unless there are grounds for believing that those values would more reliably be met in its absence. There is little reason to believe in such grounds.[48]

Schools and Parents

One might be tempted to conclude that one of the schools' major tasks is to protect children from parents, and that this conclusion contradicts what I have been saying about the importance of parental authority. I think it is true that we need schools in part to protect children from their parents: there is ample reason to fear that some children would be worse off if their parents had full control of their upbringing and education. This does not detract from my position that parents should be respected unless they have demonstrated their inadequacy.

It may also seem that I have been peering at the schools through rose-colored glasses. This is not the case. As we all know, there are bad teachers who do not know their subject matter, indoctrinate, or are burned out. There are also bad counselors who channel kids into courses, tracks, and programs on the basis of stereotypes. Other

45. Naturally, it does not follow that we must all agree about everything in order to live together.

46. Tolerance is, of course, a two-edged sword, as extreme tolerance permits oppression of third parties. The exact definition of the limits of tolerance is obviously of major importance. For further development of the political aims of education and the constraints they place on the school system, see Gutmann, *Democratic Education.*

47. This is, of course, a contested assertion, for which I will be arguing later. What it entails also depends on how "equality" and "justice" are defined. Interminable squabbling about the details of such concepts, however, can be an excuse for failure to act even when there are clear cases.

48. For further discussion of this issue, see Ivan Illich, *Deschooling Society* (New York: Harper & Row, 1971), and Arthur Pearl, "The Case for Schooling America," *Social Policy* 2 (March–April 1972): 51–52.

problems occur because of insufficient funding, stupidity, incompetence, and political pressures. Our current academic curriculum certainly needs scrutiny, as does the mix of practical and scholastic activities; perhaps we even need to reconsider whether full-time schooling should be compulsory at every level. In addition, I think there is a case for children having more rights within the context of the school.[49]

In short, to argue for universal required schooling is not to say that our present system is ideal. It is to say that we need more than one institution to help keep children on track. Let the best possible circumstances occur as often as possible: loving, responsible, intelligent parents providing what children need, and their schools reinforcing and complementing this care. Let the worst never occur: irresponsible, prejudiced, uncaring parents neglecting or indoctrinating their child, and schools supplying more of the same treatment. With compulsory public education, if a teacher or school is bad, we can hope that a parent will be able to salvage the situation, either by putting pressure on the educational institution or by moving the child to another. But likewise, a good school can help salvage a child who is not being well parented. As in government, it seems prudent to have a system of checks and balances. Equal rights for children would eliminate this particular system of checks and balances.

We have now begun to get a feel for what a world with equal rights for children might look like. The existence of such rights would directly or indirectly affect many areas of life that would appear upon superficial examination to remain unchanged; moreoever, exercising them—as opposed to just having them—would have far-reaching implications. These implications and possibilities would to a considerable degree depend on social arrangements as well as social norms. Economic arrangements are particularly important, and require further examination.

49. Arguing for a specific set of rights is beyond the scope of this work. However, I would not want it to be thought that because I argue against legal emancipation of minors, I think it follows that they should not be granted any particular civil rights. On the contrary, I do think that the burden of proof should be on those who would limit those rights, and that the arguments currently used to do so are indefensible. See, e.g., Justice William Rehnquist's arguments in favor of the right to remove books from school libraries in Hazelwood v. Kuhlmeier, 479 U.S. 1053, 93; L.E2d 978, 107; S.Ct. 926 (1987).

Financial Matters

The two most salient issues confronting us here are the questions of children's economic dependence and the role of work in children's lives.

I noted earlier the obvious fact that a significant difference between women and children is their economic contribution to the family: women tend to add resources, whereas children tend to subtract them. Now dependence erodes power in human relationships, at least in market economies. Perhaps no less important, we are inclined to recognize fewer rights on the part of those who make demands on us without providing anything tangible in return.

This psychological inclination is clearly an insufficient ground for denying children equal rights. A moral theory of dependence must distinguish between different types of dependence. We might reasonably start by assuming that, other things being equal, all should participate equally in work required by their own needs and the common good; exceptions are justified by morally relevant differences. So if it is true, as I have been arguing, that children develop best if they are provided with a period of learning before being expected to take on full adult responsibilities, then their general dependence is morally defensible. This fact does not, by itself, tell us much about how to deal with specific problems pertaining to their dependence, but it does suggest that it would be wrong to treat a child the way we might treat an adult who simply wants to be fed without contributing anything to the communal pot.

If, as I shall assume, children's basic dependence can be defended, then justice would not require them to work on these grounds. And if the argument for liberation based on justice fails, they don't necessarily have a right to work, either. Hence a purely consequentialist assessment of such work would be in order.

I have argued that children *do* need a period of learning before being expected to take on adult roles. This means that schooling is crucial; but, as we have seen, schooling is not easily compatible with a regular, full-time work schedule. This would, by itself, pose a serious obstacle to any plan that permitted children to engage in such work. There are additional obstacles, as well.

One apparently peripheral issue is the problem of transportation. Public transportation in the United States is often inadequate and cannot be counted on to get people where they need to go efficiently. The ability to drive, in many places, is therefore almost a prerequisite for taking on adult roles. If driving were just a matter of skill, this fact wouldn't present an insurmountable obstacle to children's working; however, driving also involves steady attentiveness and good judgment. These are not traits for which children, even teenagers, are noted. If children's right to work were a matter of justice, we would be required to remedy this problem; doing so would, in any case, be desirable on other grounds.[50] However, children's right to work is not a matter of justice. And if tens of thousands of deaths a year doesn't move government to provide good public transportation, we could hardly hope that the demand for justice for children would do so. It would therefore be utopian for proponents of equal rights to brush off this difficulty as a mere practical detail.

In addition, children would, I am convinced, contrary to Harris and other liberationists, be all too easy to exploit.[51] Knowledge, experience, and prudence help protect us from exploitation; but, as we have seen, it is in these areas that children are most deficient. Many might be willing to work grueling hours for inadequate wages, trapped in dead-end jobs.

Some might be willing to take health risks they would later regret. They might not know enough to protect themselves from toxic chemicals, radiation, or dangerous machinery. The lure of a car bought with hazard pay might well outweigh any serious concern about the future. This is an especially serious problem for a population where the inability to imagine oneself at twenty-five, let alone fifty, is common.[52] Children are also likely to be more vulnerable

50. We need better public transportation for several reasons. First, many people need it because they are too poor to own cars or cannot drive for some other reason. Second, the current system is inefficient in terms of natural resources and contributes to global warming. Third, it is absurdly dangerous to life and limb.

51. Harris, "Political Status of Children," p. 50. For some descriptions of how children are currently being exploited, see Dinah Lee, "Long, Hard Days—at Pennies an Hour," *Business Week*, Industrial/Technical ed., October 31, 1988, pp. 46–47; and Assefa Bequele and Jo Boyden, "Working Children: Current Trends and Policy Responses," *International Labour Review* 127, no. 2 (1988): 153–72.

52. If children had equal rights and were living independently, other serious problems would loom. They might, for example, have problems managing their wages. Perhaps they would learn to do so quickly, with no serious harm. But what about more threatening possibilities? Suppose a child spent money on flashy electronics rather than health insurance. Unless we, as a society, begin to provide more services of this kind, a larger fraction

than the average adult to con men. Liberated children might also, I suspect, be even more prime targets for drug pushers than they are today. Children (even teenagers), because of their general immaturity, are substantially more defenseless against the risks described here than the average adult. It would therefore be cruel to fail to protect them from the risks they run.

Furthermore, it doesn't take an overactive imagination to posit significant increases in the number of children living on the fringes of society, earning, like contemporary runaways, their daily bread by pushing drugs, prostitution, and violent crime. Formally repealing limits on children's work might open up some new opportunities, but unless there were fairly radical changes in the economy, few lucrative jobs would be available to children. If an increase in this way of life is the price of freedom, it is a type of freedom we can surely do without. It would, in any case, be short-lived as we had recourse to repressive law-and-order measures to contain the consequences.[53]

A final serious problem with full-time work for children is that our society, as it is now constituted, is often unable to absorb significantly more workers without serious dislocation.[54] Even if teenagers could get jobs, they might well be displacing older workers who need them more.

This argument would again be, by itself, insufficient grounds to deny children a right to work. If they had such a right, it would be unjust to prevent them from exercising it; but, as we have seen, the case for equal rights is too weak to assert any right to work on children's part. Furthermore, even if it were a right, the prospects for reliable full employment would nonetheless seem slight.[55] Again,

---

of the population will be vulnerable to emergencies caused in part by such lack of prudence.

53. Thanks to Margaret Briggs for pointing out this fact.

54. At the moment there appears to be a labor shortage in some sectors of the economy, but this is a function of temporary demographic conditions. Overall unemployment is still appreciable, and is considered, in any case, to be a necessary feature of capitalism. Another recent problem is a shortage of literate workers. Clearly the schooling we are now providing is not preparing qualified workers. This is another reason why abolishing compulsory schooling without putting anything in its place is not likely to help children or society.

55. To the extent that children's liberation is linked with political libertarianism, this option would seem to be ruled out. Historically, libertarianism has been closely linked with laissez-faire capitalism, although the two are not, I think, necessarily so linked.

there appear to be compelling moral grounds for at least significantly modifying the capitalism that precludes it, yet even those grounds have failed to move the people able to make such a change; the prospect for its occurrence now seems dimmer than ever. Yet without such a change, allowing children to participate fully in the marketplace is likely to have seriously harmful consequences.

Because children's working is not a matter of justice and because of the problems we have been looking at (transportation, exploitation, social disruption, and children's need for schooling), repealing the limitations on children's right to work would be undesirable. However, this judgment needn't preclude some work on children's part, work that might pave the way for a desirable set of expanded, if not equal, rights.

Is work good for children? Would it be good for society as a whole?

Viviana A. Zelizer points out that in many circumstances children are considered an economic asset, and are expected to contribute as soon as they are able. She asserts that children take on work responsibilities sometime between five and seven in many cultures; they help with younger children and animals, and do housework. In China, for example children of five or six prepare meals, clean the house, and feed domestic animals. Are these children being abused or exploited? She suggests that we can get some sense of whether they are or not by noticing whether they are healthy, alert, and cheerful. Do they have time to play? Is work unduly displacing other learning activities or is it, on the contrary, helping them learn adult roles?

We might query further: could it be that children are harmed by not working? The answer may be surprising. Zelizer asks:

> Is it reasonable or even feasible for a working mother to retain responsibility for the "real" jobs while children are carefully reserved educational chores (and fathers only slowly and reluctantly increase their share of domestic tasks)? And is it good for the child herself or himself to remain a privileged guest who is thanked and praised for "helping out," rather than a collaborator who at a certain age is expected to assume his or her fair share of household duties?[56]

56. Zelizer, *Pricing the Priceless Child*, p. 209.

In some contemporary households, child labor is an essential part of the domestic economy. Some commentators see it as a regrettable incursion on childhood. Others believe that it is a proper recovery from an unhealthy period of rearing "sacred" children.[57]

There appears to be a good deal of evidence that some work helps children mature in desirable ways. A study done in the 1960s showed that ten- to fourteen-year-old boys who worked felt more competent and demonstrated noticeable "personality development"; they suffered no negative consequences.[58] This is not to say, of course, that children cannot be overworked or exploited, as they were during the Industrial Revolution.

Anthropological and sociological studies support this kind of psychological data. Children in farming communities became more responsible and acquired "a sense of worth and involvement in the needs of others," assert Beatrice and John Whiting, authors of *Children of Six Cultures*. Another study showed that poor children who helped out became more independent, dependable, and better at handling money. Mary Elder concludes that "being needed gives rise to a sense of belonging and place, of being committed to something larger than the self."[59]

In some circles, such participation is taken for granted. It creates a more equal division of labor and helps teach children desirable moral and social attitudes. In others, however, it is not. An analysis of American guides to childrearing (a useful source of information about childrearing ideals) showed that they emphasize each individual child's "'self-realization' through 'self-discovery' and 'self-motivated behavior.'" Others are obligated not to stand in the child's way and to assist this process: "As for the question of the child's obligations to others—especially to those not his own age—the training manuals are strangely silent."[60]

57. Ibid., p. 217.

58. Ibid., pp. 218, 220. The study cited is by Mary Engel.

59. Both studies cited in ibid., pp. 220, 222. Boocock, "Children in Contemporary Society," supports this position with additional findings. She points out that kibbutz children garden and take care of animals from very early on; during the Six-Day War, children in Jerusalem were responsible for mail delivery and garbage collection (p. 420). Elementary schools in China have workshops that participate in heavy industry, producing such items as bus components; all school-age children are expected to devote more than a month every year to work.

60. Halbert B. Robinson et al., "Early Child Care in the United States of America,"

On what grounds is it assumed that contributing to the family economy is optional, or perhaps even an unjustifiable imposition on children? It might be thought that children's basic economic dependence is justifiable, but it doesn't follow that because children have a general right to a period of protected development, it is wrong to expect them to participate in ways that do not detract from that goal.

The case for such contributions is still stronger if they encourage desirable development. Thus, if by failing to ask children to contribute we teach them that it is permissible to be self-centered and oblivious of the needs of others, then, other things being equal, we ought to make that demand.

John Holt thinks that children might positively enjoy work: "Work is novel, adventurous, another way of exploring the world. . . . Many children, often the most troublesome and unmanageable, want to be useful, to feel that they make a difference. Real work is a way to do this. Also, work is part of the mysterious and attractive world of adults. . . . When a child gets a chance to work with them, he sees a new side of them and feels a part of their world."[61] I suspect that Holt is right, and that some of the problems we have with children arise from their feelings of uselessness and exclusion from "real life."

If this reasoning is sound, then it would seem that children are not necessarily exploited by work, and that they are deprived of enjoyable and valuable experience when they do not work. Moreover, our current approach may well be reinforcing the already powerful social message that cooperation and responsibility, as well as caring for and helping others, are unimportant.

Furthermore, if children regularly engaged in appropriate work, we would, I think, be inclined to recognize more extensive rights for them. Not only would we have the general sense that they were pulling a substantial part of their own weight, but they would be more able to take on responsibility for their own decisions. As I have suggested, it would be immoral to link dependence and rights in any direct way. That there are justifiable indirect links, however, is illustrated by examples such as the following.

International Monographs on Early Child Care, no. 3, *Early Child Development and Care* 2, no. 4 (1974), cited by Boocock, p. 420.

61. John Holt, "Why Not a Bill of Rights for Children?" in Gross and Gross, *Children's Rights Movement*, p. 322.

At puberty, American teenagers tend to become compulsive bathers. But this habit depletes fossil fuels, uses up expensive hot water, and limits the access of others to the bathroom. If they had more say in the household (without responsibility for the consequences), they could indulge themselves at others' expense. This isn't equality, however, but unjustifiable privilege. To forestall this state of affairs, the responsible adults must simply set a policy that is tolerable to themselves. It can be instituted with explanations and even good humor, but there is no getting around the fact that it comes down from on high.

If children had some resources of their own from work, they could be treated more like equals, as they could be held responsible for helping to come up with a system that gave everyone a shot at the hot water and bathroom, and that, still more important, allocated to them a share of the electric bill. This responsibility would most probably cause them to moderate their demands. It would also ensure that proceeds from work were not regarded simply as pin money with which to buy luxuries, but rather as, at least in part, a means for participating responsibly in the family economy.

An apprenticeship in freedom and responsibility of this sort would go far toward both more respectful family relationships and more mature children, and is surely far more sensible from every point of view than Harris's plan to apportion out a family's home. Still unaddressed, however, is parents' role in teaching the values that do not so immediately involve self-interest, such as concern for the environment and the frugality required by more equal sharing of global resources.

The foregoing suggests that it would be possible to develop new kinds of relationships that generate some of the advantages of equal rights without their worst drawbacks. That is, children could be given the opportunity to exercise freedom and demonstrate responsibility in relatively sheltered situations. Their responsibility would engender new respect in their parents for their capacities and desires *without* requiring the parents to abdicate any serious authority for further guidance in respect to more subtle (but no less important) matters. That responsibility would, as children mature, create an expanding basis for broader freedoms.

It seems clear that a liberation program that opens the door to full-time work for children would have unacceptable consequences. A moderate amount of part-time work might well be another story.

On the one hand, it would not require ending compulsory schooling; on the other, it could promote conditions that would encourage children's maturation. A drawback is that part-time work, like full-time work, poses some risk of further widening the gulf between rich and poor and displacing needier older workers. The worst consequences of such a policy might be avoided by stringent regulation of work. One approach would be to require a minimum amount of work of every child and prohibit more than a given amount. These amounts could vary with the age of the child.

It might well be true that a carefully thought-out work policy would benefit both children and adults. It might, in fact, form the backbone of a more satisfactory social place for teenagers, in particular, bringing them more of the freedom they covet without the drawbacks of fully equal rights.

Overall in these two last chapters I have tried to lay out the more salient plausible consequences of a consistently applied scheme of equal rights for children. I have suggested that it would most probably have seriously detrimental effects in all three central areas of family, education, and work. In each it would undermine existing ways of achieving certain desirable ends without providing sufficient compensating gains.

I agree with liberationists that current policies with respect to children are far from optimum. Some problems could be ameliorated by new policies that did not carry with them the disadvantages inherent in equal rights, policies that borrowed—but not blindly—from their insights.

Chapter 6

LIBERATIONIST RESPONSES

> The weakest were soon thinned out, and the strongest survived to achieve leadership of the band. But by then they were bigger than the others, and such a leader would eventually be driven out, turned against by his fellow band members including the next in line whom he had befriended several years back, just as he himself had turned and attacked the previous leader who had been *his* "friend."
>
> Then the process starts all over again; he is driven out and forced to join the senior age band as its most junior member, the weakest and most useless of its members. Here he will meet up again with the person or people who had befriended him in the previous band, and he may or may not turn to them again. Since in this band sexual interest plays more of a part, there are alternative ways of winning friends that are by no means adjacent in age. Bila's little Nialetcha needed no prompting to learn that her eight-year-old body held all sorts of possibilities for exploitation. She is one who will survive. . . .
>
> —Colin Turnbull, *The Mountain People*

Where do we stand? I have argued that the call for equal rights for children based on an appeal to justice fails: children are not oppressed if they are refused equal rights. Moreover, as examination of the probable consequences of a consistent liberationist position shows, equal rights would in themselves be quite harmful to both children and society in general. Family life would be rendered both more difficult and less likely to succeed at its task of preparing children for adult life. Public education would be still further weakened, and one might expect not only lower levels of academic achievement but further fragmentation and conflict with respect to values. Full-time work for children would create risk of exploitation, social dislocation, and unjustified inequality. Some (but not all) of these consequences could be avoided given sufficiently comprehensive social and political changes, but they are unlikely to be made. In their absence, the status quo looks substantially more attractive than the most plausible equal rights scenario. If we, as a society, were prepared to make somewhat more limited improvements in education and welfare policies, some version of protectionism could be made still more attractive.

Let us examine two responses to these consequentialist arguments. The first is a suggestion for attempting to supply the maturity that children now lack. The second argues that their immaturity would disappear if they were treated as equals.

Child Agents

Howard Cohen recognizes that children lack certain capacities necessary for running their own lives. With the aid of child agents to supply some of those capacities, however, he believes we can bring children up to the level of ineptitude at which we accord adults the freedom to make their own choices. Since he believes that justice requires equal rights for children, he argues that creating the institution of child agents is a moral duty. As this idea appears to be analogous to such innovations as the subsidized child care necessary for women's liberation, and as Cohen is one of the few proponents of equal rights for children who seriously grapples with consequentialist objections, his suggestion deserves to be examined with some care.

Cohen points out that grownups often borrow or buy expertise they need. This practice illustrates the fact that we do not always need to have a given capacity in order to exercise the corresponding right. Cohen's insight that we routinely use specialists to help meet our needs is well taken. Few have time to learn medicine, law, or dry cleaning; even if we did, we would not have time to do all our own work. Yet we are not therefore denied medical care, legal advice, or clean clothes.

Instead of responding to children's incapacities by supplying special help for them, we instead conclude that they ought not to be engaging in the relevant activity. But Cohen asks why we do not go the other way, arguing that children should be provided with the special help they need to exercise equal rights.[1] He argues that there is merely a difference in degree, not in kind, between the kind of help we think appropriate to procure for adults and that which would be necessary for children. But differences in degree are not morally relevant.

Putting aside for the sake of argument any discussion of the general principle that differences in degree are not morally relevant, let us consider whether the differences (whether of degree or of kind) between children and adults do make a difference here. Before concluding that child agents can simply fill the gap between children's capacities and the demands of adult life, we need to take a careful look at what is going on when we consult such experts.

Even when experts supply only instrumental knowledge, using them may require considerable knowledge and judgment. On the one hand, it is necessary to have a clear enough idea of what is involved to be able to judge whether a given expert is competent or not. In medicine, law, and even dry cleaning, practitioners have varying amounts of expertise. If we are to use them successfully, we must be able to pick out the better ones. It's not clear that children have or could quickly develop these necessary skills. Adults are not all equally adept at such choices, but I think it would be fair to say they have a better shot at success because of their greater general knowledge.

On the other hand, getting a job done often involves more or less intricate trade-offs between feasibility, cost, and completeness. That spot on my silk dress can be removed, for example, but only at the cost of fading the fabric or causing it to disintegrate. In general, achieving goals can be costly, painful, and time-consuming: deciding whether nonetheless to go ahead requires a perspective on the importance of the aim in one's overall scheme of life. But, as I have been arguing, adults are much more prone to consider the place of a particular goal in the context of their overall interests. That's why they brownbag it to save for dinner at a restaurant and get cavities filled to avoid extractions later. Children tend, instead, to focus on their immediate ends. So, for example, Rachel might prefer a lower-level math class in order to stay with her less advanced friends, even if that means losing the chance to forge ahead in math. If agents

1. Cohen, *Equal Rights for Children*, chaps. 5–6.

helped children choose such goals, satisfaction now would quite often be gained at the expense of their overall interests.[2] Powerlessness has in these kinds of cases safeguarded children's well-being; empowering them via child agents would not be beneficial.[3]

In response to this problem, Cohen seems to suggest that a good agent should keep an eye on the overall pattern of a child's choices, just as we might expect an expert hired by an adult to do in a smaller way. So if I naively order up a vasectomy for my guinea pig, the vet should let me know that such operations are not usually successful. In the same way, a good child agent should discuss various ways to reach goals as well as the longer-term implications of both means and ends. If a child wants to buy a motorcycle, her agent has a duty to point out the dangers and even to try to dissuade her. Such procedures, of course, imply clear standards for judging projects better or worse; conceding the existence of such standards places the entire burden of this liberationist position on the principle that respect for others always rules out paternalism.

Let us return again to Jenny. Under Cohen's regime, fed up with life at home, she consults her agent. But she is quite likely to give the agent a rather skewed picture of life at home. To get a clearer idea of what is going on, it would be appropriate to talk with her parents to hear what they have to say. Cohen's description of the role of agent does not exclude such consultation. As the child is supposed to be an independent client, however, not a social worker's "case," such consultation cannot be mandatory. So if Jenny is just tired of her parents' expectations of honesty, responsibility, and hard work, it is easy enough for her to elicit advice to move out by misrepresenting them as humorless ogres. Under these circumstances, agents are not really in a position to give wise advice.

One might also suppose that agents should be licensed. Otherwise anybody could hang out a shingle, and there would be no standards

2. This is not to say that intellectual goals should always take precedence over social ones. In some cases, however, sacrificing the one to the other advances an individual's interest significantly and is appropriate. Parents and teachers are often in a much better position than a child to know when this is the case.

3. Some people have serious doubts about this view. Palmeri, "Childood's End," argues that we tend to hold that children are incapable of making decisions when what we mean is that we disagree with the decisions they do make. This is just another version of the skepticism about value judgments discussed in chaps. 1 and 2. Houlgate, on the other hand, is skeptical about the empirical basis for our concern about the quality of children's value judgments. See his "Children, Paternalism, and Rights to Liberty."

for the quality of advice.[4] What would be the measure of good agents? What shall be the criteria for licensing? Francis Schrag also sees problems with Cohen's proposal. He argues that Cohen succumbs to the very paternalism he decries. Agents not only execute orders, but give opinions about their overall wisdom.[5] I don't think that this, by itself, would be paternalistic: adults, as I have been arguing, are often quite in need of and eager for such wisdom themselves. But children are less likely to face the unwelcome news that doing what they want would have heavy consequences or that the high price of some particular goal ought to be paid anyway because of its importance to their life as a whole. If they don't take the advice, then agents aren't doing what needs to be done. Agents could coerce children into doing the right thing, but that would be paternalistic and incompatible with children's having equal rights.

Consider the following sort of situation. Seven-year-old Jimmy has leukemia. He is confronted with an extremely unpleasant and somewhat risky bone marrow transplant, with a 50 percent chance of cure; the alternative is no transplant and an 80 percent chance of death in a year. Given young children's fear of pain, their tenuous grasp on the concept of death, and their sense of time, which makes a year unimaginably long, how many would go along with parents' pressure to choose treatment? Perhaps the same advice from his agent would persuade, but there is no guarantee that it would. I am not even sure how many teenagers would go along with such advice. Yet most adults would probably decide that the increased chance of a healthy life warrants some immediate suffering; those who didn't would be more likely than Jimmy to be making a realistic assessment of the relative costs of the two courses of action. As I will argue later, this greater degree of autonomy makes a difference in the way society should deal with the situation even when the benefit to be gained by coercion is otherwise equal.

Schrag's second objection to Cohen's proposal about agents is that children, unlike adults, would still have to consult an agent. Schrag concludes that Cohen thinks children should be making their

4. Whether such licensing is compatible with the general political assumptions underlying the liberationist view is questionable. But let us suppose that it might be justified on the grounds that we can temporarily restrict freedom in order to preserve it—even though the same reasoning could undermine the case for child liberation.

5. Francis Schrag, review of Howard Cohen, *Equal Rights for Children*, *Law and Philosophy* 1 (April 1987): 160.

own decisions, but is not sure that they can do so by themselves. A child "has to be both capable of making serious decisions (otherwise how could he 'hire' agents the way adults do?) yet be incapable of making them (otherwise why would he need to borrow an agent's *decision-making* capacities?)."[6] To have truly equal rights, children must be free to forgo the use of a child agent, and even to refuse to hear opinions about proposals. Schrag therefore rightly judges that agents cannot fulfill the central function Cohen requires to make his liberationist argument defensible.

What *does* emerge strongly from Cohen's argument, however, is the importance of providing better sources of advice and help for children outside the family than now exist. Although this suggestion carries with it some potential for problems, society needs to recognize that the conflicts of interest inherent in family life are real. We could do so, however, by recognizing more protective rights for children, such as much more subsidized counseling or even more and better sheltered group living arrangements. Such services could help provide children with a different, perhaps more objective view of their situation. In contrast to the help provided by equal rights, however, ultimate decision-making authority would not generally rest with the child. This way most children could be supplied with more help than at present without the drawbacks associated with equal rights.

A further problem with agents becomes evident when we note that so far the emphasis here has been on supplying children with advice about their own interests. But what about morality, which ought to play at least as great a role in decision-making as self-interest? Granted, agents could probably give children good advice about lots of garden-variety issues that are relatively uncontroversial; given the even more generally unpalatable nature of moral claims than of advice about prudence, it is even less likely to be followed, however.[7]

The matter of moral decision making leads naturally to more general questions about harm to others. Cohen believes that with the introduction of child agents he has narrowed the scope of harm that

6. Ibid, p. 161.

7. This could be an advantage, of course, with respect to controversial issues such as abortion. But the problem of getting good moral advice about such problems is a rather general one, not especially connected with the existence of agents, except insofar as they might have special power over teenaged girls.

could befall children and others. I think it has been shown that agents cannot safeguard children from the worst consequences of equal rights. Some of the same considerations suggest the same conclusion with respect to harming others: agents could only advise against, not prohibit, actions that would harm others.

Cohen responds to this concern by reminding us that if children are liberated "the harm to *others* will be minimal. We are not talking about children being able to do whatever they please. Each child's rights are circumscribed by the rights of others. . . . All the options fall within a range limited by what is socially acceptable."[8] But I believe that this way of putting the matter is misleading. To say that children ought to have equal rights is just to say that they may do anything that is not prohibited for adults. It does not follow that children may rob, rape, or murder. But it would be naive to think that this position does not leave a great deal of room for harm, for it is untrue that children would be constrained by social acceptability. Adults may now do many harmful acts that are not prohibited by law. Only their general maturity keeps such acts within the bounds required by social life. But this gap between legally regulated behavior and conduct essential for securing a decent society is enormous, something that will continue to be true so long as we desire to minimize legal intervention in our lives.

Why do we want to do this? One need not be a libertarian to see that it would be difficult to formulate and enforce laws about the kinds of behavior that are nonetheless necessary for a good society. Furthermore, the apparatus required to do so would be unbearably oppressive: do we really want "sex police" around every corner to make sure people use condoms? So instead, we must rely on shared informal standards, sporadically enforced by social pressure.

The more limited the role of the law in our lives, the more important consideration for others becomes: as Cohen stresses, "large doses of mutual good will" are critical. But, as I have argued, he underestimates the difficulties that would arise with regard to immature children, especially if their early upbringing does not particularly emphasize self-discipline or concern for others.

Cohen says that paternalists argue that

8. Cohen, *Equal Rights for Children*, p. 72.

> there are situations falling short of interference with the rights of others in which we may prevent them from doing what they want to do, or in which we cause them to do things that put them out a little. Often it is possible to exercise our rights in ways which lead to minimal disruptions in the lives of others or to exercise them in more intrusive ways. People who recognize the difference and are sensitive to the system try to do as little disrupting as possible. But children who do not have the capacity to see that there are ways and there are ways not to exercise their rights will, as often as not, cause more havoc than is necessary. The system of negative freedoms is sufficiently delicate that it needs a large dose of mutual good will to work really well to maintain a large area of civil liberty.[9]

He believes that predicating great harm to others on these facts depends on an all-or-nothing viewpoint that fails to take into account the possible role of child agents. Since those agents aren't in fact likely to be able to play the role he assumes, however, he underestimates the gravity and extent of harm that can come of activity in that unregulated zone.

I am not just talking about the adroitness required for saying the right thing about a friend's ghastly new haircut. Recall, for instance, our earlier consideration of adolescent sexual behavior. Although there are laws against such activity by minors, they are not usually enforced. Thus for the most part, sex constitutes a legally unregulated zone, and, as we have seen, sexual activity among adolescents is widespread.[10] Their immaturity and the pressures upon them, together with their fragile hold on the prerequisites for a good life, renders them especially vulnerable to the consequences of foolish choices, consequences that, as we have seen, seriously affect others.

There are some crimes, such as murder, arson, assault, and rape, that the justice system does attempt to deal with. But neither the illegality of the act nor the attention of that system necessarily suffices to deter individuals from committing them. Given the high crime rates in the United States (especially in comparison with most other societies), it is clear that neither formal nor informal restraints are currently operating adequately. To the extent that adult authority would be undermined by equal rights, it seems likely that the

9. Ibid., p. 68.
10. Consider the statistics in Elkind, *All Grown Up*, pp. 185–86.

moral (and perhaps even prudential) restraints against such criminal acts would be still further relaxed.

There are also more indirect harms that might come of equal rights for children. Cohen argues that "we may not like to see our children vote for candidates from crackpot political parties or . . . work instead of going to school, but by making these rights available to adults, we have already indicated that the fabric of society will not be ripped apart should anyone pursue these options. If we really thought it would be, we would have foreclosed them."[11]

But as I argued in chapter 2, where children typically behave differently from adults, it can be appropriate to predicate different rights for them. Thus, if it were true that children were more likely to be taken in by crackpot politicians, society might need to protect the political system by denying children the vote. This would be the case even if some individual children could be counted on to vote sensibly. If we didn't like this consequence, we could consider ways to enfranchise them by such means as competency tests.

Now, one might argue that it would be desirable to institute such tests for adults, too: given the political decisions of the last few years, it's hard to have much confidence in *their* ability to make sensible choices. The way the country is run, so the argument would go, is too important to be left in the hands of people who cannot be bothered to inform themselves or to take into account anything other than claims about their own pocketbooks.

This is a seductive argument. But the problems inherent in universal tests for voters are apparent; in particular, they have in the past been twisted to exclude on irrelevant grounds whole classes of citizens, and the same thing might well happen again.[12] So although a political competency test would, in theory, make for better decisions, the practical problems involved in administering it would probably rule out anything of the kind. It does not follow that the same would necessarily be true for children. Devising a competency test for children would require the same kinds of difficult choices about content that would arise with respect to one intended for adults. But the fact that children belong to a class for which access to the vote would be an honor, not a right, might alter the situation

11. Cohen, *Equal Rights for Children*, p. 72.

12. See, e.g., Jack Bass, "Election Laws and Their Manipulation to Exclude Minority Voters," in *The Right to Vote* (New York: Rockefeller Foundation, 1981).

in a significant way. Perhaps the smaller scope of the testing enterprise and its optional nature should make it easier to insulate from the kinds of political pressures to which a universal test would undoubtedly be subjected.

It might be true that middle- or upper-class children would be disproportionately represented among those who would pass any such test because of their superior education and the encouragement of their parents even if all discernible bias were eliminated. In that case, we would need to consider the other two options with respect to children's voting, letting all children vote or denying the vote to all of them. But the first would be vulnerable to the related objection that there is no reason to believe that adult voting patterns would not be replicated among the children, so that many more middle- and upper-class children would vote. So perhaps the best solution would be, after all, to withhold the vote from children until some specified age.

What we ultimately do about the question remains to be seen. My major point here, however, is that the characteristics of the class to which children belong might well justify limitations on its members that would not automatically apply to members of other classes, despite arguments that might otherwise appear to apply equally plausibly to both. Thus, if we could not come up with a fair and workable testing system, we could still justifiably limit children's access to the vote on utilitarian grounds.

The same is even more obviously true of compulsory schooling. Cohen argues that "we have already indicated that the fabric of society will not be ripped apart should anyone pursue" the option of working instead of going to school.[13] But because of past compulsory education, members of the class of adults can be expected to have a certain amount of schooling under their belts already when they decide whether to quit. This is not the case for children.

The general form of this debate recapitulates an earlier one by James Fitzjames Stephen and John Stuart Mill about the same issue. Mill argued that adults could be coerced only to prevent them from harming others; but this principle does not apply to children, whom he thought needed protection and education.[14] Stephen's objection

13. Cohen, *Equal Rights for Children*, p. 72.
14. Mill, *On Liberty*, chap. 4, esp. pp. 558ff.

was that this argument proved too much: society would then be able to deny those who could not pass certain tests the status of adulthood.

Stephen accuses Mill of admitting "the whole principle of interference, for it assumes that the power of society over people in their minority is and ought to be absolute, and minority and majority are questions of degree, and the line which separates them is arbitrary." He goes on to argue that Mill

> insists on the fact that society has complete control over the rising generation as a reason why it should not coerce adults into morality. This surely is the very opposite of the true conclusion. . . . How, . . . having educated people up to a certain point, can it draw a line at which education ends and perfect moral indifference begins? The fixed principles and institutions of society express not merely the present opinions of the ruling part of the community, but the accumulated results of centuries of experience, and these constitute a standard by which the conduct of individuals may be tried, and to which they are in a variety of ways, direct and indirect, compelled to conform. . . . Education never ceases . . . . All of us are continually educating each other, and in every instance this is and must be a process at once moral and more or less coercive.[15]

Stephen fails to see that the same facts can be argued either way, depending on one's moral premises.[16] Mill ranks liberty higher among moral goods than does Stephen, although not so high as do libertarians. I agree with Mill that childhood is primarily a period of apprenticeship, during which we attempt to teach children certain good habits. If they fail to acquire the relevant traits by the time most are equipped to function reasonably well, it is appropriate to admit defeat.

One reason is that further attempts of the same sort will probably founder: a new approach is needed. The restrictions inherent in the version of childhood argued for here protect from harm but, as liberationists rightly stress, sometimes also prevent learning. Some peo-

15. James Fitzjames Stephen, *Liberty, Equality, Fraternity* (1873) (Cambridge: Cambridge University Press, 1967), pp. 142, 157–58.

16. He also treats Mill rather unfairly, I think, for Mill never argued for "perfect moral indifference." He seems clearly concerned about the harm that individuals can do themselves; he was simply more worried about the harm society can do to individuals.

ple learn only the hard way, and by a certain age need to be left to muddle through. If Jason, at sixteen, still loses clothes left and right, he clearly won't learn responsibility until the cost falls on his shoulders. Only an unusually hard-nosed parent would let him go out in winter without a jacket if he could not buy himself another. Once he is on his own, however, the lesson gets driven home.

Even were this not true, there would be grounds for abandoning the apprenticeship period beyond the time we determine as optimum. A good deal of freedom is essential for satisfying adult life, even if people disagree about what trade-offs they are willing to make with respect to it.[17] Human social arrangements need (partly to motivate children to take on adult responsibilities) to mark and respect the differences between children and adults, and one obvious way to do so is to recognize a much larger measure of freedom for adults. That freedom is based in part upon the recognition that adults more often than children behave autonomously, where autonomy implies (among other things) taking responsibility for the consequences of your actions. Hence despite occasional misuse, adult welfare, to a much larger extent than that of children, depends on provision for substantial liberty. This is true for even the more demanding moral ideal of community that I and many others would like to see supersede current liberal conceptions of the good society.

Thus in many cases a standard liberal defense of restrictions on children where adults have freedom would be sound. Take, for instance, the (unlikely) case of a pleasure-inducing drug with no side effects except destroying artistic talent. Painful as it would be to watch people opt for the drug, if freedom means anything to us, it would be wrong to outlaw it.[18] But it would surely make sense to deny children access to it, on the grounds that we ought not to let them destroy what talent they have before they are able fully to envision what it might mean to them later.[19]

17. In the end, I think, this is the essential disagreement underlying differing political conceptions of the good. To the extent that we are socially constructed, within certain limits these differences may be irreconcilable; but it would be premature to conclude that they are.

18. For further discussion of drugs and related issues, see David A. J. Richards, *Sex, Drugs, Death, and the Law: An Essay on Human Rights and Overcriminalization* (Totowa, N.J.: Rowman & Littlefield, 1982), esp. chap. 4.

19. Although of course it may be difficult or impossible to keep drugs out of the hands of children if they are freely available to adults. But we know from experience that illegal

Proponents of children's liberation are dubious about this kind of defense of line drawing between children and adults. Palmeri, for instance, concedes that it is acceptable to limit children's behavior as long as they do not see its detrimental consequences. But, she goes on, "after a child understands such a relationship are we then justified in acting paternalistically? What justification could we have?"[20]

The problem is that there are many degrees of understanding. We can know that Twinkies rot our teeth without being able to imagine what it is like to have rotten teeth, and what the long-term consequences might involve. Likewise, a child might know in a somewhat abstract way that artistic talent is good without fully understanding the delight (as well as worldly success) that could accompany it. Now, as we all know, people develop this kind of understanding at different rates. Ten-year-old Martha's view of the question will most likely be better than that of her five-year-old sister, Anne, but worse than that of her seventeen-year-old brother, John. But John may have a clearer understanding than his nineteen-year-old friend Bill, or even his sixty-five-year-old grandfather, Michael.

We face here the same problem of line drawing encountered earlier, and I think that we can consistently extend the approach suggested before: let us try to find an age at which most people have a sufficiently realistic understanding of how things work to make informed judgments about the trade-offs inherent in the issues. When the question concerns harm to others, limits on children and adults work the same way: threat of a given degree of harm justifies restriction. When the question concerns harm to self, limits on children and adults work differently. I have argued that there can be good reasons for restricting children's behavior when it would be unjustifiable to restrict the same behavior in adults. Because freedom is, other things being equal, a good thing, restrictions must in both cases be justified. Because of differences between members of the two classes, however, they can more easily be supported in the case of children. On the one hand, as a rule of thumb we can more often

channels create at least the same difficulty. Overall, there are still better approaches to many problems. I think it would be important to go at the problem of drugs from two angles. First, we need to figure out why people are so susceptible to them. Second, I think it would be desirable to develop a pleasurable but harmless somalike drug. For speculation about the first issue, see my "Are Pregnant Women Fetal Containers?" *Bioethics* 4 (October 1990): 271–93.

20. Palmeri, "Childhood's End," p. 113.

reasonably suppose that children are deficient in either knowledge or self-control, so that their actions are not sufficiently autonomous to warrant free reign. On the other, they are at a stage in life at which more can go irretrievably wrong.

Naturally, as children grow older, these assumptions must get weaker, and it therefore takes a correspondingly stronger argument to restrict. At the same time, it must be acknowledged that this approach leaves unprotected unusually ignorant or impulsive adults. Whether, and to what extent, we might want to protect such adults by paternalistic policies need not be resolved here, however. The answer would, in any case, depend to a considerable degree on the extent to which their situations could be distinguished from that of the average competent adult.

The stepwise, piecemeal approach to rights suggested by this strategy has both advantages and disadvantages over the much attenuated legal version of it we now adopt. On the one hand, it poses new and more difficult decisions about the (still somewhat arbitrary) boundaries dividing those with a given right and those without it. On the other, it would more accurately reflect children's development and would undermine the case for equal rights based on the lack of difference in individuals a day before and a day after their eighteenth birthday. It also would have the crucial benefit of placing the burden of proof on those who would restrict, so that existing harmful paternalistic practices would more likely be eradicated. I think it would be a good idea, however, to save some freedoms for full adulthood on the aforementioned grounds that adult status must be seen to be worth striving for. The decision as to what they would be would have to take into account both the need to avoid unnecessary restriction and the need for a meaningful difference.

Compromise approaches such as this preserve important values, even if they are not as "clean" as more obviously attractive all-or-nothing solutions that according to one dimension are consistent, but that according to others treat very unlike cases alike. Other things being equal, freedom can reign; when they are not, we face the difficult task of making reasoned choices among the competing values.

The proposal to supply children with agents amounts to the claim that even though the consequences of endowing children with equal rights might not be very good, they could be rendered sufficiently acceptable to justify those rights. But I think it has been shown that child agents cannot protect children or society at large from the harmful consequences of unwise decisions.

Does the control of children on the kinds of grounds suggested here justify paternalistic treatment of adults nearly as readily as for children? I have argued that we can both protect children and reaffirm adult freedom by settling for boundaries justified by careful generalizations. Although this approach has an arbitrary element, it can in some cases be circumvented. In any case, it seems far preferable to the exceptionless (and therefore overly inclusive) categories recommended by liberationists.

Children's Nature

Now, what about the liberationist argument that children would successfully adapt if they were granted the same freedom as adults?

I have been arguing that mature behavior is in large part learned. At the least, there is good reason to suppose that children do not automatically develop the kinds of self-control essential for prudent and moral behavior. These claims follow from rejection of the growth metaphor and the positive considerations offered in support of a learning model. In chapter 3 we saw that the formula more freedom = better development is not borne out by experience. It may be true that in some situations children would benefit from greater freedom; however, there is no evidence for the claim that the kind of freedom recommended by the growth model and inherent in laissez-faire permissiveness is desirable. On the contrary, there is a good deal of evidence in favor of the view that children need a protected and controlled period of learning to mature, a period when they are not free to do as they see fit in the ways open to adults.

We have just been considering one argument that concedes children's need for help but attempts to supply the missing maturity by providing children with adult advisers. I think it has been shown, however, that this approach is not likely to compensate for children's relatively undeveloped capacities of judgment or self-controlled behavior. A different tack would be to object that I have underestimated the degree to which children would be capable of changing to meet the challenge of liberation. It, too, would concede children's current inability to function adequately in the adult world, but would emphasize the socially constructed nature of childhood and contend that children would soon develop the necessary traits if they were granted the freedom to act independently, together with the responsibility for consequences that goes with it.[21] In short, it could be denied that children's immaturity is an inevitable feature of human development, and argued that it is instead a consequence of their oppressed state: the freedom denied them causes their inadequacies rather than the reverse. This is, of course, an empirical claim, and nothing short of full-scale experimental trials would definitively prove it true or false.

This question is complicated by the various possible theses that liberationists might hold but which are rarely distinguished from one another in the literature. The first is that existing children of every age would adapt: all we have to do is repeal any legal references to children. A second is that only children who grow up under the new regime would be able to adapt: it would seem to follow that the law should at first be implemented in steps. The third is that children would adapt, but only if there are other concurrent changes in society. This thesis is most persuasive if adult status is predicated of children only after a given age, and only if it is accompanied by both democratic permissiveness in early childrearing and a far more forgiving and protective social environment for us all.

Let us take a closer look at the idea that our current conception of children's nature is so colored by unfounded popular assumptions about their incompetence that we might still reasonably expect them to flourish if they were fully liberated. It seems to me that, given what we have seen so far, only the third thesis (that successful liberation would require substantial social change) is at all plausible; furthermore, in light of all the foregoing evidence, the burden of proof must surely be on liberationists to provide solid support for their case.

As we have seen, the growth metaphor could not by itself support such a position; however, perhaps the opposing extreme social constructionist view holds out some promise here: this thesis would be that children are so flexible that they can function well in a wide

21. For appeals of this sort, see Franklin, *Rights of Children*, and Harris, "Political Status of Children."

variety of circumstances.[22] At issue is the extent to which children are able to thrive in any environment and whether there are developmental stages that cannot be bypassed.

Skepticism about the reality of babies' and young children's current immaturity seems more unwarranted than doubts about the proper nature and status of older children. Nowhere do they behave like adults; if they had the potential to do so, it would be surprising if some group had not discovered it. Babies and very young children are everywhere given special protective treatment. Certainly the vision of Ik children offered us by Colin Turnbull fails to inspire confidence in the thesis that they would do fine on their own.[23] It is only between five and seven years of age that many societies recognize a milestone of development, after which children are expected to engage in formal education, take on responsibility, and generally respond to reason.[24] However, many cultures recognize an additional extended period of learning before children are expected to take on adult roles. It is predicated on the assumption that youngsters are not ready to assume such roles until much later.

Is older children's apparent inability to behave maturely a necessary feature of human development or could it be altered by changes in our behavior toward them? As we have seen, some historians and other social scientists contend that we create childhood. Philippe Ariès, for example, maintains that in the Middle Ages, children went to work without any formal education.[25] Others, such as John Sommerville, argue that a deliberate social decision was made in the nineteenth century to prolong childhood, creating adolescence. Teenagers "were excused from participation in the larger society while they concentrated on personal growth." Before that time,

22. One's opinion here will be influenced by the details of the assumptions about children's nature upon which it is based. Despite their apparently radically Lockean approach, these contentions may, in fact, be based on a growth model that holds that children are internally programmed in such a way that certain adult traits will emerge no matter what the environment. This view contrasts with the one we examined earlier, that such traits will emerge only in a noncoercive environment.

23. Colin Turnbull, *The Mountain People* (New York: Simon & Schuster, 1972).

24. Barbara Rogoff, Martha Julia Sellers, Sergio Pirrotta, Nathan Fox, and Sheldon H. White, "Age of Assignment of Roles and Responsibilities to Children: A Cross-Cultural Survey," in Skolnick, *Rethinking Childhood*, pp. 249–68. Even Richard Lindley, who argues quite persuasively for the liberation of teenagers, agrees that there is no need for serious debate about this point: "Teenagers and Other Children," p. 78.

25. Philippe Ariès, "A Prison of Love," in Gross and Gross, *Children's Rights Movement.*

"youth was a time of preparation for adult life, when young people took on increasing rights and duties."[26] According to him, the change was intended primarily to meet adults' perceived social needs but the net result was a harmful limiting of young people's freedom. This thought is echoed by John Harris, who emphasizes the great utility to adults of children's alleged moral obligation to obey their parents and go to school.[27] Feminist thinkers such as Shulamith Firestone have also suggested that children's prolonged dependence is part of the net of oppression that has deformed women's lives. Restricting women to the private sphere requires compelling reasons to keep them there; prolonging childhood provides such justification.[28]

Cross-cultural studies reveal an amazing array of different conceptions, practices, and behavior with respect to older children. Among the several cultural systems described by the anthropologist Ruth Benedict, the Canadian Ojibwa, for instance, expected many twelve-year-old boys to spend months on their own trapping animals.[29]

Observations of Chinese children were thought-provoking indeed for the educator William Kessen, who found them "unnaturally" well behaved: "The shock for American observers is to see how smoothly and without symptom Chinese children meet the expectations of adults and become socially adept, calm, and dutiful school children who amaze the Western visitor." He attributes their development to a coherent cultural environment: the Chinese, unlike us, have "*a shared sense of what a child is.*" We, on the contrary, "live in a zoo of variety, with relatives, physicians, psychologists, novelists, journalists, and television all providing different—sometimes even contradictory—messages about the nature of children."[30] Our diverse accounts of childhood are astounding: "No other animal species has been catalogued by responsible scholars in so many wildly discrepant forms, forms that a perceptive extraterrestrial could never see as reflecting the same beast."[31]

26. Sommerville, *Rise and Fall of Childhood*, p. 179.

27. Harris, "Political Status of Children," p. 45.

28. Firestone, *Dialectic of Sex*, chap. 4, especially the beginning.

29. Ruth Benedict, "Continuities and Discontinuities in Cultural Conditioning," in Skolnick, *Rethinking Childhood*, p. 22.

30. William Kessen, "The Chinese Paradox," in Aiken and LaFollette, *Whose Child?* p. 76.

31. William Kessen, "The American Child and Other Cultural Inventions," in Kessel and Siegal, *Child and Other Cultural Inventions*, p. 262.

Even in "developed" Western cultures, assumptions about children and how they should be treated differ significantly. Wallace Lambert and his colleagues found substantial diversity in childrearing practices in the ten national or ethnic groups they studied; interestingly, Americans were by far the most permissive.[32] As we saw, for example, the Danes are stricter with young children and more permissive with adolescents than Americans are. Their teenagers are more self-disciplined and autonomous than their American peers, suggesting that early strictness causes children to internalize controls, enabling them to enjoy greater freedom and less *Sturm und Drang* later on, during adolescence.[33]

Not only is American popular opinion a stew of conflicting ideas, but so, it turns out, is the academic discipline of child psychology. Some child psychologists incline toward the view that there are ineradicable constraints on development; others see the environment as more influential in children's growth. Although the first conception draws strength from popular conceptions of Rousseau, the second from Locke's tabula rasa, careful contemporary thinking generally concedes considerable importance to both nature and nurture. Both could, in principle, be used to argue for differences between children and adults.

More fundamentally still, proponents of the view that we construct childhood, such as Kessen, press the point that "not only are American *children* shaped and marked by the larger cultural forces of political maneuverings, practical economics, and implicit ideological commitments (a new enough recognition), *child psychology* is itself a peculiar cultural invention that moves with the tidal sweeps of the larger culture in ways that we understand at best dimly and often ignore." Thus, given the individualistic bent of American culture, it is understandable how the field of child development has assumed that we can understand human development by studying individual children. But this activity ignores the extent to which they are created by the influences to which they are exposed.[34] Soviet theory, on the contrary, would be more likely to emphasize just these

32. Lambert et al., *Child-Rearing Values*, pp. 345–55. The groups studied were American, English-Canadian, French-Canadian, English, French, French-Belgian, Dutch-Belgian, Italian, Greek, and Portuguese.

33. Kandel and Lesser, "Parent-Adolescent Relationships," pp. 635–40.

34. Kessen, "American Child," p. 262.

aspects at the expense of individualistic assumptions. This line of reasoning is carefully developed by such scholars as Urie Bronfenbrenner and Jerome Kagan.[35]

The most influential contemporary growth theory that posits major internal limits on development is Jean Piaget's model of human nature. Piaget argues that children's thinking goes through three major stages before adolescence, when they are able to reason, judge, and make decisions like adults. These stages are the "sensorimotor," the "preoperational," and the "concrete operational." The final stage, during which adult mental operations are achieved, is the "formal operational."[36]

Infants are in the "sensorimotor" phase, wherein the major intellectual, social, and emotional developments are constructing a world of constant objects, attaching themselves to others, and establishing trust. During the next, "preoperational" period (from about two to six), children learn to use symbols and can use them to reason in a simple way and express their wants. They make characteristic mistakes in using them, confusing questions about one and many, and taking symbols for what they represent. "Magical thinking" is common. From the end of this period till early adolescence (at eleven or twelve) children pass through the "concrete operational" stage. They develop facility at manipulating symbols; particularly important is the ability to classify objects and create hierarchies. Concrete operations help the child develop the capacity to act according to rules. They also cause the child to begin to think critically about parents, the beginning of separation from them. At the "formal operational" stage, adolescents attain essentially adult intellectual powers, with the advent of second-order manipulation of symbols. Emotional, intellectual, and social independence is greatly increased, with all that

35. Urie Bronfenbrenner, "A Theoretical Perspective for Research on Human Development," in Skolnick, *Rethinking Childhood*, pp. 108–27; Jerome Kagan, "On the Need for Relativism," in ibid., pp. 40–57.

36. See Bärbel Inhelder and Jean Piaget, *The Growth of Logical Thinking from Childhood to Adolescence: An Essay on the Construction of Formal Operational Procedures*, trans. Ann Parsons and Stanley Milgram (New York: Basic Books, 1958). Among those who respect his views are Eleanor Maccoby, Lawrence Kohlberg, and David Elkind. For a recent discussion of the stages of development described here, see Elizabeth Hall, Michael E. Lamb, and Marion Perlmutter, *Child Psychology Today*, 2d ed. (New York: Random House, 1986), pp. 32–33, 314–30.

this implies. Thus this theory suggests that both the content and form of children's thinking depends on their age.

Piaget's views are widely considered to be at least partially verified. David Elkind, for instance, argues that cross-cultural studies confirm the existence of his posited stages.[37] Eleanor Maccoby qualifies this view somewhat, maintaining that while not all the details of Piaget's work have been empirically confirmed, his general themes have been. As Maccoby notes, there is an important difference between classical growth models and Piaget. Piaget allows for—indeed requires—environmental influence: without environmental stimulation growth is retarded.[38] How much the environment can alter outcomes is still unclear, however.

The role of environment in determining behavior is considered much greater by the intellectual descendants of Locke. More than adherents of other schools, they see humans as substantially malleable; they are convinced that children's behavior responds to the expectations expressed for it. Thus, if we believe that adolescents will be moody and rude, our children are likely to comply; if we relegate them to a social holding pattern, they will adopt the general characteristics of powerlessness.

That the discipline of child psychology, as well as the children it studies, is influenced by cultural assumptions seems beyond doubt. But then, what is to be made of these conflicting views about the plasticity of development? It would hardly be feasible to attempt a grand synthesis of these positions.[39] Rather, I think we need to take various findings as warnings and guidelines.

37. Elkind, *All Grown Up*.

38. Maccoby, *Social Development*, pp. 20–21.

39. It may be that the apparently conflicting views about the fixity of development are not quite so far apart as they now seem. In particular, it seems that relativists—those who conceive of human nature as relative to its environment—are not carrying their considerations to the most radical conclusions possible. To do so, in fact, would be to give up any nonhypothetical judgments in child psychology: there is no fixed "nature" for them to study, only hypothetical cases of *X* treatment causing *Y* result. Social constructionists recognize, however, that the implications of their arguments do not necessarily go so far as that. Wolfgang Edelstein writes:

> On the surface, at least, the differences between relativist and non-relativist accounts of childhood in historical perspective do not appear as important as we might have anticipated. The non-relativist no longer adopts a Platonic stance beyond history and the relativist apparently does not reject a potentially comprehensible transcontextual order. Both positions agree that the life-world as well as the cognitive and affective

Piaget's work suggests certain limits on children's possibilities, although the environmentally controlled component of development creates some room for diversity.[40] The extent of such variability is up in the air, however. Most important for us here are questions such as whether and to what extent physical conditions or education alter the timetable. Again, proponents of children's rights tend to be sanguine about children's potential for rapid learning and development, a position that may be in considerable tension with the contrasting assumptions of the growth model that tends to undergird their work.[41]

What about physical conditions or special teaching? Is there reason to believe that physical conditions alter children's mental development? We do know that malnutrition causes mental retardation, and that good nutrition promotes general physical growth.[42] But is there any evidence that optimum physical conditions speed up mental development? And what, if anything, can we say about the efficacy of education? Could it be true, for example, that if we systematically taught children basic reasoning skills early on, Piaget's conclusions about the development of reasoning would be shown to be faulty? Or if we made teaching self-control, enabling virtues, or moral development high priority, might children mature earlier?[43] What we have seen so far is that failing to make the relevant de-

---

> character of children are profoundly historical in nature. Both positions operate on the assumption of substantive contextual dependencies, affecting the totality of children's lives. ("Cultural Constraints on Development and the Vicissitudes of Progress," in Kessel and Siegal, *Child and Other Cultural Inventions*, p. 76)

Kessen, too, concedes that "the argument for cultural invention is not what Nagel has called a malicious philosophy of science that substitutes a kind of genteel know-nothingism or radical relativism for empirical analysis and verification. The argument, however, does call for reconstruction. It does call for the scientific enterprise, certainly the child-psychological enterprise, to be constantly under review and revision": " American Child," p. 33.

40. Especially since even biological development can be altered to some extent by environmental stimulation, both physical and mental.

41. M. D. A. Freeman, one of the few protectionists to address the issue head on, concedes the force of studies such as those cited here, but then goes on to assert that research shows that before the age of ten or twelve, children lack the knowledge and judgment necessary for adult functioning: *Rights and Wrongs of Children*, p. 46.

42. See, e.g., David E. Barrett and Deborah Frank, *The Effects of Undernutrition on Children's Behavior* (New York: Gordon & Breach Science Publishers, 1987); John Dobbing, ed., *Early Nutrition and Later Achievement* (London: Academic Press, 1987).

43. See, e.g., Margaret Donaldson, *Children's Minds* (London: Fontana, 1978). Donaldson contends, contrary to Piaget, that young children are capable of taking into account other people's points of view.

mands seems to undermine development, whereas making them seems to be associated with satisfactory progress. Discovering the answers to such questions is essential if we are to have a realistic idea of children's true potential.

Even the information we have cannot be added to our premises without critical assessment. We cannot, for example, infer adolescence's nonexistence from a given society's failure to recognize it: individuals at a given stage of development may have needs that are being ignored. Nor can we infer from a recognized phase of adolescence that it is either necessary or desirable: it may be convenient, as Somerville suggests, to emphasize or mold a group's characteristics to suit perceived social needs.

Different societies need different kinds of people. These needs are likely to affect the relevant assumptions, practices, and values. Thus, for instance, a feudal agricultural society needs people with rather different characteristics than a highly technological one. It would not therefore be too surprising to find many differences between such societies, including conceptions of childhood and maturity.

Kenneth Keniston has done some interesting speculation about this subject. He maintains that psychological development is less determined than physical development, and suggests that "both folk wisdom and clinical studies indicate that there are physically mature individuals with the psychology of children, and precocious biological children who possess adult developmental characteristics." Human development is *contingent* upon a variety of factors. He thinks that perhaps society would disintegrate if we did not provide the conditions needed for psychological development up to the six- or seven-year-old level, but that after that "we begin to discover a series of truly developmental changes that may or may not occur." For example, the ability to engage in formal operational thought may never develop: with it, "the intellect breaks free from the concrete world into the realm of hypotheses, ideals, and contra-factual conjectures." Without these capacities many of our unique intellectual projects could hardly proceed. Human societies could exist in the absence of such thought, but they would be very different from our own.[44]

44. Kenneth Keniston, "Psychological Development and Historical Change," in Skolnick, *Rethinking Childhood*, pp. 194, 196, 198.

The fact that not every society recognizes adolescence as a distinct stage might have significant implications both for our general theory of human nature and for our thinking about desirable societies. As Keniston states his hypothesis in what he calls its "most extreme and provocative form":

> Some societies may "create" stages of life that do not exist in other societies; some societies may "stop" human development in some sectors far earlier than other societies "choose" to do so. If, therefore, a given stage of life or developmental change is not recognized in a given society, we should seriously entertain the possibility that it simply does not occur in that society. And, if this is the case, then in societies where adolescence does not occur many of the psychological characteristics which we consider the results of an adolescent experience should be extremely rare: For example, a high degree of emancipation from family, a well-developed self-identity, a belief system based upon a reexamination of the cultural assumptions learned in childhood, and, perhaps, the cognitive capacity for formal operation.[45]

Speculation of this sort opens up a whole world of fascinating possibilities; were their reality born out by further research, it would force us to recognize and bear responsibility for more fundamental choices about how to live than we have ever before faced. Pinning down the possibilities here will require much hard labor, however, as broad generalizations require both accurate empirical work and large inductive leaps; as such, they are vulnerable to both unconscious and conscious bias.

Where does all this leave us with respect to the question whether our current treatment of children responds to their necessary and inevitable patterns of development? Do we instead create immature children by practices that retard and deform their development? Remember that upon the answer to this question rests the plausibility of the liberationist case for equal rights. If the liberationists' belief were true, then one precondition of their platform would exist.

The case for substantial molding of behavior by environmental pressures seems undeniable. I and I'm sure many others have certainly watched parents shape their little girls into manipulative flirts by treating them like pretty pets, and their little boys into unruly

45. Ibid., pp. 200–201.

monsters by acting as though they were uncontrollable. Many more such stories would not be hard to find.

In short, there *are* powerful arguments in favor of a less rigid view of human development than our culture usually assumes. If, historically, children could function in the adult world much earlier than they do now, we must rethink the necessity of their current roles. If, in other cultures, children develop without the crises we take for granted, then we know that under some conditions the crises are unnecessary. If children's behavior is now at least in part conditioned by our expectations, then different expectations may lead to different behavior. And if our expectations are influenced by theories that are in turn conditioned by culture, then it would seem that we have a large hand in constructing childhood: we are not, in our dealings with children, merely reacting to "reality." This position is supported by some of the issues so far examined. If early firmness encourages adolescent responsibility, and laissez-faire permissiveness retards it, then we can to some extent control the age at which children might operate well independently. Likewise, if some work experience has a maturing effect, then it could be built into the norms for childhood.

Some unusual adolescents may already approach the level of adults in their reasoning and behavior. Not only should their decisions be accorded comparable respect, but they might well be a fruitful source of information about the conditions that led to their mature state. It would not be too surprising to learn, for instance, that their home life included emphasis on thoughtful assessment of ideas and events, as well as firm, loving guidance that at an early age helped them learn such enabling virtues as self-discipline and foresight. If their environments—whatever they may turn out to have been—were to become common, this might well change the face of childhood and confound our expectations about the amount of time offspring need to learn the complexities of the adult world. My own suspicion is that under optimum conditions, many children might become capable of operating quite independently shortly after puberty. One's impression is that in a few short months the child comes to see the world from an entirely new perspective. Perhaps a major contributor to this change is the conscious experiencing of sexuality in a new and forceful way; if nothing else, this experience provides an emotional grasp of the workings of human relations which is hidden until that point. If Piaget is on the right track, the new reasoning skills that develop at this point would provide another reason for choosing adolescence.

The possibilities are all the more tantalizing when we consider the kinds of obstacles many vulnerable children have had to contend with. Their heads have been filled with religious, political, racial, and sexual beliefs for which there is no shred of evidence; they have been forced to swallow hurtful and untrue beliefs about both themselves and others. Making sure fewer children are subjected to such abuse would be analogous to lifting the foot of oppression off women's necks: we cannot know in advance just how far-reaching the consequences would be.

Does any of this imply that children are infinitely malleable, given the appropriate environment? That they can play any role, be anything? We have seen that there seems to be good evidence to the contrary. It wouldn't be unreasonable, for example, to conclude that in the absence of fairly strict early preparation, most teenagers cannot handle the kind of sexual freedom they now have in American society. That they might be able to handle it under different conditions, however, is suggested by the high rates of sexual activity *unaccompanied* by pregnancy in other developed societies.[46] What this sort of example suggests is that early freedom is likely to lead to undesirable consequences, whereas early restriction of the right kind makes responsible freedom possible somewhat later. And, to the extent that Piaget's theories have been confirmed, we face limits. If, for example, children in general show little ability to think in a principled way about political systems before the age of eleven, then perhaps they should not be participating as political equals before that age.[47]

Our wariness before such "facts" cannot falter, however. We must apply our increasingly sophisticated understanding of the interactions between nature and nurture to them as sensitively as possible.[48] It will therefore require systematic investigation and experi-

46. See "Risking the Future: A Symposium on the National Academy of Sciences Report on Teenage Pregnancy," *Family Planning Perspectives* 19 (May/June 1987): 119.

47. Lindley, "Teenagers and Other Children," suggests that both ignorance and volatile emotions would justifiably disqualify young children from political participation.

48. We need attention parallel to that now being directed by feminists to research on sex differences. Alison M. Jaggar gives a persuasive account of the interaction between

mentation to determine whether such findings merely reflect common cultural practices or whether they could be changed by different ones. Thus, for example, it may be that no one now helps children understand the issues and that a systematic political education program (perhaps starting at a very young age) would have surprising results.

As we think about how best to proceed in the absence of certain knowledge about either what kind of people we want our children to become or the prerequisites for their becoming them, it is tempting to conclude that we have a completely free hand. This is not the case.

First, I believe that despite the lack of certainty, there are some clear guidelines about both these matters. We know well enough that we don't want children to lack the control necessary to achieve desirable ends, nor do we want them to be feckless about their own future or unmindful of the interests of others.[49] Furthermore, although a good deal of empirical work clearly remains to be done on the causal prerequisites for these desirable traits, the best available evidence points pretty clearly in the direction of early loving but firm control of children, control that is, of course, sensitive to differences

---

biology and culture, even for such apparent "brute facts" as the physical differences between women and men:

> It is also easy to see how certain physical differences between women and men are affected by social inequalities. These differences may sometimes be quite gross, as in the case of Chinese footbinding or as in the contemporary deformation of women's feet, tendons and backs by high-heeled shoes. Different forms of exercise also encourage different muscular development in males and females, with males tending toward greater development of the upper body. Even differences in height are affected by such social factors as diet and exercise. When the diet of girls is less adequate nutritionally than that of boys, it is predictable that girls will remain smaller. But even in societies where both boys and girls receive an adequate diet, the physical training of girls influences their adult height. The onset of puberty in girls, unlike its onset in boys, dramatically slows female growth. However, since the onset of puberty depends in part on the ratio of fat to body weight, it tends to occur later in girls who are more athletic and so have less body fat. Other things being equal, athletic girls thus tend to grow taller than girls who are less athletic—and how athletic girls are encouraged to be of course is generally a function of social attitudes. ("Sex Inequality and Bias in Sex Differences Research," in Hanen and Nielsen, *Science, Morality, and Feminist Theory*, p. 34)

49. I realize that there can be disagreement about whether a given course of action is appropriately assertive or merely selfish, but it doesn't follow that there aren't clear cases of each kind of action or that we have major difficulties in telling the two apart in everyday life.

among children and circumstances. This fact leads me to a second point that needs to be made here, that different strategies of child-rearing are, in effect, experimentation on children. It would therefore be irresponsible to pursue in a wholesale way unpromising approaches. Thus if the best available evidence suggests that letting young children go free of adult-imposed control unfits them for life in anything like our contemporary society (or perhaps any feasible society at all), then it would be immoral to rear them in that manner. The case is, I would contend, comparable to certain notorious medical experiments such as the Jewish Chronic Disease Hospital case or the more recent New Zealand cervical cancer experiments.[50] As there is much less certainty, however, about specific types of control and freedom, it would not be immoral to try out different policies with respect to them. Thus, for instance, it would surely be reasonable to let a child choose what to wear, or her name, or any number of other things that are now generally decided by parents, as soon as she can express an opinion about them.

50. See, e.g., Jay Katz, *Experimentation with Human Beings* (New York: Russell Sage Foundation, 1972), for accounts of egregious failure to obtain informed consent, as in the Jewish Chronic Disease Hospital case. For a more recent example of women left untreated for cervical carcinoma in situ *without* informed consent, see Alastair V. Campbell, "A Report from New Zealand: An 'Unfortunate Experiment,'" *Bioethics* 3 (January 1989): 59–66.

CONCLUSION

> The final *rite de passage* is into manhood and womanhood, at the age of twelve or thirteen, depending on how long the candidate for adult status has been able to fight off the attacks of his competitors. By now he has learned the wisdom of acting on his own, for his own good, while acknowledging that on occasion it is profitable to associate temporarily with others. That such associations must be temporary he has had plenty of opportunity to observe as he has grown from junior member to senior member of each band, from the bullied and beaten to the bully and beater.
>
> —Colin Turnbull, *The Mountain People*

Should children have equal rights?

Let us briefly recapitulate the arguments about such rights. At present different rights are recognized for adults and children. Some of adults' rights free them to act in accordance with their own judgment; they are considered competent to make a wide variety of decisions ranging from what to wear to whom to marry. Children, on the contrary, are denied these rights on the grounds that children are irrational. Their alleged irrationality justifies protecting them in ways that also limit their freedom.

Proponents of equal rights contend, however, that in reality children are no more irrational than the least competent adult. Hence there is no morally relevant difference between the two classes, and the divergent laws that apply to children constitute unjust discrimination, discrimination that oppresses children.

This thesis about oppression has often been quite uncritically embraced—or equally unceremoniously dismissed. The philosophical discussion has so far been inconclusive and unsatisfying. Despite its challenge to common sense, the liberationist argument has a good deal of intuitive appeal. Liberationists quite reasonably place the burden of proof on those who would limit freedom; when they fail to find a morally relevant difference between those favored with the freedom to pursue their own conception of the good and those denied it, they conclude that the distinction is unjustifiable. They may also rightly challenge the view that if children cannot now cope with equal rights, it is unthinkable that they could ever do so. In support of their position, they argue that giving children more freedom would breed the requisite responsibility. Children could also cope better, they say, if certain social changes were made.

In response, protectionists have rightly (to some extent) tended to focus on the question whether children truly *are* irrational in the important ways, and the extent to which irrationality undermines claims to freedom. Protectionists also tend to rely on theories of human development that characterize it as a succession of necessary stages, which cannot, because they are at least partially biologically based, be greatly speeded up.

Although I have been arguing against the liberationist position, I have considerable sympathy with some of its assumptions. One is that, other things being equal, freedom is a good thing that ought to be promoted: within wide margins, people should be free to live their lives as they see fit.[1] Another is that although I think we will eventually discover for sure that there are certain, perhaps biologically determined, limits on human development, the evidence in favor of substantial flexibility and responsiveness to conditions can hardly be denied.

However, proponents of equal rights for children tend to be far more prone than I am in any given case to judge that all other things *are* equal and that therefore freedom should prevail over other conflicting values. Most appear to be liberals for whom the threat (or reality) of harm is relatively immaterial in comparison with the value of freedom; those who call themselves utilitarians are nonetheless more prone to value freedom over avoiding harm when the two might clash.[2] Sometimes they underestimate the probability of harm arising from children's rights; often, however, they simply attribute to freedom more weight than I think is warranted.

Choosing between conflicting values is notoriously difficult as there may be good arguments on all sides. I have argued here that

1. This includes parents, whose freedom would be enhanced were childhood shorter.
2. Richard Lindley, for instance ("Teenagers and Other Children").

the overridingly high valuation of freedom implied by the liberation argument is untenable. Generalizing the principles that motivate the case for equal rights for children by setting it within the context of a wider moral theory demonstrates the inadequacy of the theory and hence of this application to it. So unless there is something about the situation of children that justifies freedom for them apart from that libertarian theory, liberation founders at the outset. Only a consequentialist appeal or an independent appeal to justice could provide the necessary support.

Good consequences, however, are an unlikely source of support of equal rights for children. It is true that protection of children is sometimes bought at the cost of some freedom. I believe that some of this lost freedom is not inextricably connected with desirable protectionist policies and could therefore be retrieved for children. Thus, on the face of it, I see no need for linking guardians' or schools' supportive duties with authority to determine dress or censor reading materials. Certainly, legal sanctioning of such authority should, wherever possible, be eradicated and its moral basis denied. However, there is no doubt that protection sometimes requires limits on freedom, and these limits sometimes cause frustration and unhappiness.

Protection, nevertheless, can secure immediate advantages, like being shielded from physical danger or exploitation, having a relatively settled family life, or just having free time to play. Protection can also increase both freedom and other values, such as equality and utility. Thus, for example, it can promote freedom by safeguarding certain types of choices that would otherwise not exist. So a law requiring school attendance for children apparently narrows their choices; at the same time, though, it protects a choice that would probably disappear altogether for some children—getting an education. And, for all children, as liberal opponents of equal rights emphasize, some kinds of limits make possible a wider range of choices later, choices that may both be intrinsically valuable and also advance other desirable states of affairs. A math requirement, for instance, can help foster equality by making sure that all children have the prerequisites for interesting and well-paid occupations.[3]

3. See Sells, "Mathematics Filter." Such a requirement is obviously only a necessary condition for equality, not a sufficient one.

In response to such arguments, liberationists emphasize how many children are being reared under inadequate conditions, conditions that would be remedied if children had equal rights. It is true that many children are not being raised under good conditions. Poverty undermines the advantages inherent in protectionist policies; others, for various reasons, are not being properly cared for.[4] At present a few of these children are being helped by being taken out of the hands of their families and reared by other adults. As liberationists point out, these kinds of policies have not always been well administered and children aren't necessarily better off as a result of them; *their* solution is to empower children to escape adult control altogether. But there seems to be no reason to think that adult rights for children are necessary or sufficient to improve this situation. Better educational and social welfare policies are quite likely to ameliorate these kinds of problems without the disadvantages of equal rights.

I have argued that the probable disadvantages of children's liberation would outweigh whatever advantages it might bring for both these children and more normally situated ones. First, by severing the asymmetrical legal ties that now bind parents and children together, equal rights would weaken appropriate parental authority. Two critically important consequences could be expected to follow. One is that parents would be more reluctant to provide for their children the kind of early training that now appears to be necessary for responsible and moral behavior later. The other is that adolescents would be less likely to take their parents' guidance seriously. Both of these consequences could reasonably be expected to have detrimental effects not only on children's own well-being but on their ability to participate constructively in a good society. A consistently interpreted liberationist policy could also leave children stranded without parents; to the extent that the condition of contemporary runaways reflects what would await such children, it should be avoided at almost any cost.

Second, equal rights would require abolition of compulsory schooling. While it is obvious that there is a good deal the matter with the schools at present, it doesn't follow that what is the matter could best be gotten rid of by undermining their authority in this way.

4. Shulamith Firestone notwithstanding, it doesn't seem likely that they are therefore getting the advantages of equal rights. See her *Dialectic of Sex*, chap. 4.

Compulsory public schooling constitutes, if nothing else, a safety net for children who might otherwise get little or no education. It can also help transmit fundamental social values.

Third, equal rights would propel many children into the workplace at an early age, where, without education, they would be prepared for only the most menial jobs. There they would be subject to the uncertainties of fluctuating demand and might survive only by exposing themselves to various hazards or underbidding other needy workers. This state of affairs might reasonably be expected to increase still further the gap between rich and poor.

These claims are supported by a realistic assessment of the differences between children and adults. Liberationists, as we saw, tend to concentrate on showing that children are not irrational: they can think logically and are by no means dunces at getting what they want. I have argued that these capacities are not sufficient grounds for awarding adult rights, however: you need not be irrational in any narrow sense, or even unable to satisfy your immediate desires, to be relatively unable to know or act upon your own interests or those of others. Doing the latter requires, in addition to basic reasoning skills, a good stock of general background knowledge as well as certain hard-earned character traits. Liberationists often acknowledge the importance of these things, but rely for their case on the indubitable fact that not every adult manifests them either. In response, I have argued that it hardly makes sense to let the lowest functioning adult set the standard for acceptable behavior. One might as well argue that because some adults are illiterate, it is unjust to require children to learn to read. Only extreme skepticism about the possibility of wisdom or a libertarian moral theory could extricate proponents of equal rights from this awkward corner. But neither escape route is very attractive.

Liberationist responses to the problems created by children's deficiencies are unsatisfactory. Cohen's institution of child agents sounds promising, but upon further reflection it appears that they could not help children enough to matter unless they too exercised authority over them incompatible with equal rights. Nor is there any particular reason to suppose that if children were granted freedom tomorrow, they would magically develop the maturity necessary to operate even as well as the least capable free adult, let alone in a more desirable way. On the contrary, the best available evidence suggests that adequate functioning depends on an early childhood environment incompatible with equal rights for children.

Despite the power of these arguments, they might be trumped by a compelling appeal to justice. As we saw, however, the claim that protectionism is necessarily unjust is unconvincing, although specific components of our treatment of children may well be so. Hence the decision about what policies are best ought to be made on consequentialist grounds—as even Cohen in the end must concede.

What seems clear to me, in light of the foregoing considerations, is that the disadvantages of equal rights for children would most likely far outweigh the advantages. Part, though not all, of the problem here is the nature of our own society. Contemporary American society bears the dubious distinction of being one of the most unsupportive and violent cultures now in existence. Racism, sexism, and elitism, among other undesirable attitudes and practices, are common, and lead to many serious problems for both adults and children. Hence not every serious difficulty children face arises from the refusal to let them choose their own path within the limits faced by adults.

It might nonetheless be true that although the problems do not arise because of protectionism, abolishing it could help solve them. However, there is no reason to think that either the process of freeing children or the product, "free" children, would necessarily change such discriminatory practices. Imperfect though these protective institutions are, they are for the most part more helpful in preparing children to cope with and change the adult world than the alternative would be. There is something of the noble savage underlying the liberationist picture of untainted children sallying forth to make their way in the world. Their contemplated success there, however, seems to me to owe more to wishful thinking on the part of liberationists than to a coolheaded prediction of likely consequences. It is true that crusades by idealistic young people may well have played a significant role in some social change; it would be rash, on this basis, to extrapolate their successes to the revolution in attitudes and practices necessary for children's liberation. The nature of our society not only makes life difficult for adults, but, it seems to me, renders the prospect of equal rights for less mature people almost unthinkable. If we had a safer, more consistently caring world, it would be easier to envision releasing fledglings into it somewhat earlier.[5]

I agree that the kinds of social changes recommended by liberationists would in general be desirable. For example, more protective labor legislation, subsidies for schooling at any age, and guaranteed minimum incomes would go far toward improving life for all, as well as making it possible for vulnerable children to function more independently. While the blueprint for a better society is a project for a different book, there are clearly minimum requirements for human welfare that are not now being met by our society. Desirable as having them would be, however, there is in any case no sign of their coming anytime soon. Granting immature children equal rights in the absence of an appropriately supportive environment would be analogous to releasing mental patients from state hospitals without alternative provision for them.[6]

The liberationist case predicated on these changes is also, in any case, exposed to the fundamental objection that if we followed such policies now, many of the problems motivating the call for equal rights would evaporate. A more egalitarian and caring society would, after all, provide for families in ways that eliminated the stresses resulting in child abuse, provide more outside support to deal with such abuse when it did occur, provide a school system free of the biases that now make "education" such a profitless trial for many children, and so forth. Addressing these issues directly would seem much more efficient than helping children out of the coercive frying pan into the hierarchical fire.

Even if we created a society in which children of a given age would be able to move more freely, this goal wouldn't necessarily justify its creation, despite the value of freedom. First, unless the proposed new society also addressed the political and environmental challenges to human survival, it would be unacceptable. Second, we might have other defensible goals that would be in conflict with the

5. Doing so might run the risk of arresting their development in such a way as to render them less able to maintain or enhance those very characteristics once they became full members of society. But that would remain to be seen.

6. The consequences of releasing the mentally ill from those hospitals without adequate provision for their welfare has been disastrous and was unanticipated by the well-meaning advocates of release in the name of freedom.

aim of earlier freedom for children. Thus, for example, if we wanted to continue to enjoy a technologically advanced society, it would probably be necessary to demand ever more self-discipline and training of children. Or we, as a culture, might prefer certain characteristics in adults that are unlikely to develop if children are granted adult freedoms too early, such as the egalitarian practices that exclude racism or sexism, or even the kind of "high" artistic culture that is acquired only over time. Some such goals would no doubt, as liberationists contend, constitute unjustified subordination of legitimate freedom, but the claim that they all do is implausible and would require much more argument. Liberationists avoid these questions, for the most part, by refusing to acknowledge that more freedom for children may be in serious conflict with other highly desirable values.

Before going on to consider the implications of these points, let us therefore bid adieu to the idea that children should have the same rights as adults: neither justice nor good consequences support it. Even its most radical proponents have trouble sticking to a consistent interpretation of it, and it cannot be made to fit any acceptable moral theory. In short, we can regard this particular swimming pool as safely fenced in.[7]

What else has been accomplished? By showing that a policy of equal rights for children is untenable, we should have reassured those who fear that they are wronging their children whenever they set limits for them, although they still need reasons for thinking that any particular limit is justifiable. "New breed" parents also need to come to terms with the considerations raised here. Despite the fact that my proposition that young children need loving but firm handling if they are to develop self-control is to a considerable degree dependent on the validity of empirical studies, it would be irresponsible to dismiss it as therefore inconclusive. The proposition is coherent and well enough supported to place the burden of proof on those who prefer a different approach to show why it is defensible. Hence, although the conclusion reached here is negative, in the sense that it denies the soundness of arguments for equal rights for children, it constitutes a major step forward in helping us think about how to deal with children.

7. Thanks to Daniel Little for this vivid way of putting the matter.

Every point in the argument against liberation adds to the base of knowledge that helps us move on to construct a just and livable policy. The chief implication of the argument is that some form of protectionism is morally acceptable: it can be right to limit children's freedom against their will even when it would be wrong to limit an adult in the same way. The second is that we must have some idea of specific instances in which such limitation is appropriate. Thus, for example, common-sense expectations that children ought to treat others with respect, help around the house, and take their own intellectual development seriously are defensible. It is therefore not wrong to make such demands of children and is, in fact, wrong *not* to do so.

It is true that the precise applications of this principle will vary according to child and circumstances. No matter how much more we come to know, I suspect that childrearing will continue, in considerable part, to be something we do by the seat of our pants. This will be the case not only because of the notorious problems involved in applying general principles to specific situations, but because, as we all know, children develop gradually, unevenly, and at their own rates; their personalities also vary hugely. This state of affairs is likely to persist even if we narrow the limits of variability by applying what we know about the causal links to valued traits. Moreover, children's development will continue to be strongly influenced by factors outside parents' control, and parents' reaction to the consequences of this state of affairs will have to be tailored to the circumstances.

Given the world into which the next generation is emerging, together with the things that will be necessary to make it a better one, what would we want to require of children before they assume full adult rights? I have been arguing that they should be solidly on the path to emotional, moral, and intellectual maturity. By that I mean that their actions should have begun to manifest substantial awareness of their own long-term interests and the ability to act on those judgments. They should also be well on their way to being able to support themselves, preferably by means of a calling they enjoy and are good at.[8]

8. What this last condition would mean in practice in the case of those who hope for careers requiring long years of preparation in graduate school would remain to be seen.

I have argued that self-control is primary among the essential prerequisites for these conditions. It contributes to self-esteem, satisfaction, and many forms of worldly success; its lack is most probably at the root of much self-destructive behavior, unhappiness, and failure. Still more important, we need children to be caring individuals who can willingly subordinate their own interests to those of others. Self-control is a major prerequisite for the ability to do so. They also need to be raised so as to take pleasure in the welfare of others and to feel pain at their suffering: mere intellectual interest in doing the right thing is not enough. Only thus is there is any hope of eradicating a world where some are wrapped in fur while others, padded with rags and paper, are shivering over grates. Only thus is there any hope of making the political changes necessary to ensure human civilization beyond the next century.

It is in this respect that most of the liberation literature and the responses to it seem to me to be most inadequate: the burning question always seems to be whether children can successfully complete their own projects.[9] It is true that managing one's own freedom in this way doesn't necessarily preclude moral behavior toward others. It could be argued that respecting others' rights and showing moral concern is built into that very notion of autonomous freedom. But the nature and tone of the discussion suggest that this dimension of the issue is not foremost in people's minds. My point is that, given the social nature of our lives, moral behavior is at least as important as our ability to act in consonance with our own enlightened self-interest, if not more so.

No doubt, we have a lot to learn about how to create such warm people. But we ought not to underestimate what those who deal with children professionally already know. As I have been arguing, we are not starting from scratch: there is a substantial base of information upon which to build. Making sure potential parents are apprised of it would be a step in the right direction; if nothing else, such knowledge would help provide them with the self-confidence to stand up for what they think is right and to withstand the kind of manipulation children are apt to try out on them. At the same time, naturally, it would be important to emphasize the importance of

9. Compare this question with the contemporary attitudes toward children described by Zelizer in *Pricing the Priceless Child*.

human variability and the pitfalls of applying general rules to specific cases; only in this way could we attempt to guard against overly rigid demands on parents' part.

There is an additional source of knowledge that we ought to be drawing upon. If Carol Gilligan's findings about the greater inclination of girls and women to employ a care orientation in moral reasoning have any validity, as I suspect they do, we need to start looking more carefully at how girls are raised.[10] What causes them to lean toward valuing relationships more? Why do they tend to take more for granted the importance of nurturing people? This is not to say that the traditional education of girls should be made into a model for all—any more than that of Emile. There's obviously a great deal wrong with an approach that tends to weaken women's self-esteem and render them timid and submissive.[11] Tracking down the antecedents of various traits will be laborious, but it is necessary so that we can attempt to cultivate those we value and avoid those we don't. If we are lucky, we will discover that the two can be separated; if we aren't, we may face some difficult choices.

More specifically, what could we say about possible improvements in the way children are to live as we seek to achieve the goals I have laid out here? Harris suggests the possibility of establishing for them a new social slot: "Perhaps there is a case for creating some sort of 'junior citizen' status for children with citizen's rights, but with reduced opportunities for work and increased opportunities and incentives for undertaking education (but not compulsion). . . ."[12] This approach would recognize children's special needs while still treating them as equals, since treating people as equals doesn't necessarily require identical treatment. This seems a sensible suggestion, although the precise rules fixed upon would determine whether it were an improvement or not.

Those rules would depend on the principles governing them. In

10. Gilligan, *In a Different Voice*. If Sandra Harding is right that Africans are also more likely to manifest this kind of moral orientation, we will also need to explore its antecedents. See Harding, "The Curious Coincidence of Feminine and African Moralities: Challenges for Feminist Theory," in *Women and Moral Theory*, ed. Eva Feder Kittay and Diana T. Meyers (Totowa, N.J.: Rowman & Littlefield, 1987).

11. Some percentage of these tendencies obviously arises directly from women's status as second-class citizens; but feminists have also been documenting how traits can plausibly be linked to treatment of girls. See, e.g., Paige Porter, ed., *Gender and Education: Sociology of the School* (Victoria, Australia: Deakin University Press, 1986).

12. Harris, "Political Status of Children," p. 50.

theory, Harris would, of course, refuse to adopt any protectionist precepts, but given the foregoing, that axiom needn't cramp us. The points that can profitably be drawn from the liberationist case are, it seems to me, the following: first, the importance of freedom, second, the necessity for justifying limits on it. Taking these points to heart, without thereby swallowing the whole case, we might plausibly adopt the following approach. Age should be a suspect classification, and the burden of proof rests on the shoulders of those who would limit liberty. Notice, however, that it does not follow from this position that freedom should automatically prevail when values conflict—that would be a much stronger thesis, one firmly squelched by the case against liberation. On the contrary, in many cases an individual's liberty must be limited when it threatens serious harm to others. I would also like to see more emphasis on promoting such goods as equality and general well-being, even at the cost of some freedom. Thus the mayhem attributable to certain liberties such as unrestricted gun ownership should suffice to justify their prohibition; also, taxation to provide a welfare floor and public education are clearly defensible limits on freedom.

Threat of harm to others would, by itself, in some cases, also justifiably restrict children's freedom; thus the bad consequences for others would support the case for compulsory education, even if children's own well-being did not depend on it. However, and this point is where the reasoning with respect to adults and children differs, consideration of children's own welfare does justify restrictions of their liberty, restrictions that would be paternalistic if they were imposed on adults. Thus children's freedom should, among other things, be limited when it seriously interferes with the prerequisites for their future development. This position should also be understood as requiring solid evidence that it would so seriously interfere, not mere speculation: it is not an infinitely elastic criterion that will expand to justify any proposed restriction on children.

As we have seen, this principle provides clear guidance in some cases, such as compulsory schooling. Unfortunately, of course, the optimal course of action is by no means so clear in many situations. On the one hand, short of trying out a given freedom, our assessment of its probable consequences must inevitably be underdetermined by the evidence. On the other, once we get beyond the clear cases, notions about what constitutes harm vary considerably.[13] These are problems common to every consequentialism, but a retreat to deontological judgments hardly seems to me to be a feasible alternative: as is so often the case in life, we must simply do the best we can. Part of the solution is, I think, that once reason, evidence, and argument have run their course, political negotiation will in some cases have to determine what is to be done.

What about the legal tools for creating limits? Two basic approaches are at our disposal. One is the age-based blanket approach; the other is a competency-based approach that attempts to match right to ability. At present in the United States, we have a mixed system, with the preponderance of the first kind of law. This approach restricts children below the age of sixteen, for example, to certain kinds and amounts of work. It also fixes eighteen as the age of majority. However, there are significant exceptions to this way of doing things. Thus from sixteen on, children may be free to try to show their competency to drive; they can also attempt to demonstrate their general competency in emancipation hearings.[14]

Each approach has disadvantages. Age-based laws inevitably have an arbitrary element and may therefore be under- or overinclusive. Competency tests require us to agree on what and how to test, and open the door to political manipulation.[15] A satisfactory children's policy will most probably continue to use both kinds of limits. Judging which is best for a given type of situation will require case-by-case analysis to decide not only whether any restriction at all is justifiable but also what type is optimal. Working out a comprehensive policy on children would therefore require interdisciplinary teams, and would extend beyond the scope of this work. However, it is worth looking briefly at a few areas.

13. For example, are children harmed by not being exposed to classical music, if we assume that such exposure is a prerequisite for later love of it? Or are they merely being deprived of a benefit? Is the loss (whichever it may be) serious? One criterion for deciding these kinds of issues would be whether children are sorry later about what happened. But that doesn't quite do the job. If a child never develops a taste for Bartok, say, then she may be sorry that she had to suffer through the exposure. And if she is not exposed, she won't know what she missed. For a thorough discussion of harm, see Joel Feinberg, *Harm to Others* (Oxford: Oxford University Press, 1984).

14. See Robert M. Horowitz and Howard A. Davidson, eds., *Legal Rights of Children* (New York: McGraw-Hill, 1984), secs. 4.06 and 4.19.

15. For a discussion of the disadvantages see Cohen, *Equal Rights for Children.*

Let us start by considering living arrangements. Proponents of equal rights for children are concerned not only about children caught in abusive or otherwise substandard households, but about the conflicts of interest that can arise between child and parent in otherwise satisfactory families. I have argued that although these problems do exist, the answer to them is not children's liberation: helping children acquire equal power in the household or letting them leave it altogether is not likely to be in their best interest. Yet liberationists are right, there are real problems here that need new solutions.

I argued against equal rights for children because they empower children not only to escape abuse but to escape responsibility in a way detrimental to their long-term well-being and that of society in general. One way to meet children's legitimate needs without making it possible to evade legitimate demands on them would be to create group living arrangements that they, perhaps after a certain age, could choose to join. Not only might this be one constructive solution for children who are being abused in various ways, but it could help children and parents who are experiencing serious conflict (both conflicts of interest and simple disagreements) to resolve it in a positive manner. Choosing to live in such a "children's house" could not be an escape from responsibility, however. That is, the adult members of the house would have to make sure that those living there complied with the same basic kinds of rules provided by good parents. Only thus could we avoid undermining appropriate parental authority.

A well-run home of this sort would be expensive, for to work well it would have to be much more than a minimally provisioned warehouse for unhappy children. Therefore, no such proposal could be realized without outside support. Parents could be asked to contribute a part of the cost, although requiring such a contribution would prevent some children from choosing such an option. To avoid this outcome, other sources of support would be necessary. Children themselves could provide some of it in the form of the labor necessary to maintain the house. If, as might be desirable, children were also required to engage in specified amounts of paid work, they could also be expected to pay in a percentage of their wage. Probably, however, tax subsidies would still be necessary; for this reason, a plan of this kind might be rejected as utopian. However, it seems to me a more feasible *and* more sensible way of resolving some of the problems now facing families than instituting equal rights for children.

What about work and education? I have argued that compulsory education is highly desirable and ought not to be sacrificed to free children to work, even though some work for them would probably be beneficial. Any such alteration of current arrangements would naturally have to be organized with great care. Foremost among our concerns would have to be ensuring that any reduction in required schooling did not undermine schools' benefits. Another would be regulating work in such a way as to ensure that no child worked too much and that each did about the same amount; only thus could we hope to prevent further widening of the gap between rich and poor.

It should be clear that the changes I am suggesting aren't only liberatory: they may also involve new duties on children's part, duties that constitute reasonable approaches to the problem of helping children develop the self-control and moral behavior necessary to maintain and improve our joint lives. Although, by themselves, they may seem to limit children still more than those imposed at present, it isn't clear that this would be the net effect of a more sensible children's policy. Overall, I suspect that if children had both more duties *and* more choices, some of our current problems with them would disappear, without the disadvantages of children's liberation.

A better policy would, I believe, recognize children's increasing desire for freedom as they grow, as well as their developing capacity to exercise it well, by partially or wholly granting them some adult rights earlier. I think it might be reasonable, for example, to expand their sexual and reproductive rights, and some civil rights.

Some courts have recognized minors' right to an abortion without parental consent, although this trend may be reversed after the 1989 *Webster* decision. Access to abortion without parental consent is, I think, fully appropriate. A driving force behind the liberalization of laws regulating abortion and contraception has been the general recognition that parenthood is a serious responsibility and one that ought to be voluntarily undertaken, not just the unintended result of sexual activity. Another has been the concern of women, in particular, to have more control over their own bodies and lives.[16]

16. Probably, of course, increasing awareness of the problems of overpopulation have also driven the changes in law and attitudes. Witness the changing policies in various countries, depending on whether over- or underpopulation is feared.

The burden of proof should be on opponents of such access to show why the same arguments don't justify these similar rights for girls. Parental consent requirements are allegedly designed to encourage girls to talk with their parents about the pregnancy, but don't in fact work that way.[17] Statistics suggest that the existence of such a law won't encourage a frightened girl to talk to her parents and merely prevents her from getting the abortion she desires.[18]

Such laws usually contain escape clauses that provide for a hearing at which a judge determines whether a girl is mature enough to make the decision to have an abortion, and if not, whether an abortion is in her best interest. But if she is not mature enough to make *that* decision, what kind of mother could she be? And, as we have seen, a clear-eyed look at the consequences of early childbearing would in virtually all cases favor abortion if we were trying to minimize harm. So if a young woman wants an abortion, there is no good reason to prevent her from having it and good reason to encourage her to do so. Proponents of prohibition or control might argue that we have a right to try to prevent minors from behaving immorally. That may be true in clear cases such as harassment, rape, assault, or murder, but not in such contested cases as this.

Oddly enough, the case for required consultation with an informed adult is far stronger if a girl wants to stay pregnant and put the baby up for adoption or keep it. The situations of deciding for abortion and deciding for continued pregnancy are importantly asymmetrical. *Pace* pro-lifers, in the first case no person but the girl herself is directly affected by the decision; in the second, her decision creates a person who *is* directly affected by her decision. Given the assumption that fetuses don't have an overriding right to life, deciding for abortion is chiefly self-regarding, and a parental veto would constitute unwarranted paternalism. A decision for continued preg-

17. Consider how few parents get around to sex education; even fewer discuss contraception. On these subjects, see Clay Warren and Michael Neer, "Family Sex Communication Orientation," *Journal of Applied Communication Research* 14 (Fall 1986): 86–107; and Steven E. Landfried, "Talking to Kids about Things That Matter," *Educational Leadership* 45 (May 1988): 32–35.

18. See Patricia Donovan, "Your Parents or the Judge: Massachusetts' New Abortion Consent Law," *Family Planning Perspectives* 13 (September/October 1981): 224–28, for a discussion of the effect of such laws. Fewer girls appear to seek abortions, and those who do so experience risky delays and harassment. Lawrence H. Tribe describes a number of absurd or tragic situations caused by such laws: *Abortion: The Clash of Absolutes* (New York: Norton, 1990), pp. 199–203.

nancy becomes a matter of morality because of the future existence of a second person.

Many people have rightly worried about the problem of girls prevented from having abortions they desire by parents, medical personnel, or judges. Although this is a serious concern, the converse case of a girl who refuses abortion elicits little discussion. Surely girls should be informed about the probable consequences of early motherhood on their own long-term happiness and that of the child. We know, however, that teenagers are generally even more deaf to what they do not want to hear than most grownups. Once a baby is born, however, reality begins to be driven home, and the girl may dump the child on her own unwilling mother to raise.[19] This act is surely seriously immoral, and when it is probable, it would be reasonable to apply pressure in favor of either abortion or adoption at birth.[20] Equal rights would free girls to have abortions without imposing upon them responsibility for any new life they create; a more protectionist approach would seek ways to do both. The same protectionism would be unwarranted for adult women because they are much less likely to fail to take responsibility for babies and those babies are somewhat less likely to worsen their life prospects significantly.

Similar considerations would govern children's sexual and contraceptive rights. I have argued against children's liberation on the grounds that they are unready for the freedom it would bring. It does not follow that we should not attempt to find more satisfactory ways to enable them to meet their needs. Sexual frustration is in itself a significant source of misery, especially for the young. Our current policies (and those that would be promoted by equal rights) leave them fairly free to seek sexual satisfaction, but, again, fail to help them behave prudently and morally. A protectionist policy that recognizes the validity of their desires and our mutual interest in

19. As I suggested earlier, this solution is no doubt better for the child, but it can be awfully unfair to the individual selected for another round of childrearing when she may wish to devote her life to other things.

20. After all, one of the basic arguments for abortion in the first place is that people ought not, other things being equal, to be forced to become parents against their will. Of course, when the mother is very immature, troubled, or dependent, adoption will be better for the child. But it makes sense to try to avoid the need for such a solution. Unfortunately, required consultation might be no more effective here than with abortion; schools might be able to run useful programs, however.

their responsible behavior might find ways to satisfy both. That this approach is realistic is suggested by the fact that most other developed countries have lower rates of teenage pregnancy, abortion, and childbearing than the United States.[21] Sex educators no doubt have good suggestions about how to proceed, but truly realistic sex education, discussion of moral issues, and free contraception couldn't hurt.

Success here, as elsewhere, might well require fundamental social change. For example, girls often fail to use contraception, even when it is available; they may be similarly reluctant to insist on safe sex. Underlying such behavior may be an accurate assessment of their inferior and dependent position vis-à-vis boys and men; helping them to behave more responsibly would therefore entail gender equality.[22]

This approach to sexuality would also raise difficult questions about the age of consent, relationships with adults, and ultimately our attitude toward sex in general—questions on which it would be most difficult to get a consensus. These problems, however, are no greater than the ones that would be raised by equal rights.

There would be equally good reason, I suspect, to recognize many civil rights for children from an early age. Here, too, the burden of

21. These lower rates exist despite similar statistics with respect to age at first intercourse and rate of subsequent activity. The most shocking bit of information is that American fifteen-year-olds are five times more likely to have babies than their counterparts in any other developed country on which we have information. See "Risking the Future: A Symposium on the National Academy of Sciences Report on Teenage Pregnancy," *Family Planning Perspectives* 19 (May/June 1987): 119.

22. Caroline Whitbeck elaborates on this point:

> We still live with the legacy of the view expressed by Rousseau that women should not be educated to make responsible decisions but to learn 'to bear the yoke.' While factions quarrel over *which yoke* the young teenage girl should bear, the present situation will continue. On the one hand, those who would forbid the young teenager heterosexual intercourse have often convinced her that premeditated contraceptive preparation shows that she is cheap, that is, too available. . . . On the other hand, societal arrangements that make the girl dependent on pleasing men pressure her into sexual intercourse at an early age. As long as we are content to leave girls subject to pressures, and simply try to see that the 'right' yoke is placed upon them, rather than support the development of their capacity to make decisions they can live with concerning their lives in general and sexual activity in particular, the only alternatives to increased maternity (and resulting morbidity and mortality) among teenagers, will be the grim options of legal abortion or illegal abortion." (Caroline Whitbeck, "The Moral Implications of Regarding Women as People: New Perspectives on Pregnancy and Personhood," in *Abortion and the Status of the Fetus*, ed. William Bondeson, H. Tristram Engelhardt, Jr., Stuart Spicker, and Daniel Winship [Dordrecht: Reidel, 1983], pp. 265–66)

proof should be on those who would limit such rights to show that special harm would ensue if children had them. Because there are so many civil rights, they obviously cannot be covered in detail here, as they would have to be looked at on a case-by-case basis. Even when it turns out to be a good idea to restrict a given civil right, the bias toward freedom should help us find ways to minimize the negative impact. If having a right is not likely to cause harm, then, as Cohen suggests, there would be no reason to withhold it, even if it were not exercised until a later date. If it is likely to harm, a compromise such as competency tests might limit harm while promoting liberty. Still other rights might need an entirely novel strategy. For example, it seems that the criminal justice system has not yet found a way to recognize children's immaturity without increasing their risk of being subjected to harsher or more arbitrary treatment than would have been the case had they been considered adults; yet treating them like adults is hardly the solution.[23] A protectionist approach cognizant of the value of freedom should be able to get beyond the either/or reasoning (individuals are either fully incompetent or fully responsible) that has tended to plague the legal treatment of children.

One question raised by the attempt to create a more consistent policy with respect to children's rights is whether it would be appropriate, in addition to reviewing particular rights, to lower the age of majority altogether. If children had more freedom earlier, this matter might, of course, be less urgent than it now seems. In general, however, the answer would have to depend on whether we intend to hold to the standards of maturity I laid out earlier. If so, then the timetable would, I suspect, be at least in part a function of how singlemindedly we made that goal a priority.

Up to a certain point, it is plausible to believe that the extent to which we are willing and able to subordinate children's present desires to their long-term interests determines when they are able to manage adult rights. As we all know, however, children are not just lumps of clay. They have a life apart from their preparation for adulthood, and one component of the equal rights controversy is how much of their present happiness should be sacrificed for their future well-being.

This dichotomy is, at least in part, a false one, as control and

23. See Cohen's arguments about this matter, in *Equal Rights for Children*, chap. 9.

happiness don't always preclude each other; sometimes, however, they do. One of Rousseau's arguments in favor of children's freedom was that their chance of dying was so great that it wasn't fair to deprive them now for the sake of benefits they might well not live to enjoy.[24] In many cases, the argument for early freedom can, of course, no longer depend on this consideration.[25] Despite my contention that preparation for adulthood should play a much larger role in the lives of many children than it now does, it doesn't seem reasonable to let such preparation fully determine those lives. Setting policy with respect to children's rights and duties will require much thoughtful discussion of the trade-offs between enjoyment and preparation that we, as a society, are prepared to make. It could very well be that a number of different mixes are justifiable. In general, it is probable that the less we emphasize preparation, the later children will mature; there may, however, be a floor of preparation below which they never do so adequately.

This issue raises once again the fundamental questions discussed in chapter 6. How flexible are children? What kind of society do we want? What is the relationship between these two questions?

With respect to knowledge about children's potential, a priori reasoning will take us only so far; to get an accurate idea of possible limits we must look to history and other cultures. As we have seen, there are grounds for supposing that children are more flexible than many people have thought. Careful observation and experimentation might have surprising things to tell us.[26] We must also, however, take very seriously warnings about limits implied by some of the material examined here: children may be much more flexible than we have thought, but it doesn't follow that there are no causal relationships between the way they are treated and the way they turn out.

Children's possibilities raise again, with greater force, the question what kind of society we want. Again, we are obviously constrained by the social nature of human life, the physical requirements of the earth that sustains us, and the prerequisites for desirable human de-

24. See Rousseau, *Emile*, p. 79.

25. This is not quite so true, however, for segments of the American population suffering from high infant and child mortality rates. I fear that those populations are still not in a position to take Rousseau's advice if they are to improve their social position.

26. The limits of moral experimentation here remain to be delineated, of course.

velopment. These constraints provide boundaries, but a variety of ways of life are possible within them. Such choices mean that decisions about how to deal with children are value-laden at the core, as they depend on our relative weightings of such basic values as freedom, equality, and welfare, as well as on what we regard as worthwhile pursuits. As I have argued, decisions about children therefore cannot be independent of more general decisions about what kind of society to have.

Some people dream of Polynesian paradises, where fruit floats onto our plates and life is a succession of enjoyments. Were reality like this, children could no doubt run free very early. That way of life is not available to most of us, however, and could not be made so even if we desired it. Realism therefore requires of us some hard thinking about the kinds of society we could have and would want. I have argued for a more communally oriented society, one where more is asked of us for the sake of others, but where more is also offered in return. Such a society would, I think, help us live much more satisfying lives than those that now are customary. It precludes equal rights for children, but given what we have seen, that seems a small price to pay.

Last Words

At the outset of this investigation no final word on how to treat children was promised; nor have I delivered any. The foregoing does suggest tentative paths for those who want guidance now, as well as for those who want to take up the challenge of further inquiry.

There is good reason to think that, despite its appealing conceptual simplicity, a policy of granting children equal rights wouldn't be the best way to resolve the problems we face. Some version of protectionism is far more promising. Discerning the best version of protectionism will require us to confront fundamental questions about the good life and to engage in thoroughgoing intellectual inquiry about what is necessary to achieve it.

What seems clear is that implementing a better protectionism would require fairly major social changes. This is not a call for further sacrifice on the part of parents, not a call for more of the traditional scrimping, so familiar to the middle class, for such "advantages" as summer camp. Parents, however, would have consistently to respond to children's need for love, concern, and discipline. Devoting such attention to children needn't be a sacrifice, of course: it should be, most of the time, a pleasure. Nevertheless, the precondition for its being a pleasure is considerable change in the way society is organized. Such change is necessary not only to ensure that attention to children does not, once again, become an occupation to which women are expected to sacrifice all else, but to ensure for each child the conditions necessary for a decent life.

These are, unfortunately, radical demands. They require equality between the sexes, and reorganizing the work world so that everybody has access to a job that pays a living wage and allows for enough leisure to parent successfully. These states of affairs should be among our foremost goals, not only for the sake of our children, but for our own.

I have in this work tackled the question of children's place in society, without assuming significant improvements in basic social arrangements. My emphasis on individual development might therefore seem to be a case of blaming the victim, of attempting to lay responsibility for society's problems on parents and children. This is not true, as I have repeatedly pointed out how social conditions create or aggravate problems families face, and how social changes could alleviate them. Society is not going to improve by itself, however: "society" is composed of people, and if it is to change, people will make the changes. Thus we are faced with the necessity of simultaneous pressure on several fronts. Furthermore, no matter how ideal a society we have, no matter how it facilitates desirable development, each of us will still surely have to learn some self-control and other good traits. Eating educated planaria didn't turn out to be an easy road to wisdom, and it is doubtful whether any similarly effortless route to virtue will ever be found.

Another reason for going ahead with an investigation of children's place regardless of the kind of society we have is to explore what we do know. Not only may that help us develop better policies for now, but it might help us get clearer about what a better society might require. And even if we had that better society, we wouldn't, in the absence of such analysis, necessarily know what to do about children: intuitions about such matters, even in the best society, aren't enough.

Finally, the outcome of such examination reinforces once again the necessity for reshaping society to fit human needs more adequately. Children's liberation is, in some sense, a Band-Aid: it addresses problems children are having now without looking deeply enough at the social arrangements that create or exacerbate them. It takes those social arrangements for granted and proposes a solution that—because it ignores the gradualness of human maturation—is likely to create serious new problems. In the end it recognizes the need for some basic social change, but only in order to prevent the worst of those new problems. How much more sensible it would be to address first the issues—poverty, discrimination, bad education, and the like—that are at the root of many children's contemporary difficulties. If these problems were corrected and more reasonable protectionist policies of the sort I have sketched out instituted, the difficulties inherent in growing up would be reduced to the minimum and conditions created for fruitful and happy development. This line of reasoning should, if we care about our children, provide yet another incentive to fight for this kind of world.

Appendix

MORAL THEORY

Applying philosophical method to practical problems violates the Cartesian requirement that we progress to specific judgments only when foundations are secure. Although the demand for such rigor is often legitimate, it may be inappropriately applied—just as when physics becomes the model for all science.[1] Additionally, in ethics and political philosophy, we must often do the best we can even if our conceptual apparatus is not quite yet in working order: problems won't wait.

How is it possible to proceed sensibly? It seems to me that the best approach is whenever possible to assume the minimum and to adopt vocabulary neutral with respect to essentially contested notions. Obviously, though, there's a limit to how successful this strategy can be, as so many issues in philosophy are still in that category.

Consequently, it could be argued that it's a waste of time to do this kind of work because its problem-solving value evaporates as readers bail out when they encounter denials of their own favorite assumptions or assertions of ones they detest. It seems to me that it would be a shame to come to this conclusion. In general, we have

1. Our approach to topics must be consonant with their nature and demands. (See Aristotle!) Also, consider that much valuable work has been done on higher-order topics without the kind of theoretical agreement we would all like. Such philosophers as Plato, Aristotle, and Aquinas addressed a huge variety of practical issues in the course of their work.

much to learn by watching how theses are developed even if we disagree with certain assumptions; if nothing else, the experience compels us to think through how our own assumptions would alter the conclusion. But more important, many interesting issues may arise apart from these difficulties.

Consider problems in ethics, in particular.[2] Many of us who've been in the trenches trying to teach and apply ethical theories are having doubts about the usefulness of anything like currently accepted approaches. As we are all acutely aware, there are several such theories. Their conclusions about a given case are often incompatible; even when conclusions coincide, justifications tend to diverge. We are therefore compelled to pick a single theory if we wish to ensure consistent answers. But which to choose, and why? Although a few seem to me to be downright untenable, there are serious problems with all: whichever we choose opens us up to reproach on theoretical grounds even before we attempt to apply it. Complicating the picture further is the obscurity, and even inconsistency, of some moral theorists (take Kant or Rousseau, for example), so that radically different interpretations of any given theory may be possible. The interpretation once chosen, we may discover that there is, even so, no guarantee of help with the particular problem we wish to address. So although we still march our students through the traditional theories and make token bows in their direction in research on practical problems, their link with moral problem solving seems ever more tenuous.

One might react by pulling out, retreating to the theoretical. Ethics as an intellectual game. . . . Philosophers have quite often succumbed to that temptation. But who then will address the moral, social, and political problems now threatening us? Journalists? Politicians? Diplomats? Generals? And, equally serious, notice that there is no salvation from the slippery slide that pulls not only applied ethics but ethical theory itself from our grasp. The latter, after all, requires debatable assumptions in such fields as philosophy of mind and language, not to mention empirical knowledge about how we function. Of course, these assumptions depend in turn upon further debatable assumptions in logic, epistemology, and metaphysics. So

2. Some of the following material is based on my "Feminists Healing Ethics," *Hypatia* 4 (Summer 1989): 9–14.

to be consistent, we might have to withdraw from all but the most basic areas of philosophy.

So: back to the drawing board. But how to proceed? Most of us choose the least problematic moral theory—the one whose costs we are least reluctant to pay. In so doing, we adopt a set of principles, arranged neatly in our preferred pecking order. But it's often hard to have much confidence in that particular ranking. I myself, for example, am drawn to utilitarianism. I think that too much has been made of some of its problems, that there are acceptable solutions to others. Some can be resolved—at the cost of importing into the theory conflicts that otherwise arise only at its margins—by positing utility for such values as freedom and justice. Other people are drawn by liberal theories, say contractarianism or Kant; I think they often find themselves smuggling in assumptions about utility. So our practical reasoning about specific issues often is less divergent than one might have expected. I think that's what happens when we think about why recognizing equal rights for children wouldn't be a good idea. The liberal argument suggests that children need protection so they won't make decisions that diminish future autonomy, whereas the utilitarian argument is about the reduction of future utility. But autonomy and utility are so closely related that the reasoning in both cases is often quite similar.

This blurring of boundaries makes it easier to achieve some kind of consensus, although it is difficult to escape the suspicion that it is a result not of the accurate application of particular moral theories but of ideas that were already floating in the air. This same problem affects a more principle-oriented approach to ethical problem solving such as the one espoused by Tom Beauchamp and James Childress. In their excellent text *Principles of Biomedical Ethics* they lay out a number of general moral principles, declining to align them in any hierarchical order that would clarify what to do when they conflict.[3] While the resulting flexibility is appealing, it seems to import into the core of decision making a disturbing degree of relativism. For these reasons, despite its promise of practical guidance, moral theory seems to leave us in the lurch just when we need it most.

3. Tom L. Beauchamp and James F. Childress, *The Principles of Biomedical Ethics*, 3d ed. (Oxford: Oxford University Press, 1989).

Whether this state of affairs is the "temporary" result of our inability to develop an adequate universal theory or a perhaps irremediable reflection of reality, as Tristram Engelhardt seems to assert, remains to be seen.[4]

The fact that traditional theories often fail to provide much guidance for practice is both a problem and a possible exit from this apparent impasse. Attempting to resolve concrete problems brings us nose to nose with problems for which the standard theories have no wisdom. What kind of situation are we dealing with? How is it most appropriately described, and what criterion can we use to tell? Who is to count in the moral deliberations and why? What are the most relevant facts and what are the grounds for deciding? As we grapple with such matters, the question which moral principle should ultimately prevail may recede almost to the vanishing point, while texture and context are in the forefront.

Is there any handhold to help pull ourselves out of this confusion? Especially promising is recent feminist work in ethics, work that is exploring new ways of thinking about human relationships. Among its useful premises is the idea that it may be more fruitful to concentrate on the context and details of problematic situations, not to try to deduce what ought to be done from highly abstract and general principles. This approach seems to me to be a possible way out of the aforementioned difficulties, and given the block we have come to on that other road, one well worth investigating.

The problem, it seems to me, is that this new road, by itself, is likely to generate serious problems of its own. Concentrating on particular situations, without the benefit of underlying principles, will leave us forever unable to resolve many conflicts or to generalize from one case to another.

Take, for example, the promising emphasis on notions of caring and preserving relationships. It helps keep our feet on the ground as we deliberate about how to live. Often enough, if we care about others, it will be obvious what ought to be done. Many, perhaps most, situations calling for moral decision making involve choosing between our own selfish desires and others' welfare. Should a doctor

4. H. Tristram Engelhardt, "Applied Philosophy in the Post-Modern Age," *Journal of Social Philosophy* 20 (Spring/Fall 1989): 42–48.

lie to cover up negligence? Should a parent squelch a kid's natural curiosity because answering questions gets tiresome? Everybody knows the answers: do we care enough to do the right thing?

I have argued elsewhere that feminist work of this kind has a great deal in common with an intelligent utilitarianism.[5] For example, in a pioneering paper, "A Feminist Approach to Ethics," Susan Sherwin urges upon us an ethic that "rejects the predatory conception of human interaction inherent in any theory that is essentially concerned with preserving the separateness of persons." A good theory will, on the contrary, assume empathy and promote emotional and political bonds.[6] In a similar vein, Caroline Whitbeck has argued for what she calls a "responsibilities view," a morality that exhorts us to contribute to others' welfare. This approach entrusts us with certain tasks, together with the discretion required for carrying them out.[7] We may, Virginia Held emphasizes, be responsible for individuals with whom our relationship is not voluntary.[8] Our "central preoccupation," say Eva Feden Kitay and Diana T. Meyers, "is a responsiveness to others that dictates providing care, preventing harm, and maintaining relationships."[9] The assumption here, again, is that if we care about others, what needs to be done will be clear. The same assumption, it seems to me, underlies the practice of utilitarianism: the needs of others are obvious and it is our duty to try to meet them. Furthermore, a feminist ethic implies equal attention to the welfare of all affected parties, and utilitarianism seems to be the only theory that takes such attention for granted.

Despite these clear affinities, utilitarianism has been rejected by many feminist theorists, although not for the traditional reasons.[10] The more I see of the new work, the more puzzled I get about this

5. Laura M. Purdy, "Do Feminists Need a New Moral Theory?" paper presented at the conference Explorations in Feminist Ethics, Duluth, Minn., October 1988. Some of the following text is taken from this paper.

6. Susan Sherwin, "A Feminist Approach to Ethics," *Dalhousie Review* 64 (Winter 1984–85): 711.

7. Caroline Whitbeck, "A Different Reality: Feminist Ontology," in *Beyond Domination*, ed. Carol C. Gould (Totowa, N.J.: Rowman & Allenheld, 1984), p. 79.

8. Virginia Held, "Non-contractual Society," in Hanen and Nielsen, *Science, Morality, and Feminist Theory*, pp. 111–37.

9. Eva Feder Kittay and Diana T. Meyers, "Introduction," in *Women and Moral Theory* (Totowa, N.J.: Rowman & Allenheld, 1987), p. 3.

10. The traditional objections are that utilitarianism ignores justice, is too demanding and involves dubious comparisons of interpersonal preferences.

antipathy. For example, diminishing suffering is one of utilitarianism's most urgent charges. We are to achieve this end by choosing actions and social policies entailing the least possible suffering.[11] Such a program corresponds, so far as I can tell, in all important respects exactly with Sheila Mullett's proposals for moral sensitivity, ontological shock, and praxis. The first is "painful awareness of suffering"; the second is commitment to awareness and action; the third involves a shift from individualistic perspectives to collective ones.[12]

Feminist ethics adamantly opposes all forms of egoism and selfish individualism. So does utilitarianism. Its motto, "the greatest happiness of the greatest number,"[13] is intended to convey its concern with everyone's welfare. Such a charge involves responsibilities toward all on the basis of need rather than contract. But this concern is no theoretical, duty-driven affair. Mill argues that

> education and opinion . . . should so use that power [over human character] as to establish in the mind of every individual an indissoluble association between his own happiness and the good of the whole—especially between his own happiness and the practice of such modes of conduct, negative and positive, as regard for the universal happiness prescribes; so that not only he may be unable to conceive the possibility of happiness to himself, consistently with conduct opposed to the general good, but also that a direct impulse to promote the general good may be in every individual one of the habitual modes of action, and the sentiments connected therewith may fill a large and prominent place in every human being's sentient existence.[14]

This emotional linking of interests is by far the best guarantee against the kind of individualism feminist theory rightly condemns.

Sandra Harding excoriates contemporary moral theory for its fas-

11. See Jeremy Bentham, *Principles of Morals and Legislation*, in *Works of Jeremy Bentham*; and Mill, *Utilitarianism*, esp. chap. 2, where he writes: ". . . the happiness which forms the utilitarian standard of what is right in conduct, is not the agent's own happiness, but that of all concerned. . . . As the means of making the nearest approach to this ideal, utility would enjoin, first, that laws and social arrangements should place the happiness, or . . . the interest, of every individual, as nearly as possible in harmony with the interest of the whole. . . ." (p. 418).

12. Sheila Mullett, "Shifting Perspective: A New Approach to Ethics," in *Feminist Perspectives: Philosophical Essays on Method and Morals*, ed. Lorraine Code, Sheila Mullett, and Christine Overall (Toronto: University of Toronto Press, 1988), pp. 114–16.

13. Despite its logical incoherence.

14. Mill, *Utilitarianism*, pp. 418–19.

cination with justice at the expense of human welfare: "To the observer armed with gender theory, egoism, utilitarianism, and formalism all appear to address characteristically masculine problems of how to elaborate rules for adjudicating competing rights and duties between generalized autonomous individuals. None takes as an equally important problem how to elaborate ways of resolving conflicting responsibilities to dependent particular others." She goes on to ask: "Should moral theory take the development of a concept of justice and political theory the project of constructing the just state as central when these goals, even if achieved, would not by themselves bring about greater social welfare? Is justice sufficient to maximize social welfare?"[15]

It is ironic that Harding should castigate utilitarianism for insisting on justice at the expense of social welfare, as that is precisely what it refuses to do. The price for utilitarianism, as it is likely to be for feminist ethics, is rejection by many members of the philosophical establishment.[16] In both cases the charge is unwarranted, and, I think, for similar reasons.

Formal justice, in the guise of a carefully drawn account of universalizability, must surely be espoused by both. Although the appropriateness of universalizability for feminist ethics has been the subject of hot debate, and some accounts of act-utilitarianism seem to try to do without it, I believe that it is a minimum requirement for any ethic. Of course, nothing follows about how narrowly distinctions should be drawn or what characteristics of a situation should be considered morally relevant.

Nor are the demands of material justice overlooked. Mill's comments about material justice are often thought to be inconsistent with his adherence to the principle of utility, but careful reading of chapter 5 of *Utilitarianism* suggests that this idea is mistaken. There he argues that justice is simply a set of the most general and important dictates of utility.[17] Proponents of other theories of justice appear to be unable to recognize this concept as justice.

15. Sandra Harding, "Is Gender a Variable in Conceptions of Rationality? A Survey of Issues," in Gould, *Beyond Domination*, p. 56.

16. See various contemporary critiques of utilitarianism, as well as comments about women's moral capacities by such "great" philosophers as Kant and Rousseau; see also Lawrence Kohlberg's work.

17. For example, he mentions our need for security. This view assumes certain facts about human nature, which might be different. If they were different, then the dictates of justice would be different, too.

"Care" reasoning, however, seems to me to follow a similar logic. Take the notorious Heinz case: a man's wife will die unless he steals medicine from a druggist.[18] The boy Jake's analysis is that he should of course steal, as life is more important than property. His decision that life has priority over property is deemed to demonstrate a sophisticated understanding of justice. But is it anything more than recognition that property is meaningless without life—clearly a utility-maximizing judgment?

The girl Amy is unwilling to declare so unambiguously that Heinz should steal the drug: What are the likely consequences of that course of action? she asks. Her analysis seems to me frankly utilitarian, as she appears to be concerned mainly with averting suffering, although Gilligan describes what she proposes as "maintaining relationships." But I don't think this distinction makes a big difference: if, as recent feminist work has rightly emphasized, relationships are essential for survival (let alone happiness), then the practice of having relationships has utility. Averting suffering tends to nourish relationships and therefore has utility.

The difference between Amy and Jake's analysis seems to me to be mainly in her unwillingness to put up with the terms of the puzzle since she sees that bad consequences will follow no matter which course is chosen. The boy's willingness to accept the lesser evil is taken as a sign of his intellectual and moral maturity, even though it results in unnecessary suffering avoided by her less theoretical, more down-to-earth approach.

It is exactly this kind of vision and flexibility that is desirable in feminist ethics. Susan Sherwin urges us to consider not just the immediate features of a given case. At least as important are the assumptions underlying particular solutions, as well as their long-term consequences, especially political consequences.[19] Thus decisions must take into account not only the interplay of principles immediately involved (say, autonomy and nonmaleficence) but the ultimate consequences of choosing one or the other in our society.

Sherwin is fearful of theories, such as utilitarianism, that compel us to separate the intrinsic morality of technologies from questions

18. See Gilligan, *In a Different Voice.*

19. Susan Sherwin, "Feminist Ethics and In Vitro Fertilization," in Hanen and Nielsen, *Science, Morality, and Feminist Theory*, pp. 281–83.

about their particular applications.[20] But this objection is, I think, inconsistent with her desire for context-sensitive judgments. She is rightly concerned to ensure that what we might call "deep" context gets taken into account. Doing so for a given situation or society, however, tells us nothing about other ones.

Furthermore, only consequentialist theories require such distinctions of us, as they demand the fullest and most sensitive understanding of social conditions. Most important, perhaps, they must take power asymmetries into account; otherwise the intent to rectify imbalances is impotent and suffering caused by them continues.

Consider, for example, the question of surrogate motherhood. I think that in some worlds the practice would lead to more happiness than suffering. Practiced in our own sexist, racist, capitalist world, the possibility of harm is so great that we must stringently regulate it or perhaps even ban it altogether.[21] Only distinguishing necessary from contingent features of the practice (the latter arising from the context within which practice occurs) allows us to make this bifurcated judgment. Failure to differentiate these features deprives us of the use of beneficial technologies when circumstances preclude the envisioned harm. It is the rights- and justice-based theories Sherwin objects to that ignore the realities of deep context by attempting to focus on isolated actions.

Similar kinds of comment are appropriate in response to objections that utilitarianism allows for neither special relationships nor concern with specific individuals. The theory could hardly ignore the psychological facts of human existence. One of these facts is that we form attachments to particular individuals, whose welfare is specially important to us. No judgment could therefore possibly maximize utility unless it takes seriously this fact about our relationships with others. So long as there are clear rules about the boundaries of such special relationships, utilitarianism can incorporate them without violating universalizability.[22]

20. I am using "intrinsic" here in a slightly odd way. By it I mean an evaluation of the consequences that necessarily follow from the fixed features of an act. This is compatible with an act's having no intrinsic morality.

21. Laura M. Purdy, "Surrogate Mothering: Exploitation or Empowerment?" and "A Response to Dodds and Jones," *Bioethics* 3 (January 1989): 18–34 and 40–44.

22. As Kai Nielsen rightly points out in "Afterword: Feminist Theory—Some Twistings and Turnings," in Hanen and Nielsen, *Science, Morality, and Feminist Theory.* He

Attention to context is thus mandatory for any decent analysis; context dictates where special provisions, such as affirmative action, are appropriate. This same point justifies devoting ourselves to particular causes, such as the feminist movement. There are many injustices in the world, and it probably makes sense to allocate effort where we feel the most emotional pull, so long as all serious problems get addressed by somebody. The immediate utility of fighting women's oppression may sometimes seem to benefit women less than their oppressors, but this can hardly be true in the long run. However, urgent threats not in our particular bailiwick may require us to drop our commitments temporarily. Examples might be widespread homelessness, a life-threatening epidemic, an invasion from outer space.[23]

Feminist thinkers are right, I think, in their insistence that we need to pay attention to the needs and desires of others, not as exemplars of the human condition but as idiosyncratic selves. Utilitarianism,

---

says:

> To recognize that *my* friends have a special claim on me that others do not is to recognize, for someone who understands what morality is, that *your* friends also have a similar claim on you . . . unless there is some morally relevant and in turn universalizable difference between you, your friends or your situation and me. It also involves believing that the moral point of view at crucial junctures requires impartiality. But again such a commitment to impartiality and universalizability does not require and should not require, moral agents to be, what they cannot be anyway, to wit, detached, identityless atomic individuals." (p. 390)

Mill, too, addresses this and related points quite fully. He argues that

> those among them who entertain anything like a just idea of its [utilitarianism's] disinterested character sometimes find fault with its standard as being too high for humanity. They say it is exacting too much to require that people shall always act from the inducement of promoting the general interests of society. But this is to mistake the very meaning of a standard of morals, and confound the rule of action with the motive of it. It is the business of ethics to tell us what are our duties, or by what test we may know them; but no system of ethics requires that the sole motive of all we do shall be a feeling of duty. . . . It is the more unjust to utilitarianism that this particular misapprehension should be made a ground of objection to it, inasmuch as utilitarian moralists have gone beyond almost all others in affirming that the motive has nothing to do with the morality of the action, though much with the worth of the agent. . . . The great majority of good actions are intended not for the benefit of the world, but for that of individuals, of which the good of the world is made up; and the thoughts of the most virtuous man need not on these occasions travel beyond the particular persons concerned, except so far as is necessary to assure himself that in benefitting them he is not violating the rights, that is, the legitimate and authorized expectations, of anyone else. . . . (*Utilitarianism*, pp. 419–20)

23. These points address some of Sherwin's comments in "A Feminist Approach to Ethics."

unlike any other moral theory, again requires precisely the same thing. The only way to increase happiness is to get people what they really need and want.

The need to supply what people want rather than what they need sometimes conflicts with the requirements of justice. In a utilitarian world, however, the conflict conforms with concerns advanced by feminist ethics. What people want now may interfere with what will make them happy in the long run. This can be the outcome either when current desires are satisfied at the expense of future ones or when development is deflected from the most ultimately satisfying deployment of our talents. Furthermore, we can sometimes justifiably be asked to forgo our own satisfaction on behalf of others. Therefore one of the most pressing tasks of any decent moral theory is to find the right mix of preference satisfaction and concern for long-term personal and social interests. Mill's psychology, by encouraging some desires at the expense of others, is designed to make the job easier.

Where feminist thinkers seem to diverge from utilitarianism most strongly is on the questions about the nature of the self and about the proper theoretical structure with which I started this discussion. Many feminists conceive of the self as socially constituted, not merely as strongly influenced by social factors. Since Mill's psychology is a variation on the latter theme, these feminists reject it. It seems to me, however, that this relational notion of the self remains to be elucidated in a fully clear and persuasive manner, and I am as yet unconvinced that it would dissolve or otherwise lessen the importance of most of the interpersonal conflicts that now constitute many of the critical moral questions now facing us.

With respect to theoretical structure, I think that moral theory must have some of the logical organization supplied by a theory such as utilitarianism. First, not every problem can be resolved by caring or nourishing relationships. "Caring" cannot show us when we may legitimately say no to preserve our own well-being, or how to resolve a genuine conflict of interests. Moreover, not every relationship is worth preserving. Caring will compel us to consider the kinds of communication, compromise, and concern about long-term effects now sorely lacking in much moral decision making. It should help us rule out practices that belittle or ignore suffering. But if it is focused too narrowly on particular others with whom we have relationships, it might also have some tendency to narrow our vision to exclude awareness of the broader kinds of social and political context crucial to good moral reasoning. Second, unless we can formulate principles that help us apply our insights about caring to more general contexts and get beyond preoccupation with particular cases, we are no better off than proponents of situation ethics. Also, as people have been pointing out, if this approach is not adopted by all, we simply perpetuate the status quo, in which women are expected to do and in fact do most of the caring.[24]

There are other difficulties as well. This approach grows out of Carol Gilligan's findings that women are more likely than men to think in terms of caring. Regardless of the epistemological adequacy of her claims, the mere fact of difference doesn't automatically transform them into a *moral* theory.[25]

As I have suggested, serious objections can be raised to some of the uses to which the corresponding "moral theory" is being put. Others could be raised where its recommendations conflict with other theories. Some of these objections parallel disagreements between traditional theories. Utilitarians, for instance, require concern for all sentient creatures; contractarians might, on the contrary, be reluctant to sacrifice for beings not party to the original contract.[26] They might therefore be unmoved by utilitarian appeals to end factory farming of animals or starvation in India. Arguments for sacrifice required by caring are in danger of meeting a similar fate unless

24. E.g., Claudia Card, "Women's Voices and Ethical Ideals: Must We Mean What We Say?" *Ethics* 99 (October 1988): 125–35.

25. Gilligan's work has atttracted a great deal of attention and comment. Among the more interesting criticisms are Sandra Harding's interesting piece comparing African and "women's" morality, which raises questions about the link between caring and women, and Dianne Romain's paper "Care and Confusion" (presented at the conference Explorations in Feminist Ethics, Duluth, Minn., October 1989), which raises more general issues than Gilligan's work.

Despite considerable initial skepticism, I find myself now more inclined to believe that there are significant differences in the way women and men think about moral problems. After teaching women exclusively for nine years, I have recently been teaching at a coed institution. There is no doubt that when someone denies the existence of noncontractual moral obligation, it is a man; it is the women who respond by asserting that there are certain ways you just can't treat people regardless of prior agreement. Admittedly, this is anecdotal evidence, but it is nonetheless quite compelling. How this difference connects up with moral theorizing is another problem. (For an excellent discussion of this and other aspects of Gilligan's work, see Romain, "Care and Confusion.")

26. The more sophisticated the contractarianism, the more inclusive it is likely to become. See Rawls, *Theory of Justice.*

they are bolstered by considerations such as those provided in chapter 2.

Where does all this leave us? My sense is that at this point the best we can do is attempt to cobble together the results of the two disparate activities in applied ethics, investigating the details of specific problems and theorizing. If we succeed, the outcome will, I think, be more than the development of merely "parochial" moral accounts, and should, on the contrary, illuminate and enlighten more generally. Even if, because of the aforementioned difficulties, few works in applied ethics will be definitive, they should nonetheless help us think more clearly about how to ameliorate moral problems.

SELECTED BIBLIOGRAPHY

Ackerman, Bruce. *Social Justice in the Liberal State*. New Haven, Conn.: Yale University Press, 1980.

Adelson, Joseph, and Robert P. O'Neill. "Growth of Political Ideas in Adolescence: The Sense of Community." In Conger, *Contemporary Issues in Adolescent Development*, (1975).

Aiken, William, and Hugh LaFollette, eds. *Whose Child?: Children's Rights, Parental Authority, and State Power*. Totowa, N.J.: Rowman & Allenheld, 1980.

Ariès, Philippe. "A Prison of Love." In Gross and Gross, *Children's Rights Movement* (1977).

Aristotle. *Nichomachean Ethics*. In *The Basic Works of Aristotle*, ed. Richard McKeon. New York: Random House, 1968.

——. *Politics. In The Basic Works of Aristotle*, ed. Richard McKeon. New York: Random House, 1968.

Austin, John. *The Province of Jurisprudence Determined* (1832). New York: Noonday Press, 1954.

Baier, Annette. *Postures of the Mind*. Minneapolis: University of Minnesota Press, 1985.

——. "The Need for More than Justice." In Hanen and Nielsen, *Science, Morality, and Feminist Theory* (1987).

Bakan, David. "Adolescence in America: From Ideal to Social Fact." In Skolnick, *Rethinking Childhood* (1976).

Barry, Brian. *Theories of Justice*. Berkeley: University of California Press, 1989.

Baumrind, Diana. "Child Care Practices Anteceding Three Patterns of Preschool Behavior." *Genetic Psychology Monographs* 75 (1967): 43–88.

——. "Current Patterns of Parental Authority." *Developmental Psychology Monographs*, 4, no. 1 (1971): pt. 2.

——. "Some Thoughts about Childrearing." In Bronfenbrenner, *Influences on Human Development* (1972).

Baumrind, Diana. "Authoritarian vs. Authoritative Parental Control." In Conger, *Contemporary Issues in Adolescent Development* (1975).

——. "Socialization Determinants of Personal Agency." Paper presented at the biennial meetings of the Society for Research in Child Development, New Orleans, 1977.

——. "Reciprocal Rights and Responsibilities in Parent-Child Relations." *Journal of Social Issues* 34, no. 2 (1978): 179–96.

Beauchamp, Tom L., and James F. Childress. *The Principles of Biomedical Ethics*, 3d ed. Oxford: Oxford University Press, 1989.

Becker, Wesley. "Consequences of Different Kinds of Parental Discipline." In *Review of Child Development Research*, ed. Martin L. Hoffman and Lois Wladis Hoffman, vol.1. New York: Russell Sage Foundation, 1964.

Bellah, Robert. *Varieties of Civil Religion*. San Francisco: Harper & Row, 1980.

Benderly, Beryl Lieff. *The Myth of Two Minds*. New York: Doubleday, 1987.

Benedict, Ruth. "Continuities and Discontinuities in Cultural Conditioning" (1938). In Skolnick, *Rethinking Childhood* (1976).

Benn, S. I., and R. S. Peters. *Social Principles and the Democratic State*. London: Allen & Unwin, 1959.

Bentham, Jeremy. *The Works of Jeremy Bentham*, ed. John Bowring. Edinburgh: W. Tait, 1838–1843.

Berger, Brigitte, and Peter Berger. *The War over the Family*. New York: Anchor/Doubleday, 1983.

Black, Max. "Ambiguities of Rationality." *In Naturalism and Rationality*, ed. Newton Garver and Peter H. Hare. Buffalo, N.Y.: Prometheus, 1986.

Block, Jeanne H., Norma Haan, and M. Brewster Smith. "Socialization Correlates of Student Activism." In Bronfenbrenner, *Influences on Human Development* (1972).

Bloom, Benjamin. *Developing Talent in Young People*. New York: Ballantine, 1985.

Blustein, Jeffrey. "Children and Family Interests." In O'Neill and Ruddick, *Having Children* (1979).

——. *Parents and Children: The Ethics of the Family*. Oxford: Oxford University Press, 1982.

Boocock, Sarane Spence. "Children in Contemporary Society." In Skolnick, *Rethinking Childhood* (1976).

Brake, Michael. *Comparative Youth Culture*. London: Routledge & Kegan Paul, 1985.

Brandt, R. B., ed. *Social Justice*. Englewood Cliffs, N.J.: Prentice-Hall, 1962.

Bronfenbrenner, Urie. "The Roots of Alienation." In Bronfenbrenner, *Influences on Human Development* (1972).

——. *Two Worlds of Childhood: U.S. and U.S.S.R.* New York: Pocket Books, 1973.

——. "A Theoretical Perspective for Research on Human Development." In Skolnick, *Rethinking Childhood* (1976).

——. ed. *Influences on Human Development*. Hinsdale, Ill.: Dryden, 1972.

Bunge, Mario. "Seven Desiderata for Rationality." In *Rationality: The Critical View*, ed. Joseph Agassi and Ian Charles Jarvie. The Hague: Martinus Nijhoff, 1987.

Card, Claudia. "Women's Voices and Ethical Ideals: Must We Mean What We Say?" *Ethics* 99 (October 1988): 125–35.

Chambers, John. *The Achievement of Education*. New York: Harper & Row, 1983.

Clarke, L., and L. Lange. *The Sexism of Social and Political Theory*. Toronto: University of Toronto Press, 1979.

Clifford, William K. "The Ethics of Belief." In Clifford, *Lectures and Essays*. London: Macmillan, 1879.

Cohen, Howard. *Equal Rights for Children*. Totowa, N.J.: Littlefield, Adams, 1980.

Cohen, Sol. "In the Name of the Prevention of Neurosis: The Search for a Psychoanalytic Pedagogy in Europe, 1905–1938." In *Regulated Children, Liberated Children: Education in Psychoanalytical Perspective*, ed. Barbara Finkelstein. New York: Psychohistory Press, 1979.

Coleman, James S. *The Adolescent Society: The Social Life of the Teenager and Its Impact on Education*. New York: Free Press of Glencoe, 1961.

——. and Torsten Husen. *Becoming Adult in a Changing Society*. N.p.: Organization for Economic Co-operation and Development, 1985.

Condry, John, and Michael L. Siman. "Characteristics of Peer- and Adult-Oriented Children." *Journal of Marriage and the Family* 36 (August 1974): 543–54.

Conger, John Janeway. "A World They Never Knew: The Family and Social Change." In Conger, *Contemporary Issues in Adolescent Development* (1975).

——. *Contemporary Issues in Adolescent Development*. New York: Harper & Row, 1975.

Coopersmith, S. "Studies in Self-esteem." *Scientific American*, 218, no. 2 (1968): 96–106.

Dammann, Erik. *The Future in Our Hands*. Oxford: Pergamon, 1979.

de Man, Anton Frans. "Autonomy-Control Variation in Childrearing and Aspects of Personality in Young Adults." Dissertation, Rijksuniversitat, Leiden, 1982.

DeMause, Lloyd. "The Evolution of Childhood." In *The History of Childhood*. New York: Psychohistory Press, 1974.

Donaldson, Margaret. *Children's Minds*. London: Fontana, 1978.

Douvan, Elizabeth. "What Happens to Parents." In *From Youth to Constructive Adult Life: The Role of the Public School*, ed. Ralph W. Tyler. Berkeley: McCutcheon, 1978.

——. "The Age of Narcissism, 1963–1982." In Hawes and Hiner, *American Childhood* (1985).

Duck, Lloyd. *Teaching with Charisma*. Boston: Allyn & Bacon, 1981.

Dworkin, Gerald. *The Theory and Practice of Autonomy*. Cambridge: Cambridge University Press, 1988.

Dworkin, Ronald. "Liberalism." In *Public and Private Morality*, ed. Stuart Hampshire. Cambridge: Cambridge University Press, 1978.

Edelstein, Wolfgang. "Cultural Constraints on Development and the Vicissitudes of Progress." In Kessel and Siegal, *Child and Other Cultural Inventions* (1981).

Elkind, David. *All Grown Up and No Place to Go: Teenagers in Crisis* Reading, Mass.: Addison-Wesley, 1984.

Elshtain, Jean Bethke. "The Family, Democratic Politics and the Question of Authority." In Scarre, *Children, Parents and Politics* (1989).

Engelhardt, H. Tristram. "Applied Philosophy in the Post-Modern Age." *Journal of Social Philosophy* 20 (Spring/Fall 1989): 42–48.

Filmer, Robert. *Patriarcha*. In John Locke, *Two Treatises of Government*, ed. Thomas I. Cook. New York: Hafner, 1947.

Firestone, Shulamith. *The Dialectic of Sex*. New York: Bantam, 1970.

Flacks, Richard. "Growing Up Confused: Cultural Crisis and Individual Character." In Skolnick and Skolnick, *Intimacy, Family, and Society* (1974).

Franklin, Bob. *The Rights of Children*. Oxford: Basil Blackwell, 1986.

Freeman, M. D. A. *The Rights and Wrongs of Children*. London: Frances Pinter, 1983.

Freud, Anna. *The Ego and the Mechanisms of Defense*. New York: International Universities Press, 1946.

Friedman, Marilyn. "Feminism and Modern Friendship: Dislocating the Community." *Ethics* 99 (January 1989): 275–90.

Gewirth, Alan. "Can Utilitarianism Justify Any Moral Rights?" In Gewirth, *Human Rights: Essays on Justification and Applications*. Chicago: University of Chicago Press, 1982.

Gibson, Mary. "Rationality." *Philosophy and Public Affairs* 6, no. 3 (1977): 193–225.

Gilligan, Carol. *In a Different Voice*. Cambridge: Harvard University Press, 1982.

Glazer, Nona Y. "Questioning Eclectic Practice in Curriculum Change: A Marxist Perspective." *Signs* 12, no. 2 (1987): 293–304.

Goldstein, Leslie Friedman. *The Constitutional Rights of Women*. New York: Longman, 1979.

Goodman, Paul. "Reflections on Children's Rights." In Gross and Gross, *Children's Rights Movement* (1977).

Gould, Carol C., ed. *Beyond Domination*. Totowa, N.J.: Rowman & Allenheld, 1984.

Grimshaw, Jean. *Philosophy and Feminist Thinking*. Minneapolis: University of Minnesota Press, 1986.

Gross, Beatrice, and Ronald Gross, eds. *The Children's Rights Movement: Overcoming the Oppression of Young People.* New York: Anchor/Doubleday, 1977.

Gutmann, Amy. "Children, Paternalism, and Education: A Liberal Argument." *Philosophy and Public Affairs* 9, no. 4 (1980): 338–56.

——. *Democratic Education.* Princeton: Princeton University Press, 1987.

Hafen, Bruce C. "Puberty, Privacy, and Protection: The Risks of Children's 'Rights.'" *American Bar Association Journal* 63 (October 1977): 1383–88.

Hanen, Marsha, and Kai Nielsen, eds. *Science, Morality, and Feminist Theory. Canadian Journal of Philosophy* 13, suppl. (1987).

Harding, Sandra. "Is Gender a Variable in Conceptions of Rationality? A Survey of Issues." In Gould, *Beyond Domination* (1984).

Hardyment, Christina. *Dream Babies: Three Centuries of Good Advice on Child Care.* New York: Harper & Row, 1983.

Hare, R. M. *Freedom and Reason.* Oxford: Clarendon, 1963.

Harris, John. "The Political Status of Children." In *Contemporary Political Philosophy: Radical Studies*, ed. Keith Graham. Cambridge: Cambridge University Press, 1982.

Hartmann, Heinz. *Ego Psychology and the Problem of Adaptation.* New York: International Universities Press, 1958.

Havighurst, J. "More Youth than Jobs." In *From Youth to Constructive Adult Life: The Role of the Public School*, ed. Ralph W. Tyler. Berkeley: McCutcheon, 1978.

Hawes, Joseph M., and N. Ray Hiner, eds. *American Childhood: A Research Guide and Historical Handbook.* Westport, Conn.: Greenwood, 1985.

Healy, Jane M. *Endangered Minds.* New York: Simon & Schuster, 1990.

Held, Virginia. *Rights and Goods: Justifying Social Action.* New York: Free Press, 1984.

——. "Non-contractual Society." In Hanen and Nielsen, *Science, Morality, and Feminist Theory* (1987), pp. 111–37.

Hoffer, Willie. "Psychoanalytic Education." *Psychoanalytic Study of the Child* 1 (1945): 301.

Hohfeld, Wesley. *Fundamental Legal Conceptions* (1919). New Haven: Yale University Press, 1964.

Holt, John. "Why Not a Bill of Rights for Children?" In Gross and Gross, *Children's Rights* (1977).

Horowitz, Robert M., and Howard A. Davidson, eds. *Legal Rights of Children.* New York: McGraw-Hill, 1984.

Hospers, John. "What Libertarianism Is." In Machan, *Libertarian Alternative* (1977).

Houlgate, Laurence D. "Children, Paternalism, and Rights to Liberty." In O'Neill and Ruddick, *Having Children* (1979).

——. *The Child and the State: A Normative Theory of Juvenile Rights.* Baltimore: Johns Hopkins University Press, 1980.

Hughes, Judith. "Thinking About Children." In Scarre, *Children, Parents, and Politics* (1989).

Hume, David. *An Enquiry Concerning Human Understanding*. Oxford: Clarendon, 1748.

Illich, Ivan. *Deschooling Society*. New York: Harper & Row, 1971.

Inhelder, Bärbel, and Jean Piaget. *The Growth of Logical Thinking from Childhood to Adolescence: An Essay on the Construction of Formal Operational Procedures*. Trans. Ann Parsons and Stanley Milgram. New York: Basic Books, 1958.

Jaggar, Alison. *Feminist Politics and Human Nature*. Totowa, N.J.: Rowman & Allenheld, 1983.

——. "Sex Inequality and Bias in Sex Differences Research." In Hanen and Nielsen, *Science, Morality, and Feminist Theory* (1987).

Kagan, Jerome. "On the Need for Relativism." In Skolnick, *Rethinking Childhood* (1976).

Kandel, Denise, and Gerald S. Lesser. "Parent-Adolescent Relationships and Adolescent Independence in the U.S. and Denmark." In Bronfenbrenner, *Inflences on Human Development* (1972).

Keniston, Kenneth. "Psychological Development and Historical Change." In Skolnick, *Rethinking Childhood* (1976).

Kent, N., and D. R. Davis. "Discipline in the Home and Intellectual Environment." In Bronfenbrenner, *Influences on Human Behavior* (1972).

Kessel, Frank S., and Alexander W. Siegal, eds. *The Child and Other Cultural Inventions*. New York: Praeger, 1981.

Kessen, William. "The Chinese Paradox." In Aiken and LaFollette, *Whose Child?* (1980).

——. "The American Child and Other Cultural Inventions." In Kessel and Siegal, *Child and Other Cultural Inventions* (1981).

Kitcher, Philip. *Vaulting Ambition: Sociobiology and the Quest for Human Nature*. Cambridge, Mass.: MIT Press, 1985.

Kittay, Eva Feder, and Diana T. Meyers. "Introduction." In *Women and Moral Theory*. Totowa, N.J.: Rowman & Allenheld, 1987.

LaFollette, Hugh. "Licensing Parents." *Philosophy and Public Affairs* 9 (Winter 1980): 182–97.

Lambert, Wallace E., Josiane F. Hamers, and Nancy Frasure-Smith. *Child-Rearing Values: A Cross-National Study*. New York: Praeger, 1979.

Leishman, Katie. "Heterosexuals and AIDS." *Atlantic*, February 1987, pp. 39–58.

Levy, David M. "The Deprived and the Indulged Forms of Psychopathic Behavior." *American Journal of Orthopsychiatry* 21 (1951): 250–54.

Liebert, Robert M., Joyce N. Sprafkin, and Emily S. Davidson. *The Early Window: Effects of Television on Children and Youth*. Oxford: Pergamon, 1982.

Liljestrom, Rita. "The Public Child, the Commercial Child, and Our Child." In Kessel and Siegal, *Child and Other Cultural Inventions* (1981).

Lindley, Richard. "Teenagers and Other Children." In Scarre, 1989.
Lipman, Matthew. *Philosophy Goes to School*. Philadelphia: Temple University Press, 1988.
Locke, John. *An Essay Concerning Human Understanding* (1690). Ed. A. C. Fraser. Oxford: Clarendon, 1894.
——. *Two Treatises of Government* (1689). Ed. Peter Laslett. Cambridge: Cambridge University Press, 1960.
——. *The Educational Writings*. Ed. James L. Axtell. Cambridge: Cambridge University Press, 1968.
Lomasky, Loren. *Persons, Rights, and the Moral Community*. Oxford: Oxford University Press, 1987.
Lyons, David. "Utility and Rights." In *Theories of Rights*, ed. Jeremy Waldron. Oxford: Oxford University Press, 1984.
Maccoby, Eleanor. *Social Development: Psychological Growth and the Parent-Child Relationship*. San Diego: Harcourt Brace Jovanovich, 1980.
Machan, Tibor. "The Schools Ain't What They Used to Be and Never Was." In Tibor Machan, *Libertarian Alternative* (1977).
——, ed. *The Libertarian Alternative*. Chicago: Nelson-Hall, 1974.
MacIntyre, Alasdair. *After Virtue*. Notre Dame, Ind.: University of Notre Dame Press, 1981.
——. *Whose Justice, Which Rationality?* Notre Dame, Ind.: University of Notre Dame Press, 1988.
Martin, Jane Roland. *Reclaiming a Conversation*. New Haven: Yale University Press, 1985.
Mill, John Stuart. *On Liberty* (1859). In *The Utilitarians*. New York: Dolphin, 1961.
——. *Utilitarianism* (1863). In *The Utilitarians*. New York: Dolphin, 1961.
Minow, Martha. "Rights for the Next Generation: A Feminist Approach to Children's Rights." *Harvard Women's Law Journal* 9 (1986): 1–24.
Mullett, Sheila. "Shifting Perspective: A New Approach to Ethics." In *Feminist Perspectives: Philosophical Essays on Method and Morals*, ed. Lorraine Code, Sheila Mullett, and Christine Overall. Toronto: University of Toronto Press, 1988.
Nagel, Thomas. "Libertarianism without Foundations." In Paul, *Reading Nozick* (1981).
Nash, Paul. *Authority and Freedom in Education*. New York: Wiley, 1966.
Nielsen, Kai. "Afterword: Feminist Theory—Some Twistings and Turnings." In Hanen and Nielsen, *Science, Morality, and Feminist Theory* (1987).
Noddings, Nell. *Caring: A Feminine Approach to Ethics and Moral Education*. Berkeley: University of California Press, 1986.
Nozick, Robert. *Anarchy, State, and Utopia*. New York: Basic Books, 1974.
Okin, Susan Moller. *Women in Western Political Thought*. Princeton: Princeton University Press, 1979.

O'Neill, Onora, and William Ruddick. *Having Children: Philosophical and Legal Reflections on Parenthood*. Oxford: Oxford University Press, 1979.

Orwell, George. "Politics and the English Language." In Orwell, *A Collection of Essays*. New York: Doubleday, 1954.

Packard, Vance. *Our Endangered Children*. Boston: Little, Brown, 1983.

Palmeri, Ann. "Childhood's End: Toward the Liberation of Children." In Aiken and LaFollette, *Whose Child?* (1980).

Parke, Ross D. "Some Effects of Punishment on Children's Behavior." In Bronfenbrenner, *Influences on Human Development* (1972).

Paul, Ellen Frankel, Jeffrey Paul, and Fred D. Miller, Jr. *Human Rights*. Oxford: Basil Blackwell, 1984.

Paul, Jeffrey, ed. *Reading Nozick*. Totowa, N.J.: Rowman & Littlefield, 1981.

Peak, Lois. "Training Learning Skills and Attitudes in Japanese Early Educational Settings." In *Early Experience and the Development of Competence*, ed. William Fowler. San Francisco: Jossey-Bass, 1986.

Pearl, Arthur. "The Case for Schooling America." *Social Policy* 2 (March–April 1972): 51–52.

Pierce, Christine. "Natural Law Language and Women." In *Sex Equality*, ed. Jane English. Engelwood Cliffs, N.J.: Prentice-Hall, 1977.

Plato. *The Republic*. In *The Collected Dialogues of Plato*, ed. Edith Hamilton and Huntington Cairns. Princeton: Princeton University Press, 1963.

Purdy, Laura M. "Educating the Gifted." Unpublished paper.

——. "Do Feminists Need a New Moral Theory?" Paper presented at the conference Explorations in Feminist Ethics, Duluth, Minn., October 1988.

——. "Feminists Healing Ethics." *Hypatia* 4 (Summer 1989): 9–14.

——. "A Response to Dodds and Jones." *Bioethics* 3 (January 1989): 40–44.

——. "Surrogate Mothering: Exploitation or Empowerment?" *Bioethics*, 3 (January 1989): 18–34.

Rawls, John. *A Theory of Justice*. Cambridge: Harvard University Press, 1971.

Rescher, Nicholas. *Distributive Justice*. Indianapolis: Bobbs-Merrill, 1966.

——. *Rationality*. Oxford: Clarendon, 1988.

Robinson, Halbert, et al. "Early Child Care in the United States of America." International Monographs on Early Child Care, no. 3. *Early Child Development and Care* 2, no. 4 (1974).

Rogoff, Barbara, Martha Julia Sellers, Sergio Pirrotta, Nathan Fox, and Sheldon H. White. "Age of Assignment of Roles and Responsibilities to Children: A Cross-Cultural Survey." In Skolnick, *Rethinking Childhood* (1976).

Ross, W. D. *The Right and the Good*. Oxford: Clarendon, 1930.

Roszak, Theodore. *The Making of a Counterculture*. New York: Anchor/Doubleday, 1969.

Rousseau, Jean-Jacques. *Emile, or On Education* (1762). Trans. Allan Bloom. New York: Basic Books, 1979.

Sabine, George. *A History of Political Theory*. New York: Henry Holt, 1950.

Sandel, Michael. *Liberalism and the Limits of Justice*. Cambridge: Cambridge University Press, 1982.

——. "Introduction." In Sandel, *Liberalism and Its Critics*. New York: New York University Press, 1984.

Satris, Stephen. "Student Relativism." *Teaching Philosophy* 9, no. 3 (1986): 193–205.

Scarre, Geoffrey. "Children and Paternalism." *Philosophy* 55 (1980):117–24.

——, ed. *Children, Parents, and Politics*. Cambridge: Cambridge University Press, 1989.

Schrag, Francis. "The Child in the Moral Order." *Philosophy* 52 (1977):167–77.

——. "Children: Their Rights and Needs." In Aiken and LaFollette, *Whose Child?* (1980).

——. Review of Howard Cohen, *Equal Rights for Children*. In *Law and Philosophy* 1 (April 1987): 159–62.

Scribner, Sylvia, and Michael Cole. "Cognitive Consequences of Formal and Informal Education." In Skolnick, *Rethinking Childhood* (1976).

Sells, Lucy. "The Mathematics Filter and the Education of Women." In *Women and the Mathematical Mystique*, ed. Lynn H. Fox, Linda Brody, and Dianne Tobin. Baltimore: Johns Hopkins University Press, 1980.

Sen, A. K. "Rational Fools: A Critique of the Behavioral Foundations of Economic Theory." *Philosophy and Public Affairs* 6, no. 4 (1977): 317–44.

Sher, George. "Three Grades of Social Involvement." *Philosophy and Public Affairs* 18, no. 2 (1989): 132–57.

Sherwin, Susan. "Feminist Ethics and In Vitro Fertilization." In Hanen and Nielsen, *Science, Morality, and Feminist Theory* (1987).

——. "A Feminist Approach to Ethics." *Dalhousie Review* 64 (Winter 1984–85): 704–13.

Singer, Peter. "Famine, Affluence, and Morality." *Philosophy and Public Affairs* 1, no. 3 (1972).

Skolnick, Arlene, ed. *Rethinking Childhood: Perspectives on Development and Society*. Boston: Little, Brown, 1976.

—— and Jerome H. Skolnick, eds. *Intimacy, Family, and Society*. Boston: Little, Brown, 1974.

Snyder, Martha, Ross Snyder, and Ross Snyder, Jr. *The Young Child as Person*. New York: Human Sciences Press, 1980.

Somerville, John. *The Rise and Fall of Childhood*. Beverly Hills, Calif.: Sage, 1982.

Stephen, James Fitzjames. *Liberty, Equality, Fraternity* (1873). Cambridge: Cambridge University Press, 1967.

Strickland, Charles E., and Andrew M. Ambrose. "The Baby Boom, Prosperity, and the Changing Worlds of Children, 1945–1963." In Hawes and Hiner, *American Childhood* (1985).

Tamny, Martin, and K. D. Irani. *Rationality in Thought and Action.* Westport, Conn.: Greenwood, 1986.

Trigg, Roger. *Reason and Commitment.* Cambridge: Cambridge University Press, 1973.

Tulkin, S. R., and M. J. Konner. "Alternative Conceptions of Intellectual Functioning." In Skolnick, *Rethinking Childhood* (1976).

Wald, Michael S. "Children's Rights: A Framework for Analysis." *University of California at Davis Law Review,* 12, no. 2 (1979): 255–82.

Walzer, Michael. *Spheres of Justice.* New York: Basic Books, 1983.

Weber, Max. *The Protestant Ethic and the Spirit of Capitalism.* New York: Scribner's, 1958.

Welsh, Patrick. *Tales Out of School.* New York: Viking, 1986.

Wendell, Susan. "A (Qualified) Defense of Liberal Feminism." *Hypatia* 2, no. 2 (1987): 65–93.

Whitbeck, Caroline. "A Different Reality: Feminist Ontology." In Gould, *Beyond Domination* (1984).

White, Patricia. *Beyond Domination: An Essay in the Political Philosophy of Education.* London: Routledge & Kegan Paul, 1983.

White House Conference on Children. *Report to the President.* Washington, D.C.: U.S. Government Printing Office, 1970.

Winn, Marie. *Children without Childhood.* New York: Pantheon, 1983.

Yolton, John W. *John Locke and Education.* New York: Random House, 1971.

Zelizer, Viviana A. *Pricing the Priceless Child.* New York: Basic Books, 1985.

Zimring, Franklin E. *The Changing Legal World of Adolescence.* New York: Free Press, 1982.

INDEX